T0305038

Highways and Hierarchies

New Mobilities in Asia

In the 21st century, human mobility will increasingly have an Asian face. Migration from, to, and within Asia is not new, but it is undergoing profound transformations. Unskilled labour migration from the Philippines, China, India, Burma, Indonesia, and Central Asia to the West, the Gulf, Russia, Singapore, Malaysia, and Thailand continues apace. Yet industrialization in Bangladesh, Cambodia, and India, the opening of Burma, and urbanization in China is creating massive new flows of internal migration. China is fast becoming a magnet for international migration from Asia and beyond.

Meanwhile, Asian students top study-abroad charts; Chinese and Indian managers and technicians are becoming a new mobile global elite as foreign investment from those countries grows; and Asian tourists are fast becoming the biggest travellers and the biggest spenders, both in their own countries and abroad.

These new mobilities reflect profound transformations of Asian societies and their relationship to the world, impacting national identities and creating new migration policy regimes, modes of transnational politics, consumption practices, and ideas of modernity. This series brings together studies by historians, anthropologists, geographers, and political scientists that systematically explore these changes.

Highways and Hierarchies

*Ethnographies of Mobility from
the Himalaya to the Indian Ocean*

*Edited by
Luke Heslop and
Galen Murton*

Amsterdam University Press

Cover illustration: Yangtsa – Nepal road scene
Photo by Galen Murton

Cover design: Coördesign, Leiden
Lay-out: Crius Group, Hulshout

ISBN   978 94 6372 304 6
e-ISBN   978 90 4855 251 1 (pdf)
DOI   10.5117/9789463723046
NUR   740

Printed and bound by CPI Group (UK) Ltd, Croydon, CR0 4YY

Table of Contents

List of figures

Acknowledgements

Putting this volume together has been a journey. In compiling a book that covers such an expansive terrain, we have amassed a great number of debts to an incredibly wide array of individuals, communities, and institutions. From the mountain plateaus of the Tibetan Himalaya to the coralline shores of Maldivian islands, all of our authors have been supported, sheltered, fed and humoured by countless individuals met on the roads we have studied so closely. And for that we are all grateful.

As co-editors, we would like to pay a special thanks to Professor Yongming Zhou, who was the first person to put us all around a table at the 2nd International 'Roadology' Workshop convened in December 2017 at Southern University of Science and Technology (SUSTech) in Shenzhen, China. This book was finalized in an era of online conferences only, making the friendly and collegial environment in which we all initially gathered feel even more important as a catalyst for this collective work. For their mentorship, encouragement and support, we would also like to thank Ed Simpson and Katharine Rankin, who led the respective research projects on roads which brought us to work on this book together in the first place. We would also like to thank Saskia Gieling at Amsterdam University Press and the anonymous reviewers of earlier manifestations of the chapters and original manuscript. And, finally, we would like to acknowledge our authors who have stuck with us on this long and occasionally bumpy road.

There are, of course, far too many names to mention to adequately do justice – at least in any readable fashion – to all those who have had a hand in making the research possible and bringing this volume into fruition. However, as a small gesture of gratitude to our supportive networks, we would particularly like to thank:

Adam Saprinsanga, Agnieszka Joniak-Lüthi, Amtei, Andrea Pia, Ashok Sukumaran, Buddhika, Carolyn Charlton, Debbie Menezes, Deena Shareef, Durga Hasta, Elsie Lewison, Faree Shareef, Francesca Ratnatunga, Gaveem, Ilona Bowyer, Jakob Klein, Julia Brodacki, Kanchana Ruwanpura, Khalid Chauhan, Lagan Rai, Liz Hingley, Lubna Hawwa, M.C. Goswami, Marloes Janson, Martin Saxer, Nadine Plachta, Niamh Collard, Nicole Roughton, Pushpa Hamal, Rebecca Rotter, Rita Lalremruati, Samjhana Nepali, Sanjukta Ghosh, Sara Shneiderman, Shaina Anand, Shanta Thapa, Shyam Kunwar, Srinivas Chokkakula, Thoiba Saeedh, U Hminga Libra, Tsering Gurung, U Puia, Yaman Sardar, Yangjin Bista, Ashoka University as well as the community members of Lwangtlai, Zochachhuah, and Paletwa.

The project has been supported by numerous research grants and institutions: Marie S. Curie Individual Action Fellowship from the European Commission Horizon 2020 Programme (Grant no. 751131, 2018-2019); the Highland Asia Research Group (Remoteness and Connectivity: Highland Asia in the World, ERC Starting Grant no. 637764); the US Department of Education; and the Social Science Research Council for an International Dissertation Research Fellowship. The research leading to the results presented in Chapters 6, 7, and 8 received funding from the European Research Council under the European Union's Seventh Framework Programme (FP/2007-2013)/ ERC Grant Agreement no. 616393. The research leading to the findings in Chapters 2 and 8 were also supported through funding from the Social Sciences and Humanities Research Council of Canada (SSHRC Grant no. 435-2014-1883, 2014-2020).

Preface

Thinking with roads

Penny Harvey

The anthropology of roads has flourished in recent years in tandem with the expansion of road-construction projects across the planet.[1] Confronted by the ways in which road-construction and infrastructural investments appear as instruments of economic growth, ethnographers have begun to pay close attention to diverse modes and scales of alignment that play out in specific times and places. Ethnographic research, such as is exemplified in the chapters collected here, challenges the assumptions of linear alignment and of enhanced prosperity. Looking in detail at how such large-scale infrastructure projects land in people's lives raises questions about the many different modes of engagement that emerge across the diverse scales that roads articulate.

The chapters gathered in the *Highways and Hierarchies* collection attend to the grounded effects of major road-building projects such as the Chinese state Belt and Road Initiative (BRI), designed to promote and support infrastructural development in countries right across Asia and Eastern Europe. The mega-investments of the BRI build on the symbolism of ancient trade routes. They are promoted by the Chinese state as a gift to the region, motivated by the desire to enhance regional connectivity through the facilitation of economic exchange and the promise of economic growth. China has a unique capacity to fund infrastructural initiatives at this scale, and the source of economic possibility is also always a source of political concern. In particular, the BRI is a challenge to India's interests and influence in the region. As terrestrial trade corridors are opened up through Bangladesh, Myanmar, Pakistan and Nepal, and maritime trade facilitated by the enhancement of the ports of the Maldives and Sri Lanka,

---

[1] Recent anthropological monographs on the subject of roads include Beck, Klaeber, and Stasik 2017; Dalakoglou 2017; Filippello 2017; Harvey and Knox 2015; Uribe 2017; Simpson 2021.

Heslop, Luke, and Galen Murton (eds), *Highways and Hierarchies: Ethnographies of Mobility from the Himalaya to the Indian Ocean*. Amsterdam, Amsterdam University Press 2021
DOI: 10.5117/9789463723046_PREFACE

the geopolitics of global circulation across both land and sea are reshaped. Borderlands are especially sensitive as physical and political proximities shift with the arrival of new and faster access routes to marginal areas and disputed territories. In these circumstances, roads appear as ambiguous and problematic gifts, technologies of development for some, of diplomatic provocation and asymmetrical integration for others. Either way, they impact on the lives of local people across the region who find themselves inextricably entangled in the materialities and the imaginaries of global expansion.

The chapters in this volume follow the unexpected ways in which roads change lives. They explore the notion of asymmetrical connectivity and the effects of differential inclusion. They look at how roads act as liberal modes of governance, channelling and filtering circulation, regulating movement. The ethnographic focus on how local people struggle to find ways to negotiate, resist and profit from these infrastructural projects suggest that 'enhanced connectivity' is far from straightforward. On the ground the BRI appears less monumental and more piecemeal. Every road has its own strategic implications for the territories it touches, connecting diverse local, regional and national interests. Close up we find less of a network and more of a meshwork of complex and incomplete alignments, many of which were already underway, while others address interests that diverge, often in significant ways, from the major geopolitical narratives of the wider 'project'. Indeed, the image of the BRI as a singular project is itself a rhetorical technology of alignment, an example of an idea that might help to build a road, as Rankin and Simpson suggest (this volume). More broadly still, this collection raises the question of how exactly road construction brings prosperity, and to whom, at a time when so many places are experiencing the fragility of environmental change, and the need for a carbon politics that does not simply aim to connect people and places but also to protect them.

In his recent book *Down to Earth: Politics in the New Climatic Regime* (2018), Bruno Latour argues that human beings need to find new ways to inhabit the Earth in order to survive. The challenge, he suggests, is to rethink and to redescribe what 'belonging to a territory' entails. The hope is that such thinking will produce a new awareness of the material conditions of human lives at a time when relentless modernization, deregulated extraction and the ever more frantic demands for globalized economic growth have deprived so many people of a secure 'place to land' as he puts it (Latour 2018: 5). With so many people and things on the move, as migrants, as refugees or as components of vast intersecting supply chains, the fundamental social and political challenge of our time is to find ways to conceive a common world, where connection to the Earth includes a commitment to the grounded relations of place *and* to the extensive relations through which places, ecologies and climates are brought into being. In this short essay, and as a preface to the essays that follow, I want to propose that thinking through infrastructures in general, and through roads in particular, offers one useful starting point for this latest inflection of political anthropology. What place do roads have in a world that has already exceeded its capacity to sustain continued economic growth? As massive infrastructure programmes are projected for roll out across the planet, the abrupt stalling of circulation that the 2020 global pandemic produced offers us a timely reminder of how current modes of connectivity, long taken for granted by those able to travel without a second thought, are also overwhelming the capacity to provide sufficient ground for settled ways of life.

Roads are perhaps unlikely focal points for attempting to think in positive ways about how to address the relationship between human beings and the material conditions of their lives. In terms of environmental futures, roads are generally seen as harmful technologies, and for good reason. Major road-construction projects – and indeed many minor road-building initiatives – are associated with the invasion of territories for extractive purposes, the securing of territories for military or administrative control, and the destruction of fragile ecologies as aspirations for connectivity cut into spaces where other established life worlds are not valued, or even recognized. Once built, roads invariably produce an intensified circulation of vehicles, for such is their purpose. Increased circulation brings environmental pollution, a surge in accidents and fatalities, and the displacement or destruction of the life forms, and forms of life that stand in the way. Their histories are testimony to the effects of globalization, the explosion of inequalities, and the scope and rapidity of deregulation designed to speed up extraction, circulation, and accumulation of wealth for the few.

But roads are also, and perhaps almost always, built in the name of a greater good, supported by calculations that demonstrate possibilities for development, social inclusion and well-being – across all scales, local, regional, national and international. As these possibilities are questioned, roads offer important vantage points from which to investigate the histories of how we got to where we are, and from which to think with others (of many kinds) about viable alternatives in fuller awareness of what is at stake. It is the specific spatio-temporal quality of roads that affords these possibilities for thought.

Roads draw together multiple relational systems. They both comprise the ground of specific places and extend beyond through the open-ended possibilities that arise from connectivity to elsewhere. To invest in road construction is to speculate on these possibilities in the process of seeking to bring new relational dynamics into play. The contributors to this volume look in detail at how such transformations can lead to the disruption of established social, political and economic relations but also frequently reinforce existing hierarchies. In every case, however, the intention is to transform existing social possibilities by reconfiguring the material ground of relationality. These projects of transformation are intrinsically experimental. The outcome is always unpredictable, because the instigators and promoters of the transformation can never be fully aware of the multiple relations in play at the complex intersections of engineered systems and non-engineered, emergent ecologies.[2] Engineers manage such complications by limiting their focus to specific material challenges, as they work to specify the problem and articulate potential solutions. Contracted to build a stable surface, they focus first and foremost on the terrain, the instability of seismic zones, the demands of steep elevations, heavy rainfall, or perpetual drought. The contract with the client further narrows the scope and the quality of the material interventions. They rely on the political authority of their client to manage the social complications that arise. In this way, despite the huge popularity of road-construction projects, it is ultimately the powerful who are best placed to leverage the futures that they desire, with little or no interest in the desires and expectations of those who have other plans, or who do not plan at scale at all, but day by day seek to make a living from the world that takes form around them. The erasure of alternatives matters, and provokes further questions about the significance of what emerges at these sites of convergence where a specific infrastructural form becomes both the material condition of possibility for lives lived in specific places, and for connective networks that pay no heed to place.

State politics and infrastructural transformation on the ground

My starting point for conducting ethnographic research on roads grew from an attempt to think about the presence of the state in a small Andean town, where people consistently complained that they had been abandoned and

---

2   These ideas are drawn from 'Introduction: Infrastructural Complications' in Harvey et al. 2017.

forgotten by successive governments (see Harvey 2005). Here connectivity was not taken for granted, and the road was a focal point for local disquiet. The traffic from the highland city of Cusco to the lowlands of the Amazon basin was relatively frequent. The road had become an important regional trade route, and it gave some of the larger roadside settlements the status of market towns, able to provision both a wider hinterland and the steady stream of passengers who broke their journeys in need of food and accommodation. However, the compacted earth road was also quite lethal. Accidents were common as were the small roadside crosses and shrines that marked where travellers had died. Journeys were always unpredictable. Landslides and floods frequently left people stranded, sometimes unable to continue for days on end. Local people longed for an improved road and campaigned hard. Eventually, diverse interests aligned sufficiently for funds to be forthcoming. This forgotten corner of Peru was to receive a new highway. The parameters of connectivity and circulation expanded. No longer limited to the link between highlands and lowlands within a national territory, the road had been incorporated into a more extensive international imaginary. It was set to become a section of an international 'Interoceanic Highway', built to foster the flow of goods from the booming economy of Brazil to the growing markets of Asia (see Harvey and Knox 2015). This imaginary of transoceanic connection was expressed in a surprising road sign that went up at the junction where the new road forked off the existing paved highway just outside Cusco, high in the Peruvian Andes. Among other more local destinations the sign indicated that the city of São Paulo was 4601 kilometres away! São Paulo, one of the largest cities in the world is a place that nobody was ever going to travel to via this route – except perhaps the occasional backpacker with the time to spare. The Brazilian engineers working on the project frequently travelled back to their homes and offices on the east coast of Brazil, but they would always fly. The sign suggested a link to a destination that bore no relevance to the experience or the aspirations of travellers who passed by on their journeys. It marked a claim to an imaginary connection. It could just as well have marked the distance to Paris or London.

Despite the existence of this and other unlikely claims, local people were delighted by the prospect of this road, and in many ways it met their expectations. The construction process was disruptive but there were good employment possibilities. It was clear that some stood to gain more than others and there were anxious struggles over routing, and competition for access to jobs, and to the money distributed across the provisioning supply chain. The macroeconomic promise of the road was not delivered. A limited budget had compromised the choices of route and the quality of the surface. The road that emerged was too slow, steep and winding to serve the needs of major international traders. It was also not sufficiently robust to withstand the harsh climate of the high altitudes, the shifting watery ecologies of the Amazon basin, or the seismic activity of the eastern slops of the Andes. Furthermore, major corruption scandals subsequently revealed that this road had primarily served as a source of financial extraction. It was not surprising that the rhetorical promise of modernization through the facilitation of international connectivity was never materialized.

Nevertheless, the road did produce significant social transformation that came about through the changing proximity of rural settlements to urban centres. The new asphalt surface made it possible to travel in cars rather than trucks or SUVs. Transport ownership changed and collective taxis and buses began to shuttle people between the city and the rural areas. With journey times dramatically reduced people became more oriented to urban services, particularly the medical and educational possibilities. These movements redistributed populations and reoriented lifestyles. In the 1980s the large landowners with good connections to regional centres of power still controlled the local economy and the political offices. With the arrival of this new asphalted road they began to move away from the rural towns to live in the cities. They kept their lands but ceded local administrative power to a newly educated generation, familiar with urban institutions and keen to exploit the new economic opportunities that the road afforded. Electricity and mobile telephony had accompanied the road, and people from across the wider hinterland were drawn to the attractions of engineered environments. The town of Ocongate where I had lived over many years expanded rapidly and people joked that it had become 'Hong Kongate'. For many, however, life became more precarious. The changing spatial and temporal dynamics rearranged the relative advantage of different settlements. Small producers struggled to compete with the wholesale prices of urban markets. Small traders found that passengers no longer needed the services of a roadside town as journey times shrank. Roads offered possibilities, particularly for those who had capital to invest in vehicles, in stock for smarter shops, restaurants or petrol stations. Otherwise opportunities were haphazard and unevenly distributed. Livelihoods were realigned to urban values at a time when climate change further amplified the precarity of the rural poor. Are these inevitable outcomes? Perhaps. But they are not the only outcomes. There are many ways in which roads produce modes of engagement that can lead to the erasure of a sense of place, but it is also important to attend to the ways in which roads can also provide a degree of common ground for social life and social organization.

On territory and circulation

As I began to explore roads as sites from which to think ethnographically about the nature of state presence, I recalled the centrality of Radcliffe-Brown's insistence that while states do not exist in the phenomenal world (1948: xxiii), territorial structures are of critical significance to the study of political organization.

> Every human society has some sort of territorial structure. We can find clearly-defined local communities the smallest of which are linked together in a larger society, of which they are segments. This territorial structure provides the framework, not only for the political organisation, whatever it may be, but for other forms of social organisation also, such as the economic, for example. [...] In studying political organisation, we have to deal with the maintenance or establishment of social order, within a territorial framework, by the organised exercise of coercive authority through the use, or the possibility of use, of physical force. (Radcliffe-Brown. 1948: xiv)

Both the Belt and Road Initiative and the Interoceanic Highway can clearly be understood as emerging from and thus reproducing dominant forms of political organization – national states, regional administrations, local towns. At the same time, roads also reveal the effort it takes to sustain the integrity of territorial structures, because they do not stop at the borders. This visible effort suggests that such territorial structures only ever operate as partial and permeable frameworks. Roads are indeed frequently built in an attempt to integrate territory but they are also simultaneously used to disrupt and transform existing lines of political influence and control. In this respect roads both order and disorder territorial structures, as many of the contributions to this volume emphasize. Indeed, under conditions of neoliberal financing that exploit public assets for private accumulation in the name of 'progress', roads are key instruments of modes of governance that reference territory but are not bound by territory.

In our ethnographic study of the Interoceanic Highway (Harvey and Knox 2015), we learned of the multiple agendas that brought this road into being. We also unearthed the diverse forms that a long-held ideological commitment to the creation of trade routes with global reach had taken over the years. Alongside the territorializing rhetoric that conjured the image of roads as the means to enhance a national capacity to trade effectively with other nations, the road was also clearly a site of diverse speculative investments. These investments reframed territories as either more local, or far more extensive, than the national framework acknowledged. For example, there were squatter settlements where people gathered in the hope of finding work, of establishing eligibility for compensation, or best of all, for rehousing once the road appeared. These modes of speculative investment in anticipation of displacement and subsequent compensation have been beautifully described by Jeremy Campbell in his work on a highway yet to be built in the Brazilian Amazon (Campbell 2015). Widespread falsification of land titles here has led to a situation where far more land is 'legally' registered than actually exists. The possibility of a road has granted some the space to settle, for a while at least. But it is not only the poor who speculate on roads. Large construction companies aligned to ministries of state pay handsomely for lucrative contracts. Roads are built with public money, ostensibly to serve the public good. They are also the means to secure personal fortunes and private gain at all levels of the construction process. People commonly assumed that transactions in the shadow economy of large construction projects shaped access to decision makers, to materials and machinery, and to legal permissions. The rumours of endemic corruption are occasionally substantiated in high profile court cases. The fall out from the Interoceanic Highway project included the aftershocks of the indictment of the lead construction company, Odebrecht, a Brazilian organization that was found guilty of corruption and collusion with officials at the highest level of government in both Brazil and Peru.

The bordering effects of roads

The ethnography of roads had led us to an understanding of state power as both personal and institutional, with both territorializing and de-territorializing ambitions, materialized in a complex meshwork of local, national and international relations. This tension between the containment of territory and the encouragement of flow brings the importance of borders to the fore. Roads are used to produce a huge range of bordering effects, as a consequence of the ways in which they cut through otherwise continuous territory (marking a differentiated physical space) and create corridors of differentiated movement through the enforcement of exclusionary mechanisms.

The geopolitical landscapes of South Asia are dominated by the powerful territorial state influence of India and China. But these states invest in competing vectors of circulation, with the effect that a peripheral Chinese settlement might find itself more oriented to Indian centres than to Chinese ones (see Yi Huang, this volume). Imperial histories randomly produced the borders that now ground everyday life in important respects, shaping the direction that goods and taxes flow, the languages that people speak, the source of engineering expertise and the intersection of diverse modes of authority. So too in Latin America where the circulations of goods and persons also respond to wider geopolitical arrangements, with the US looming large not only in the financing arrangements, but in the bordering practices that open and close the flow of money, of labour, of drugs, of migrants, under a fluctuating and partial regime of international surveillance. The histories of roads register these fluctuations of bordering and of marginalization and the intersections of global, national, and local forces, of human design and ecological response. On the ground, at the local scale, they are also concrete sites of differentiation. Contributors to this volume describe the uneven distribution of risk, the varied experiences and modes of travel that equate to differences of status even within a single vehicle, the punctuated rhythms of journeys, the differentiations that determine who gets to stop where and why, and who chooses to continue. These are the complex intersecting rhythms of movement and stasis, of progress and delay.

The notion that modern road networks facilitate trade, by enhancing the flow of goods and money, pays insufficient attention to the ways that roads depend on 'friction' beyond that of the vehicles on the tarmac surface.[3] Borders are the foundational expression of a managed territory. Roads are used to strengthen borders because they channel flows, they make the circulation of persons and goods more legible, and they can be policed. Nevertheless, borders are also always porous, even those that are highly militarized. The ways in which roads support and/or subvert border regimes are a key dimension of territorial politics in spaces of neoliberal governance. They are the valves that open and close the flow. Bordering devices accompany most claims to territory and the counterclaims that challenge the authority of political control. Thus, while agents of the state

---

3   A point that Anna Tsing (2004) emphasizes in her work on conceptual productivity of 'friction' as a generative force.

control populations by the use of many different kinds of roadblocks (from traffic lights to physical barriers), those who seek to challenge or question the authority of state agents also turn to roadblocks as an effective means of appropriating the capacity to control the flow. Whether deployed as modes of legal protest, or as criminal acts of intimidation or theft, these unofficial bordering devices reveal the importance of the ability to display the capacity to control the flows of goods and persons. Crucially, it is not only state forces that have this capacity.

Given the ubiquity of bordering devices, most road users expect friction, and there are skills to travelling acquired when needed by those who have learned how to circumvent barriers and checkpoints. Roads are experienced as sites of encounter and circumvention, as well as dangerous spaces. In the years of the war with Shining Path (from 1980 to the mid-1990s), journeys in Peru involved running a terrifying gauntlet of army checkpoints. Those without documents were always in danger of being arrested and detained as terrorists. The drivers would anticipate the checkpoints and stop to let people jump off the trucks and run around behind the police posts to join again further along the road. Those with papers would stay aboard. Attention to bordering devices matters because they shed light on the fluctuating rhythms of politics and capitalism as registered in the bodies of those who travel, in the state of the surfaces, in the speed of movement, in the periods of waiting.

Thinking with roads

This volume invites us to think with roads in order to attend to the hierarchies that are both reproduced and challenged as large construction projects arrive and inevitably reconfigure the places through which they pass. Ethnographic analysis allows for a focus on the diverse qualities and dynamics of specific places, perhaps allowing a glimpse of the possibilities as well as the constraints that a focus on roads brings into view. Attention to relational histories also allows for an expansive investigation about what belonging to a territory entails.

Roads produce unlikely collaborations, of engineering, finance, politics, manual labour, machinery, materials and all manner of 'disruptions' as the common purpose of a contained construction 'project', at whatever scale, will also bring forth specific and incompatible interests. But even as they emerge and fail in so many ways to deliver the promised future, roads also and always become the ground on which people, machines and animals move, or simply wait as others come and go. A road, like any track, is a space that is differentiated from its surroundings in underdetermined ways. A road is a marker of difference. What matters are the differences that are marked, and what people make of that difference. For example, a stretch of tarmac can mark the change from a rough to a smooth surface, making it possible to move at more accelerated speeds. But roads can be travelled slowly, too; they can become spaces of stillness for those who are watching, or waiting, or finding themselves left behind. What these engineered spaces become and for whom is integral to their fascination.

Whether surfaces are repaired or not, modified by design or by neglect, they are also always 'unfinished' sites. In the world of the pandemic, of climate change, and the Anthropocene, where the category of the human is unsettled by other intelligences and other grounds for existence, might there be reconciliations that particular kinds of roads can provide? Highways as demarcated surfaces also produce the verges, the places ignored and left behind by those who rush by.

In Latin America roads excite passion and have what appears to be an almost unique capacity to draw people together in the expectation of a particular mode of connectivity from which everybody can benefit. Unlike a railway, a tram, underground pipes or overground cables, the road remakes the ground on which anybody can tread. The ground may or may not be policed but it can, at times, be appropriated even as it reveals the highly uneven terms of such inclusion. I am particularly drawn to the spaces that roads become when circulation stops. Projects in suspension become intriguing sites to visit, resonant with memories of past promises. Closed roads produce accessible public spaces for marches, rituals and ceremonies.

Latour refers to the 'critical zone' of the Earth, to draw attention to the fragile and threatened material relations that are the uncared-for source of life on this planet. His plea is also a call for awareness of the urgent need to create more 'common ground'. Belonging to a territory in this respect is not primarily a political ordering – although political action is desperately needed. Belonging is an affective relationship to the ground, an acknowledgement of its value. In Peru rural people make offerings to forces of the Earth as they set off on journeys. They also draw these forces into their lives when they build the foundations of a house, and when they construct roads. A curiosity as to what roads make possible and what they prevent, what they make flourish and what they kill, is a curiosity about the relational capacities of infrastructural formations, a move to further understanding of how relational possibilities can support the redescription of what 'belonging to a territory' entails.

List of works cited

Beck, K., G. Klaeber and M. Stasik (2017). *The Making of the African Road*. Leiden: Brill.

Campbell, J. (2015). *Conjuring Property: Speculation and Environmental Futures in the Brazilian Amazon*. Seattle: University of Washington Press.

Dalakoglou, D. (2017). *The Road: An Ethnography of (Im)Mobility, Space and Cross-Border Infrastructures in the Balkans*. Manchester: Manchester University Press.

Filippello, M. (2017). *The Nature of the Path: Reading a West African Road*. Minneapolis: University of Minnesota Press.

Harvey, P. (2005). 'The Materiality of State-Effects: An Ethnography of a Road in the Peruvian Andes'. In *State Formation: Anthropological Perspectives*, ed. by C. Krohn-Hansen and K.G. Nustad. Ann Arbor, MI: Pluto Press, 123-141.

Harvey, P., and H. Knox. (2015). *Roads: An Anthropology of Infrastructure and Expertise*. Ithaca, NY: Cornell University Press.

Harvey, P., C. Bruun Jensen and A. Morita, eds. (2017). *Infrastructures and Social Complexity: A Companion*. London: Routledge.

Latour, B. (2018). *Down to Earth: Politics in the New Climatic Regime*. Cambridge: Polity Press.

Radcliffe-Brown, A. (1948). 'Preface'. In *African Political Systems* by M. Fortes and E.E. Evans-Pritchard. London: Oxford University Press.

Simpson, E. (2021). *Highways to the End of the World: Roads, Roadmen and Power in South Asia*. London: Hurst Publishers.

Tsing, A. (2004). *Friction: An Ethnography of Global Connection*. Princeton, NJ: Princeton University Press.

Uribe, S. (2017). *Frontier Road: Power, History, and the Everyday State in the Colombian Amazon*. Oxford: John Wiley & Sons.

About the author

PENNY HARVEY is Professor of Social Anthropology at the University of Manchester (UK). Prof. Harvey's major works in this field are *Roads: An Anthropology of Infrastructure and Expertise* (with H. Knox) and *Infrastructures and Social Complexity* (with C.B. Jensen and A. Morita).

1   Why highways remake hierarchies

Luke Heslop and Galen Murton

Abstract
This chapter lays out the volume's documentation of many of the uneven
– and unexpected – experiences of mobility transformation as it unfolds
as a developmental imperative across vast and complex landscapes of
South Asia. Whether journeys become shorter, faster, more treacherous,
cheaper, or more costly, questions about ownership, management, access
to 'public goods', responsibility, and other critical concerns consistently
take new shape when expressed through the coming of a new road or
transportation network. We posit that roads are fragile political achievements. In response to the sweeping state promises about new mobilities
and modernization that highways are purported to deliver, the stories
comprising this volume, and outlined in this chapter, speak from other
perspectives, such as how political opportunity is routinely met with a
measure of public scepticism and at times efficacious protest.

Keywords: South Asia, roads, hierarchy, economic transformation,
geopolitics

Introduction

There is an old joke told in various configurations throughout South Asia
that goes like this:

> On a diplomatic mission to the US, a cabinet minister from (insert
> whichever South Asian country you like here) has some issue with a hotel
> booking and is offered hospitality at the home of his American political
> counterpart. In the evening they drink whisky at the American's home
> and look out over the city. 'What a beautiful home you have,' comments
> the guest. 'How did you afford such a place on a public servant's salary?'

Heslop, Luke, and Galen Murton (eds), *Highways and Hierarchies: Ethnographies of Mobility from
the Himalaya to the Indian Ocean.* Amsterdam, Amsterdam University Press 2021
DOI: 10.5117/9789463723046_CH01

The American politician points towards a bridge in the near distance and says, 'You see that bridge?' His guest nods. 'Well, you are looking at 1% of the deal.' Years later the opportunity arises for the cabinet minister to return the hospitality and host the American. In the evening, over more whisky, the American comments on the palatial home of his host and returns the question put to him years before: 'How did you afford such a place on a public servant's salary?' At this point, the politician invites the American to look out over the cityscape and observe the bridge across the river. 'You see that bridge?,' the politician asks. The American strains his eyes in the dark and says, 'No, I can't see anything.' At this point the host smiles, gestures towards his palatial home and says, 'You are looking at 100% of the deal.'

At one level, the punchline offers a satirical comment on the perception of political corruption in South Asia vis-à-vis America. At another, it confirms the material and political reality that infrastructure does not always achieve what it is initially proposed to accomplish; moreover, such projects can be – and often are – more profitable for some powerful actors than the originally intended recipients. Furthermore, it evinces the popular understanding that grand infrastructure projects that are billed to benefit the public, such as bridges and highways, are configured to benefit the powerful. This understanding amongst the recipients of infrastructure makes the allure of the road in South Asia as a developmental panacea an even more interesting phenomenon. It is the power relations embedded within and emerging through road development that are at the heart of this book.

Globally, a staggering 25 million kilometres of new roads are anticipated worldwide by 2050, which is enough to circle the earth some 600 times (see Rankin and Simpson, this volume). Growth in South Asia is central to this prediction; India alone currently has a road network of over 5.5 million kilometres and plans to double its annual infrastructure investment to $200 billion (Lama 2019). Infrastructure-focused sovereign wealth funds, though seemingly not as successful as first anticipated, have also facilitated a surge in road construction in Asia. In the face of economic slowdown, global capital investors such as AustralianSuper have stepped in to bolster developments and keep roads unfolding across the region.

At the same time, cross-border highways and regional projects are being funded at scale by the China-led Asian Infrastructure Investment Bank (AIIB), which, with more than US$100 billion designated for the Chinese government's Belt and Road Initiative (BRI), marks another significant addition to the infrastructure investment space impacting road infrastructure across the continent (Ren 2016; Yu 2017). With an estimated US$1 trillion to be invested until 2025 (Menon 2017; Joy-Perez and Scissors 2018) a US$40 billion Silk Road Fund, a US$25 billion fund for the Maritime Silk Road, and about US$800 billion earmarked by the China Development Bank and the Export-Import Bank of China for international infrastructure investments (Oliveira et al. 2020), not even the most outwardly national(istic) programmes of development in South Asia can be considered in isolation from China's rise as an influential infrastructural global power and the globally entwined infrastructure investment space (Heslop 2020).

Foregrounding the scale of expanding highways in metric terms like kilometres paved, or the funding modalities of US dollars invested, tells only one side of a story, however. In South Asia today, road developments are far more complex and uneven, and with the highways and activities that surround them come a host of social, cultural, environmental and political upheavals; inter alia displacement, resettlement, and relocation. The current and future impacts of climate change on roads and their users – such as the risks posed to a range of infrastructures and their constituents by extreme weather events related to shifting monsoon patterns as well as environmental and ecological transformations that accompany expansive road development across South Asia – remains to be fully understood. What is clear is that the changing topography that comes with blasting rocks in mountain passes, dredging sand from the ocean floor, and paving the surface of the earth with tar and asphalt significantly impacts the everyday lives of communities across South Asia. Constructing a road, conceptually and materially, is a fragile political achievement.

This volume documents many of the uneven – and unexpected – experiences of mobility transformation as it unfolds as a developmental imperative across a vast and complex landscape. Whether journeys become shorter, faster, more treacherous, cheaper, or more costly, questions about ownership, management, access to 'public goods', responsibility, and other critical concerns consistently take new shape when expressed through the coming of a new road or transportation network. In other words, *roads change lives*, but as the following chapters emphasize across an array of South Asian places and spaces, such changes are not always for the better. In response to the sweeping state promises about new mobilities and modernization that highways are purported to deliver, the stories comprising this volume speak from other perspectives, such as how political opportunity is routinely met with a measure of public scepticism and at times efficacious protest.

The journey so far

Highways and Hierarchies: Ethnographies of Mobility from the Himalaya to the Indian Ocean examines the contemporary proliferation of road-development projects in South Asia and the Tibet-Himalaya region to show how new infrastructures simultaneously create new connections and reinforce social hierarchies across a range of spatial and political scales. While the uneven outcomes of road development have been well documented for decades (Blaikie et al. 1977), government officials, construction contractors, district leaders, and community actors continue to lobby for and commit tremendous resources to the financialization and implementation of new transport systems. And yet, in innumerable instances and across a range of landscapes and demographics, the realization of new mobilities does not have a flattening effect for all constituencies; rather, the making of new roads instead (re)inscribes particular systems of order and rank, privileging some and (re)marginalizing others. From the middle-class embrace of new and exclusive social spaces in Northeast India (Gohain, this volume) to the reproduction of risk and vulnerability for already precarious populations in rural Nepal (Murton and Sigdel, this volume), the chapters that follow bear witness to common patterns of hierarchization across South Asia. By addressing the destabilizing and reinforcing effects of hierarchy – an experience that is ubiquitous across the region but also distinct and unique to each case study – the volume contributes new insights about the ways in which road development accelerates and compounds class divisions and social disruption.

'Hierarchy', as Naomi Haynes and Jason Hickel have pointed out, is rarely deployed by Western academics in positive terms (Haynes and Hickel 2016). Our use of hierarchies does not attempt to place any sort of moral directive or injunction on hierarchy itself, but rather it is in recognition that the communities we have worked with and travel through in the pages of this book are organized hierarchically and perceive themselves to be so. Moreover, not everyone in these communities perceive hierarchy to necessarily be a bad thing per se. At stake in many of the communities discussed herein is the capacity to marshal the economic and cultural processes that emplace hierarchy in particular locations, especially in moments when these become challenged by the arrival of the road and the highway.

Our use of the term 'highways' indicates that the case studies comprising the volume are concerned with major and relatively large-scale transportation infrastructure projects – often, but not always, called 'highways' – situated in country-specific contexts. For example, in the Maldives, the road dynamics under analysis are components of national development priorities complicated by geopolitical anxieties and intrigue (Heslop and Jeffery, this volume). In Pakistan, highways in Sindh are analysed because of the imagined and anticipated new middle-class 'consumer culture' they facilitate (Khan, this volume). In Tibetan borderland regions of China, the roads under examination are part of China's state-led development initiative to open up the Sichuan-Tibet Highway (Huang, this volume). Collectively, these place-based studies, while always unique analyses of particular experiences in specific localities, also reflect broader trends of capitalization, marginalization, and social transformation that resonate with other recent studies of road and infrastructure development in the social sciences (Mostowlansky 2017; Harvey and Knox 2015; Campbell 2013).

While smaller-scale roads, in both rural and urban environments, also proliferate across South Asia, this collection deliberately examines the larger-scale development of district, state-provincial, and national highways because of the significant political and social impacts they have at local, national, and international levels. According to Harvey and Knox, roads are productive for analysis because of 'what they can tell us about how infrastructural relations simultaneously make national territories, international corridors, regional circuits, and specific localities' (2015: 25). That is, road studies help to bridge macro-level analyses of international and national geopolitical and geoeconomic connections with micro-level insights about the transformations to quotidian experiences at village, household, and bodily levels both on and off of new roadways. Larkin's (2013) analyses of infrastructure further reveal the ways in which transport technologies converge into specific systems and how these systems shape fundamental dimensions of life. As 'matter that enable the movement of other matter', things like roads, rail lines, and communication technologies 'comprise the architecture of circulations [...] and they generate the ambient environment of everyday life' (Larkin 2013: 328-329). While road infrastructures enable the movement of people and goods, they also control those movements, and thus they help rewrite relations between such things, as well as between a state and its populations. Therefore, the development of roads and the socioeconomic dynamics and bureaucratic responses they set in motion allow for a particular view of and into the state without looking at the state centre itself.

At the heart of any critical understanding of road and infrastructure development is the very notion of 'development' itself. As Nustad asserts, '[d]evelopment is about planned change, and development policies are therefore revealing about how authorities see the ideal relationship between development and the state' (Nustad 2005: 80; cf. Harvey 2005). As the nation's 'development' in some machination or other across the cases elaborated here captures the raison d'etre of the politician in contemporary South Asia, the development of highways, roads, and larger transport networks make concrete particular types of state and political performance. Roads facilitate grand openings, they are invitations for politicians to come to particular places and become associated in enduring ways, and they are enticing, particularly as they provide a tangible node at which the state idea and the state apparatus meet.

In conversation with much of the social science literature on roads and mobilities, the chapters in this volume argue against authors such as Augé, who has claimed that highways lack any 'social significance' and are typical examples of 'non-places' (1995: 73-74). Employing a definition proposed by Massey (1994) and Wilson (2004), the chapters show that, 'instead of envisioning roads as neutral lines of penetration going from centre to periphery, or point a to point b, they should be visualized as stretched-out places where intersecting social relations cluster and adhere' (Wilson 2004: 529). Harvey furthermore asserts that the road itself can act 'as a key to understanding the social and physical landscape through which one is passing and also provide a concrete space for ethnographic focus' (2005: 131). In a similar vein, Dalakoglou, drawing on Lefebvre (1991: 124-125, 164), claims the road is one of the most proximate, visible and tangible consequences of otherwise abstract and distant processes (Dalakoglou 2010: 133), thus making the road an apposite site through which to analyse the more abstract notions of the state. As Fairhead's (1992) research in the Eastern Democratic Republic of Congo (then Zaire) illustrated long ago, the road, as a space of social activity, brings together an otherwise disparate collection of characters: the heads of international financial institutions like the World Bank and the International Monetary Fund, local political cadres, corrupt police, non-governmental organizations such as the Red Cross, religious institutions such as Catholic and Protestant missionaries, and, of course, people living along roads, as some of the specific targets of development and constituents of new road projects. Following Fairhead, this volume focuses on the planning, construction and use of the road to illuminate how intersecting social relations adhere and cluster, and where power is established, exercised, and challenged.

Leveraging a grounded and materialist analysis, *Highways and Hierarchies* contributes new conceptual, empirical, and regional insights to both recent and classic key works at the crossroads of international development, mobilities, and South Asian studies. While many excellent studies of infrastructure take up the political power of infrastructural connections in urban political ecological contexts (e.g. Anand 2017; Björkman 2015; Carse 2014), fewer analyses attend to the scalar dimensions of infrastructural integration (Karrar 2010) across local, national, and international levels (Shell 2015), particularly in rural and mountainous environments (Flower 2004). In addition to providing new ethnographic and empirical understandings to ongoing conversations about infrastructures, place making, and territorial power, *Highways and Hierarchies* also sheds new light on perennial debates around the connections between road development, state making, and modernity. This includes updating the established political ecological critiques of the unevenness of rural road development (Blaikie et al. 1977) as well as advancing perspectives about the ways that powerful forces of modernity travel along new roads (Mostowlansky 2017). Working across scale, the book chapters also address the positionalities of transnational political economies (Harris 2013) as well as the geopolitical priorities of international road development (Rippa 2020) in South Asia today. Moreover, the vast development of roads across the region is explored against the backdrop of China's ongoing and far-reaching commitment to 'connectivity'. In particular, chapters on Tibet, Pakistan, Nepal, and the Maldives give a unique ethnographic insight into the China effect in South Asia, and the ways these dynamics are articulated and framed through increasingly widespread discourses on Beijing's BRI (Winter 2019).

The volume was inspired by a meeting at the 2nd International 'Roadology' Workshop at Southern University of Science and Technology (SUSTech) in Shenzhen, China, in November 2017, convened by Dr. Yongming Zhou. The workshop brought together participants from three international research programmes studying roads and connective infrastructure in Asia. These projects include 'Roads and the Politics of Thought' (SOAS, University of London),[1] 'Infrastructures of Democracy' (University of Toronto), and 'Remoteness and Connectivity: Highland Asia in the World' (Ludwig Maximilian University of Munich). As workshop collections so often do, the papers and discussions offered rich material for regional comparative discussion. Drawing from and building on the early conversations in Shenzhen, our aim with this volume is to engage with and better understand the impacts of the vast and ambitious projects of 'infrastructural connectivity' that are changing the shape of the South Asian subcontinent. Importantly, we do

---

1   Roads and the Politics of Thought: ERC Grant Agreement no. 616393; Infrastructures and Democracy SSHRCC Grant no. 435-2014-1883, 2014-2020; Remoteness and Connectivity: ERC Grant Agreement no. 637764.

this in a way that offers the reader new insights on the evolving geography and political economies of the region, particularly in light of the rapid pace and scale of road development led by the governments of the world's largest countries, India and China. While the chapters speak to specific interests of the reader (both thematically and regionally), the volume as a whole provides a wide-lens perspective of the types of challenges and changes taking place in this rapidly transforming part of the world. Furthermore, the ethnographic nature of the contributions throughout the book lends it an important quality of intimacy; that is, whilst engaging with global processes at comparative regional scales, we also present and interpret the lived experiences of those constituents whose pasts, presents, and futures are variously bound up with new roads and highways in both material and imagined ways. The book thus offers a unique focus on local perceptions of pan-South Asian road construction and draws on a broad range of sources, from village fieldwork to global media propaganda.

Organization

In South Asia as elsewhere, road developments bridge social and spatial scales but are always political projects with uneven outcomes. Building on and contributing to an emerging body of 'roadology' literature – to borrow a phrase generated from the workshops in China and as articulated and conceptualized by the convener, Yongming Zhou (2016) – the central tenet that binds the chapters in this volume – and a point that the authors collectively make in various contexts – is the role of the highway in reinforcing and destabilizing social, political, and economic hierarchies. That is, road constructions are inherently political processes that function to territorialize space across scales for distinct, but often conflicting, governmental, economic, and community interests. It is thus useful to look at transportation infrastructure because 'a road invites us to explore its constitutive relations: the materials, the finance arrangements, the politics, the dreams of progress, the design [...] and the force of contingent events that routinely disrupt the best laid out plans' (Harvey 2016: 2-3).

The chapters herein explore South Asia's vast road-development projects and programmes of improvement at a number of intersections, training an ethnographic lens on the roads as they come to stand for development and modernity, operate as sites of encounter and social experience, and symbolize the means and the ends of a relationship with the global economy. Collectively, the book presents the combined work of this aforementioned international network of research programmes that have maintained a critical focus on roads, road construction, road maintenance, and road use from the Himalayan mountain passes of the Tibetan Plateau, through the borderlands of India's north-east and the deserts of Pakistan, to the low-lying coralline islands of the Maldives archipelago and beyond. Furthermore, a key consideration throughout the book, encapsulated by the title, is how new roads and new horizons for 'connectivity' create new forms of hierarchy in the landscapes they traverse. The volume explores this question in multiple ways, including paying attention to international trends and the social dynamics of access to capital and vehicles' colonization of space (Gohain; Heslop and Jeffery), the threat inherent in movement across landscapes that have suffered decades of violent conflict (Sarma; Murton and Sigdel), and the effect and power of roads and their financialization as platforms for political performance and spaces of exposure and encounter (Khan; Huang). The chapters analyse such dynamics at varying levels, from that of individual subjectivity to that of the institution, as a synecdoche for the nation, and at all points en route.

From everyday life in rural villages throughout highlands and islands of the subcontinent to the grand agenda of China's international development programmes, the chapters are ordered with specific attention to thematic flow, rather than discrete sections based on geographic region, or rigid over-arching themes. Composing the volume on these terms allows us to follow synergistic pathways and weave different threads through the chapters as we journey across the region, such as how road developments reproduce the aspirational ideologies of modernity while at the same time reconstituting established hierarchies across distant (but increasingly interconnected) societies. In so doing, the collection provides a grounded and localized view as well as an analysis of global patterns related to transportation infrastructure development.

The central aim of the volume is to illustrate how social transformation that comes with highways takes particular form and poses specific problems in different political and geological landscapes. The book examines geopolitical hierarchy through the expansion of infrastructural horizons in South Asia's larger economies (India and Pakistan), and also the impact of road building in smaller nations in the region (Maldives and Nepal) that face distinct geological and topological challenges. The vast development of roads in South Asia is further explored against the backdrop of China's ongoing and far-reaching commitment to connectivity. The work here does not so much engage directly with the Chinese BRI, but rather, and perhaps more productively, looks at what happens to road infrastructure projects when they are developed in the shadow of – and in places incorporated into – China's vast international initiatives.

Public – and to a large degree state-generated – discourse around the geopolitics of India and China creates an unstable context through which to analyse events from on the ground. It is commonly and popularly thought that there are issues at stake in road building that are strategically significant, perhaps beyond the logics of neoliberalism and which in fact return to an age-old question of empire and power (Murton and Lord 2020). A perceived threat to India's historical dominance in South Asia has been widely promulgated in the press with confrontational headlines such as, 'Asian Giants China and India Flex Muscles over Tiny Maldives' (Sanjeev and Aneez 2018) and through international conferences entitled, 'China in South Asia: Friend or Foe'. Such grand (and popular) narratives (en)frame the subcontinent and its constituent parts as a particular locality (Appadurai 1996), notably one of competitive confrontation in which certain types of social, economic, and infrastructural activity have ready-made contexts in which to fit. The ethnographic material presented in this volume pays attention to this complicated backdrop.

The book challenges state-generated discourses around what roads offer, by developing an ethnographically informed evidence base for the chaotic, counterintuitive and sometimes unpredictable ways roads actually impact on geographies and livelihoods. At another level, the book questions the assumed status of roads in popular consciousness and explores why, for many years, the position of roads in the hierarchy of development needs has been interrogated so little (for exceptions, see Campbell 2012; Blaikie et al. 1977).

Drawing on long-term field research on road building in rural Nepal, Murton and Sigdel employ Marxist and post-structuralist critiques to posit that highway development in Nepal functions as a 'liberal mode of governance' whereby both private and public actors simultaneously territorialize national space, accumulate capital, and maintain power. Through close examination of several road-construction projects in two districts of western and central Nepal, Murton and Sigdel show how the purported benefits of new transport mobilities in fact reinforce longstanding social hierarchies, create conditions for the consolidation of centralized elite power and capital, and reproduce terms of marginality and precarity for vulnerable populations in Nepal today. In particular, they focus on the collusion between government officials and the private transportation syndicates who together orchestrate where roads get built, and who can travel on them, with special attention to the hazards reproduced along the way.

In Khan's work in Pakistan, as well as Heslop and Jeffery's study in the Maldives, we see the impact of Chinese investment on national road-development projects. Here, the material and imagined forms of connectivity that come with new infrastructural allies creates a sense of being networked into powerful channels of patronage, making small islands in the Indian Ocean, as well as sandy outlands in Sindh province of Pakistan, nodes of geostrategic significance in some modern infrastructural empire. For Khan's informants – businessmen, elders, real estate agents, people who live along the road, and politicians connected with it – though a historical relationship between China and Pakistan is well recognized, new roads are thought to be 'game changers' in the pursuit of Pakistani modernity. Khan's chapter engages with both the grand narrative of infrastructural rhetoric – becoming 'the new Dubai' – as well as everyday life in the area of Tharparkar, where a restaurant on the Coal Road sets the scene for a young man, Abdul, who is in search of work along the new frontier. Although Abdul, like many pastoralists in the area, is unable to capitalize on new employment opportunities arriving with the road, the road appears to sustain the dream of a modern Pakistan.

For Heslop and Jeffery, Chinese infrastructural interest in the Maldives places even the smallest islands on the archipelago at the centre of elaborate plots of global espionage and domination. In their chapter, the built road facilitates a multitude of local encounters as people travel further and more regularly, but it is also through the road that islanders encounter the global forces of capital and construction that shape their islands. Evoking an allegorical Maldivian folk tale and anthropological literature on 'the gift' (Mauss 1954), Heslop and Jeffery illustrate how anxieties about social change endure in new forms through becoming embroiled with domestic politics and hierarchical channels of governing 'public goods', as well as hierarchies of international geopolitics.

In Huang's chapter, we see the significance of the road to a 'hidden place' (Medog) as a grand infrastructural gesture to locate Medog firmly within the Chinese side of the Tibetan-Indian borderline. Huang carves out a significant role for the highway by illustrating how national roads in rugged mountain landscapes play domestically within the Chinese national imaginary. His ethnography of the Medog Highway introduces the concepts of 'asymmetric connectivity' and the 'punctuated road' as a means to draw out the exacerbation of existing social hierarchies between Han Chinese and regional ethnic minorities, including Menba and Luoba. While Huang does a great deal to demonstrate what roads mean for people, he also shows what roads, or rather the successful construction of roads, means for the

Chinese state. Interestingly here, failure to construct a road is discussed by the state in terms of impotency and lack of health. For the Chinese state to remain 'healthy' through connection and integration afforded by road construction, it must simultaneously engage in a process of 'channelling and filtering' movement along the road. Huang argues, that channelling and filtering involves disciplining mobile citizens and is constitutive of state formation via road construction.

Continuing along this theme of state commitments to modernity and mobility but moving further south into Northeast India, Gohain's chapter extends an analysis of social hierarchy as compounded on the highway. Through a study of roadside *dhabas* and the performance of Assamese middle-classness in the spaces of 'modern' restaurants, Gohain illustrates how pervasive, intersectional and deep-rooted notions of status can be understood from the roadside; transforming projects of 'connectivity' into mechanisms for exclusion. In doing this, Gohain draws on experiences of exclusion within cosmopolitan city spaces like malls, illustrating how the roadside *dhaba* is similarly comparable as a site of distinction and identity. For the poor, the highway does not bring connection, but signifies a new site of separation and loss. Much like in Khan's example, Gohain shows that the *dhabas* and enterprise along the highways rarely provide employment for those who reside closest to them or have been most negatively impacted by the arrival of the road.

That road building enacts neoliberal, state-building ideologies, and in so doing also entrenches inequality and (re)produces the periphery, is another common thread throughout the chapters. To a degree, all of the chapters concern the ways in which the imagination, construction, management, and use of roads creates, or at least reflects, a disjuncture between statecraft and the everyday lives of citizen-subjects. At the same time, it is striking across the chapters how quickly roads lead us to borders, state enforced (e.g. India-Pakistan, China-India-Myanmar) as well as controlled borders within the nation-state (between provinces within China). This is brought into particularly sharp relief in Sarma's chapter, which focuses on the geo-political/economic logics of building roads in historically 'remote' regions of Mizoram at the borderlands of India, Myanmar, Bangladesh, and China. Here, the Kaladan multimodal highway is met with a great deal of suspicion, and fear, by those in the 'remote' state, as it cuts through areas of protracted conflict in search of new frontiers: Myanmar's resource-rich western borders. Sarma's chapter shows, again, how projects of connectivity and mobility 'fix' and regulate mobile populations. In the case of the Mizoram borderlands, this refers specifically to border crossers and migrants. In a similar way to Huang's depiction of Medog by the Chinese state as a 'hidden place' on which to enact large-scale connectivity projects, Sarma suggests that the Indian state specifically targets remote spaces with flexible border regimes, like Mizoram, to promote spectacular development initiatives for connectivity and economic growth, which simultaneously shore up and securitize national boundaries.

The final chapter provides a conceptual intervention for contemporary and future road studies. Drawing from knowledge produced by two of the major international road studies projects mentioned above ('Roads and the Politics of Thought' and 'Infrastructures of Democracy'), the authors trace past and current trends along the infrastructural turn, and make a case for why roads matter and how research on roads reveals critical insights at the intersections of infrastructure and statecraft; or, the politics of development and the environment. In particular, Rankin and Simpson show how roads have become an integral part of political thought in South Asia throughout the twentieth and twenty-first centuries. However, as the research programmes Rankin and Simpson discuss illustrate, there is a stark incompatibility between road-building agendas and initiatives to address catastrophic climate change through carbon consumption. In India, despite environmental implications, the positive outcomes of rural roads are so deeply embedded in political and popular consciousness that there is professed to be 'no counterfactual to building rural roads' (see Rankin and Simpson, this volume). Thus, reality is exhibited by some select phrases from villagers and road planners, respectively: 'A human being has no value without a road' and 'this [a large rural roads programme] is the most important and successful government policy since Independence'. Statements such as these about roads both underpin and pose a critical question which all of the chapters herein address: *How do people think about roads, and how have people come to think about roads in the ways that they do?* These are genealogical questions that the authors of this volume endeavour to answer ethnographically. Here, the imagined and seemingly heartfelt significance of the road is not lessened by whatever material realities may prevail.

Local perceptions of South Asian road construction must be seen, heard, and considered in order to critically understand the transformative effects of road development in twenty-first-century Asia. Attending to central and acute concerns of statecraft and infrastructural geopolitics, infrastructural imaginaries and future making, and the political economies of roads, the chapters comprising this volume pay attention to the ways in which new highways and modes of road connectivity do not present the same vistas for all those whose lives and livelihoods they traverse. That is, the chapters examine how the creation of a highway comes with many strings attached, weaving together a complex bundle of social change in which new forms of hierarchy manifest and older forms of hierarchy can be (re) made and (re)established in creative and surprising new ways. Focused on South Asia but speaking to more global phenomena, the chapters collectively reveal how road planning, construction, and usage routinely yield a simultaneous reinforcement and disruption of social, political, and economic relations. As a dynamic that continues to accelerate around the world with the making of every new highway, it is imperative to understand local perspectives in order to make better changes for road users today and into the future.

List of works cited

Anand, N. (2017). *Hydraulic City: Water and the Infrastructures of Citizenship in Mumbai*. Durham, NC: Duke University Press.

Appadurai, A. (1996). *Modernity at Large: Cultural Dimensions of Globalization*. Minneapolis: University of Minnesota Press.

Augé, M. (1995). *Non-Places: An Introduction to Super-Modernity*. London: Verso.

Björkman, L. (2015). *Pipe Politics: Embedded Infrastructures of Millennial Mumbai*. Durham, NC: Duke University Press.

Blaikie, P., J. Cameron and D. Seddon (1977). *The Effects of Roads in West Central Nepal: A Summary*. Norwich: University of East Anglia.

Campbell, B. (2013). 'From Remote Area to Thoroughfare of Globalisation: Shifting Territorialisations of Development and Border Peasantry in Nepal'. In *Territorial Changes and Territorial Restructurings in the Himalayas*, ed. by J. Smadja. New Delhi: Adroit Publishers, 269-285.

Campbell, M.J. (2012). 'Between the Material and the Figural Road: The Incompleteness of Colonial Geographies in Amazonia', *Mobilities* 7(4): 481-500, DOI: 10.1080/17450101.2012.718429.

Carse, A. (2014). *Beyond the Big Ditch: Politics, Ecology, and Infrastructure at the Panama Canal*. Cambridge, MA: MIT Press.

Dalakoglou, D. (2010). 'The Road: An Ethnography of the Albanian-Greek Cross-border Motorway'. *American Ethnologist* 37(1): 132-149.

Fairhead, J. (1992). 'Paths of Authority: Roads, the State and the Market in Eastern Zaire'. *European Journal of Development Research* 4(2): 17-35.

Flower, J.M. (2004). 'A Road Is Made: Roads, Temples, and Historical Memory in Ya'an County, Sichuan'. *Journal of Asian Studies* 63(3): 649-685.

Harris, T. (2013). *Geographical Diversions: Tibetan Trade, Global Transactions.*
Athens: University of Georgia Press.

Harvey, P. (2005). 'The Materiality of State-Effects: An Ethnography of a Road in
the Peruvian Andes'. In *State Formation: Anthropological Perspectives*, ed. by C.
Krohn-Hansen and K.G. Nustad. Ann Arbor, MI: Pluto Press, 123-141.

Harvey, P. (2016). 'Introduction'. In 'Attention to Infrastructure Offers a Welcome Reconfiguration of Anthropological Approaches to the Political', ed. by S. Venkatesan, L.
Bear, P. Harvey, S. Lazar, L. Rival and A. Simone, *Critique of Anthropology* 38(1): 1-50.

Harvey, P., and H. Knox (2015). *Roads: An Anthropology of Infrastructure and
Expertise*. Ithaca, NY: Cornell University Press.

Haynes, N., and J. Hickel (2016). 'Hierarchy, Value, and the Value of Hierarchy'.
Social Analysis 60(4): 1-20.

Heslop, L.A. (2020). 'A Journey through "Infraspace": The Financial Architecture
of Infrastructure'. *Economy and Society* 49(3): 364-381.

Heslop, L.A., and L. Jeffery (2020). 'Roadwork: Expertise at Work Building Roads
in the Maldives'. *Journal of the Royal Anthropological Institute* 26(2): 284-301.
DOI: 10.1111/1467-9655.13236.

Joy-Perez, C., and D. Scissors (2018). 'The Chinese State Funds Belt and Road but
Does Not Have Trillions to Spare'. American Enterprise Institute. http://www.
aei.org/wp-content/uploads/2018/03/BRI.pdf (accessed 1 October 2020).

Karrar, H. (2010). *The New Silk Road Diplomacy: China's Central Asian Foreign Policy
since the Cold War*. Vancouver: University of British Columbia Press.

Lama, P.M. (2019). 'Transforming Infrastructure in India'. *Kathmandu Post*,
14 August. https://kathmandupost.com/columns/2019/08/14/transforming-
infrastructure-in-india (accessed 1 October 2020).

Larkin, B. (2013). 'The Politics and Poetics of Infrastructure'. *Annual Review of
Anthropology* 42(1): 327-343.

Lefebvre, H. (1991). *The Production of Space*. Malden, MA: Wiley-Blackwell.

Massey, D. (1994). *Space, Place, and Gender*. Malden, MA: Polity Press.

Mauss, M. (1954). *The Gift: Forms and Functions of Exchange in Archaic Societies*.
London: Cohen and West.

Menon, S. (2017). 'The Unprecedented Promises – and Threats – of the Belt and Road
Initiative'. Brookings Institution, 28 April. https://www.brookings.edu/opinions/
the-unprecedented-promises-and-threats-of-the-belt-and-road-initiative/ (accessed 1 October 2020).

Mostowlansky, T. (2017). *Azan on the Moon: Entangling Modernity along Tajikistan's
Pamir Highway*. Pittsburgh: University of Pittsburgh Press.

Murton, G., and A. Lord (2020). 'Trans-Himalayan Power Corridors: Infrastructure
Politics and China's Belt and Road Initiative in Nepal'. *Political Geography* 77.
DOI: 10.26034/j.polgeo.2019.102100.

Nustad, K. (2005). 'State Formation through Development in Post-apartheid South Africa'. In *State Formations: Anthropological Perspectives*, ed. by C. Krohn-Hansen and K. Nustad. London: Pluto Press, 79-96.

Oliveira, G., G. Murton, A. Rippa, T. Harlan and Y. Yang (2020). 'China's Belt and Road Initiative: Views from the Ground'. *Political Geography* 82. DOI: 10.1016/j. polgeo.2020.102225.

Ren, X. (2016). 'China as an Institution-Builder: The Case of the AIIB'. *Pacific Review* 29(3): 435-442.

Rippa, A. (2020). *Borderland Infrastructures: Trade, Development, and Control in Western China*. Amsterdam: Amsterdam University Press.

Sanjeev, M., and S. Aneez (2018). 'Asian Giants China and India Flex Muscles over Tiny Maldives'. *Reuters*, 7 March. https://www.reuters.com/article/us-maldives-politics/asian-giants-china-and-india-flex-muscles-over-tiny-maldives-idUSKCN1GJ12X (accessed 10 April 2021).

Shell, J. (2015). *Transportation and Revolt: Pigeons, Mules, Canals, and the Vanishing Geographies of Subversive Mobility*. Cambridge, MA: MIT Press.

Sidaway, J., S. Rowedder, C.H. Woon, W. Lin and V. Pholsena (2020). 'Introduction: Politics and Spaces of China's Belt and Road Initiative'. *Environment and Planning C: Politics and Space* 38(5). DOI: 10.1177/2399654420911410.

Wilson, F. (2004). 'Towards a Political Economy of Roads: Experiences from Peru'. *Development and Change* 35(3): 525-546.

Winter, T. (2019). *Geocultural Power: China's Quest to Revive the Silk Roads for the Twenty-First Century*. Chicago: University of Chicago Press.

Woodworth, M., and A. Joniak-Lüthi (2020). 'Exploring China's Borderlands in an Era of BRI-Induced Change'. *Eurasian Geography and Economics*. DOI: 10.1080/15387216.2020.1727758.

Yu, H. (2017). 'Motivation Behind China's "One Belt, One Road" Initiatives and Establishment of the Asian Infrastructure Investment Bank'. *Journal of Contemporary China* 26 (105): 353-368.

Zhou, Y., ed. (2016). *Roadology: Roads, Space, and Culture* [路学: 道路、空间与文化]. Chongqing: Chongqing University Press.

About the authors

LUKE HESLOP is a Lecturer in Social Anthropology at Brunel University and a Visiting Fellow at the London School of Economics and Political Science. He specializes in trade, labour, and mercantile kinship in South Asia, and infrastructure and connectivity in the Indian Ocean.

GALEN MURTON is Assistant Professor of Geographic Science at James Madison University in Harrisonburg, Virginia, US. His work is primarily concerned with the politics of large-scale infrastructure development throughout the Himalayas and especially in the borderlands of Nepal, India, and the Tibetan regions of China.

2   Stuck on the side of the road

Mobility, marginality, and neoliberal governmentality
in Nepal

Galen Murton and Tulasi Sharan Sigdel

Abstract

This chapter examines rural road development in Nepal to understand
how the purported benefits of new transport mobilities in fact reinforce
longstanding social hierarchies, create conditions for the consolidation
of centralized elite power and capital accumulation, and reproduce terms
of marginality and precarity for vulnerable populations in highland
Nepal. The authors posit that road development in Nepal functions as a
'liberal mode of governance' (Duffield 2008) whereby both private and
public actors territorialize national space and articulate a new but still
uneven future for Nepal. More broadly, this chapter aims to illuminate
how non-state actors working in peripheral and rural regions – such as
transport syndicates and development contractors in Nepal – help to
materialize the capitalist and bureaucratic objectives of central state
authorities through liberal practices of infrastructure development.

Keywords: Nepal, mobility, marginality, governmentality, neoliberalism

Introduction

This chapter examines rural road development in Nepal to understand
how the purported benefits of new transport mobilities in fact reinforce
longstanding social hierarchies, create conditions for the consolidation of
centralized elite power and capital accumulation, and reproduce terms of
marginality and precarity for vulnerable populations in highland Nepal.
On the basis of our primary research and analysis in three districts of
Nepal – Kavre, Mugu, and Mustang – we argue that road systems and the

Heslop, Luke, and Galen Murton (eds), *Highways and Hierarchies: Ethnographies of Mobility from
the Himalaya to the Indian Ocean*. Amsterdam, Amsterdam University Press 2021
DOI: 10.5117/9789463723046_CH02

intersecting circumstances of mobility injustice and political economy
that they generate reproduce terms of social stratification for many of the
purported targets of 'rural development'. Drawing from Marxist and post-
structuralist critiques of the uneven economic outcomes and class/caste
-delineated power asymmetries generated by infrastructure development
(Blaikie et al. 1976) and neoliberal governmentality (Ferguson and Gupta
2002), this chapter posits that road development in Nepal functions as a
'liberal mode of governance' (Duffield 2008) whereby both private and
public actors simultaneously territorialize national space, accumulate
capital, and maintain power.

This collaborative study was inspired by two succinct but loaded phrases
that we heard in Mustang and Mugu districts of Nepal between 2015
and 2017: 'If you are poor, the road makes you [feel] poorer' (Nep. *Yedi
tapai garib hunuhunchha bhane sadakle jhan garib bhayejasto anubhuti
garaauchha*) and 'To travel by bus is like buying one's own death ticket'
(Nep. *Busma hidnu bhaneko paisa tirera kaal kinnu jastai ho*). While
statements like these are routinely heard around the world, the myth
and dream that road infrastructure will deliver development and uplift
the downtrodden endures. Moreover, belying pervasive comments like
these ones, elite actors in Nepal – as in many rural places where road
development has accelerated in recent years – routinely capture the
benefits of road infrastructure. We identify these so-called 'benefits' as
modes of capital accumulation that exist in political, social, and economic
forms. By foregrounding and then reflecting on these statements, and
specifically setting them in contrast to opposite perspectives on road-
making as expressed by developers, contractors, and government officials,
our intention is to reveal why such polarized experiences with mobility
exist in Nepal and how they repeatedly reproduce one another with the
building of new roads.

In both literal and figurative ways, we ask why local citizens in Nepal
are routinely left behind by development, sitting by the side of a dusty road.
In contrast to prevailing views across South Asia that promise imagined
futures delivered via new highways (Rankin and Simpson, this volume), we
show how Nepali stakeholders in fact experience the impacts of transport
infrastructures in markedly different and uneven ways. Challenging both
popular fantasies and government narratives, our research shows that the
already marginalized are consistently made more vulnerable and precarious
as a result of road-development programmes. Attention to these dynamics
is both timely and important, as countless constituents of road development, enamoured with the enchantments of infrastructure (Harvey and

Knox 2012) and imaginaries of building a 'New Nepal' (Paudel and Le Billon 2018), experience the disjunctures of anticipated futures and the realities of ongoing social exclusion. Today, such experiences are both increasingly pervasive and acute, situated amidst massive international – and increasingly Chinese – investments in transportation infrastructure, both in Nepal and abroad.

Framed with this introduction and a conclusion, our study proceeds in four historical, empirical, and analytical sections. After reviewing some key post-structuralist and Marxist critiques of development, we reflect on the 'development of development' as an ideological project of improvement, an industry with global reach, and a process of neoliberal restructuring. Following this theoretical framing and brief discussion of our methods, in the first section we review the history of road building in Nepal and analyse the ways in which infrastructural projects have been advanced and leveraged for distinct projects and processes of both state formation and geopolitical alliance. Second, we look closely at the operations of transport syndicates in Nepal and consider how they relate to larger, and ongoing, neoliberal practices which continue to consolidate wealth and power in the hands of the elite. In the third section, we reveal how development operates as a liberal mode of governance by showing that vehicular travel in rural Nepal routinely makes uninsured life more vulnerable, rather than socioeconomically uplifted. Examining how conditions and positions of precarity are reinscribed along new roadways, in the fourth section we demonstrate that uneven class and caste asymmetries in rural Nepal are rarely flattened but instead reinforced as a function of new road-based mobility practices.

Throughout our analysis, we use a blend of Marxist and post-structuralist critical theory to unravel the political, social, economic, and environmental contexts of contemporary road development in Nepal. In so doing, we draw on the work of Mark Duffield to argue that development in Nepal, as elsewhere, operates as a liberal mode of governance. Analysing the effects of road development in three illustrative districts of central and western Nepal, we reveal some of the linkages between transportation infrastructure and neoliberal governmentality. In conversation with other chapters in the volume that discuss the relationship between road development and the 'destabilizing and reinforcing effects of hierarchy', we make this argument in order to show how in Nepal 'road developments reproduce the aspirational ideologies of modernity while at the same time reconstituting established hierarchies across distant (but increasingly interconnected) societies' (Heslop and Murton, this volume).

Development and (neo)liberal modes of governance

As Richard Peet and Elaine Hartwick argue, '"development" means making a better life for everyone' (2015:1). As a relational mode of purported progress, 'development' can be viewed as an ideology, an objective, and a practice that operates to better the conditions of life for populations subject to what Tania Li refers to as the 'will to improve' (2007). Both an aspiration and an industry of international interventionism dating to post-World War II reconstruction, development has for the past several decades also been exposed to function as a liberal mode of governance. While interventions of improvement in many ways capture the overall mission of development in a broader context, 'liberal' interpretations of development particularly emphasize the ways in which external forms of power and governance (Duffield 2008) are implicated with the developmentalist aims of improvement, self-sufficiency, and, increasingly, resilience and sustainability (Reid 2012). Although development programmes in the post-Cold War globalized world are frequently recognized as liberal, if not neoliberal, development as a liberal mode of governance has a much longer history, stretching back to the early days of development in the colonial period itself.

Development as a liberal project of improvement can be traced from the Enlightenment through the Truman Doctrine to rebuild post-World War II Europe up to the modern era and our current episode of globalization. Envisioned and formulated as a process with the potential to lift the world out of poverty and combat the expansion of Soviet communism – and operationalized overwhelmingly through the functioning of capitalism – development in its liberal form is historically linked to global political economies, predicated first on the Bretton Woods system and evolving into twenty-first-century neoliberalism and its various geopolitical manifestations (Roberts et al. 2003). Moving beyond Marxist critiques on the unevenness of development (Smith 2008), structural divisions, and class struggles generated by global development projects, a critical interpretation of liberalism also calls attention to development as an *ideological and technological* project of improvement (Li 2007) which in the latter half of the twentieth century rapidly spread to and gained a dubious ubiquity throughout the Global South.

Governmentality is a key analytic with which to bring post-structural theories to bear on development. As a 'problematic of government' (Foucault 1991), the analytic of governmentality raises critical questions such as: *How to rule, how strictly, by whom, and to what end?* Taken together, these questions suggest that the role and purpose of government, through governmentality, is to 'conduct the conduct' of a population. A government conducts this conduct through numerous *dispositifs*, or apparatuses of governmentality that operate and manage subject populations as functionally economically as possible. Thus, rather than a reified 'thing', governmentality is instead a bundle of tactics, processes, practices, and relations that render governments and administrations distinct from subjects and populations; in turn, those populations are economically governed through mechanisms of security. Thus, while *security* is the control and protection of a population, governmentality can in turn be seen and experienced by the many ways in which power operates over subjects of rule: or what Gupta identifies as the triad of *sovereignty* over territory, *discipline* over bodies, *security* over populations (Gupta 2012). Framed by the triad of sovereignty-discipline-security, we deploy classifications of governmentality to contextualize and reveal how governmentality is understood in the contexts of road development in Nepal.

As a liberal mode of governance, development also works to articulate national security, territorialize state space, and mediate the relationship between a state and its populations. As these dynamics intersect and reinforce one another, they also take a more conspicuous shape in the form of the global development-security nexus. Analysing development and security in biopolitical terms, Duffield (2010) argues that the development-security nexus emerges as a space, or a *dispositif* and apparatus of governmentality, that conducts the conduct of populations subject to the operations and objectives of international development. This conduct can be directed and orchestrated – or conducted – by public and private administrators and experts such as the state, NGOs, military actors, and the private sector. Importantly, when this conduct is conducted not by force but by 'freedoms', such as through opportunities for mobility, education, and economic activity – that is, many of the fundamental aims of development – the state can then be *seen* in critical new ways (Corbridge et al. 2005). Thus, by looking through the lens of development initiatives – especially in the form of infrastructures in Nepal – we see how populations are simultaneously securitized and mobilized, rendered technical and marketable to the development-security nexus across public and private sectors.

Although the development-security nexus is more frequently implicated in military-industrial contexts of development and the proliferation of securitizing spaces that are private (Fluri 2011), public (Chandler 2007), and resource-based (Klare 2001), the nexus is not exclusive to development as security in a militarized-industrialized form.[1] Rather, what this nexus

1   Human security is a humanitarian objective as well as an international industry (in addition to an academic subdiscipline of international affairs and development studies). In the context

represents is the intersection between development as practice and security as process.[2] Especially in the current moment of pervasive neoliberal development, private actors are increasingly situated at this intersection and, as such, are central to forms of neoliberal governmentality. By influencing the ways in which people act, think, and operate, the private sector 'conducts the conduct' of populations and even forecloses spaces formerly occupied and managed by state services. In Nepal, such liberal modes of governmentality are particularly evident with respect to road-development contractors and transportation syndicates. As we examine below in the cases of Kavre, Mugu, and Mustang, collusion in the form of patronage networks (see Rankin et al. 2019) between state elites in the government and both public and private actors in the transport sectors orchestrate where roads are built, what vehicles drive them, how common citizens travel, and the hazards they are forced to face and endure on and alongside the roads travelled.

Methods

Adopting local road building as a political field and methodological entry point, we utilized a suite of qualitative and quantitative methods to generate data for this study. These include semi-structured and structured interviews, field surveys, focus groups, archival research, discourse analysis, and extensive road travel as a deliberately mobile method of participant observation. While our analysis in this study is informed primarily by research in Mugu, Mustang, and Kavre districts, our examination is also framed and contextualized by wider observations of similar patterns of

of this chapter, we place security not only in the context of militarized or state-led operations of power, but also as the privatization of formerly public services. In all of these militarized, state-led, and privatized modalities, we see development interventions routinely mobilized as a method to integrate populations into the fold and control of both the state and the market.

2   Post-structural critique complicates understandings about the powerful relationships amongst development, the state, and security. Like Duffield (2007, 2008), research by Gupta (2012) and Scott (1998) illustrates myriad ways in which the state deploys apparatuses and logics of governmentality to develop its subjects and securitize space. As Gupta's (2012) study on poverty eradication in Bihar shows, complex bureaucracies shaped by colonial legacy create configurations of government administrations and NGO workers that perpetuate systems of structural violence out of which India's rural poor can find no escape. Scott (1998) examines the ways in which the state territorializes its space and expands its sovereignty through *dispositifs* of governmentality such as cartographic knowledge, cadastral surveys, transportation infrastructure and administrative bodies. Through productions of technological space, the state increases the 'legibility' of its subjects and brings the population into purview of central rule.

development in Nepal's Rasuwa, Ramechhap, Sindupalchowk, Dolakha, Tanahun, and Syangja districts. Specifically, research on Mugu and Kavre derives from Sigdel's ongoing ethnographic inquiry for the research project 'Infrastructures of Democracy'[3] and data from Mustang was generated by Murton's ongoing research in Nepal's northern borderlands (Murton 2017, 2018, 2019). Together, the authors conducted n = 100+ interviews with local constituents, government officials, public transport entrepreneurs, restaurateurs and hoteliers, tourists, and weary travellers across a range of age, gender, class, and caste distinctions. Amongst other topics, our questions often asked about local governance processes, regional planning, existing power relations, and democratic practices with respect to rural infrastructure development.

Infrastructural politics and road building as state making in Nepal

Beginning in the 1800s, road development has long been promised and pursued as a national project of state making across Nepal. Specifically, transportation projects and other infrastructural interventions have historically been and continue to be envisioned and articulated as paths to prosperity across the country, from urban environments to the hills and mountains as well. That is, for Nepal, 'as an iconic symbol of modernity, roads continue to hold out the promise of connectivity, political power, economic growth, and cultural status' (Rankin et al. 2017: 43). More broadly, the enterprise and interconnection of road-making as state making is widely established across time and space from Himalayan to other global mountain terrains, including both rural and urban places and almost everywhere in between. In the case of this study in particular, we find that the unevenness of social landscape and spatial mobility as experienced in highland Nepal resonates strongly with Harvey and Knox's analysis of the Interoceanic Highway in Peru, in that 'far from creating a homogeneous and integrated territory, these early road-construction projects had entrenched a sense of discontinuous space and differential capacities for moving around' (2015: 39). A rich body of scholarship increasingly attends to this global dynamic, as we review below. Joining and advancing these conversations, this chapter

3   Mugu-based research was conducted under the auspices of a five-year project titled 'Infrastructures of Democracy: State Building as Everyday Practice in Nepal's Agrarian Districts', funded by the Canadian Social Sciences and Humanities Research Council (SSHRC Grant no. 435-2014-1883), https://infrastructuresofdemocracy.geog.utoronto.ca/.

aims to illuminate how non-state actors working in peripheral and rural regions – such as transport syndicates and development contractors in Nepal – help to fulfil the capitalist and bureaucratic objectives of central state authorities through liberal practices of development.

In Nepal as elsewhere, road developments bridge social and spatial scales but are always political projects with uneven outcomes (Campbell 2013; Harvey and Knox 2015; Cook and Butz 2016; Mostowlansky 2017; Wilson 2004; Flower 2004). That is, road construction and transportation are inherently political processes that function to territorialize space across scales for distinct, but often conflicting, governmental, economic, and community interests. By looking critically at transportation infrastructure, it is possible to 'see the state' (Corbridge et al. 2005) and its citizens in new ways, as 'a road invites us to explore its constitutive relations: the materials, the finance arrangements, the politics, the dreams of progress, the design [...] and the force of contingent events that routinely disrupt the best laid out plans' (Harvey 2016: 2-3).

Subscription to modernization theories and liberal development paradigms of the mid-twentieth century, as discussed above, led to regional planning frameworks that prioritized the place of roads for a more integrated, economically robust, and secure Nepal. Beginning even before Harka Gurung's highly influential 1969 national report *Regional Development Planning for Nepal* (Gurung 1969) that clearly outlined a national and modernist liberal agenda built squarely on road connectivity and directed towards large, multinational donors like the World Bank and the Asian Development Bank, road construction has been leveraged through Kathmandu as a platform of state making as well as a vector of geopolitical power and mechanism of nationwide capital accumulation. Implemented one decade apart in the 1950s-1960s, Nepal's first road projects situated the country within wider technical and diplomatic dynamics of Cold War geopolitics. A brief review of road projects from that period shows that road infrastructure development has long been a technique of both connectivity and soft power in Kathmandu with respect to Delhi and Beijing (Murton 2017). As numerous cases of road development in Nepal indicate, national state projects of improvement and competitive geopolitical interests from outside cannot be divorced from one another and instead converge and are advanced through road construction.

Beginning in the late 1960s, the purported promises of economic growth that roads were supposed to deliver were significantly challenged by empirically rich and theoretically critical political economic research on the unevenness of development. Most important to this turn was *The Effects of Roads in West Central Nepal,* conducted and published by the Overseas Research Group based at the University of East Anglia (UEA) and published in 1976 (Blaikie et al. 1976). 'Pointing to the ways in which centrally planned road projects transform existing transport networks, displace and relocate populations, accelerate rural-urban migration, encourage speculation that leads to inflated land values, and create new political economic hierarchies' (Lewison and Murton 2020: 27), the UEA report did more work than any other single study to challenge and dispel the myth of road construction as the supreme path to prosperity via development in Nepal. More importantly, and especially for our current study, the report by Blaikie et al. also revealed, at a fundamental level, 'how development opportunities like roads create enhanced opportunity for those with capital to invest, but can lead to loss of livelihood for those who do not' (Rankin et al. 2017: 72). Challenging central beliefs in the ability of road projects to positively impact economic development and social mobility, the UEA group's neo-Marxist critique of the social disruptions and political complexities caused by rural road development in Nepal also coincided with a neoliberal paradigm shift in development practice towards the small, local, private, and individual rather than the grand, national, public, and social.

Implementing roads is a highly complex process, and the engineering challenges of road construction in Nepal are exceeded perhaps only by the social disruptions that they also create. On the one hand, it is clear that road developments are not socially flattening but, rather, produce and reproduce particular terrains of social unevenness (Campbell 2010). On the other hand, while a wide gap between the aspirations entangled with road development and the actual benefits of social transformation and economic opportunity they deliver is well evidenced (Blaikie et al. 1977), road development continues to be promoted and prioritized as a path to realize the dream of modernity and national integration that has long eluded Nepal.[4] Examining the archival record of this development trajectory, Rankin et al. point out that in Nepal, 'not a single development project has been issued that does not accord priority to road building, and on average transportation and communication infrastructure has comprised 24 percent of the national budget over the thirteen plans that have been issued since 1956' (2017: 43). Dating back to mid-century global liberalization programmes led by the World Bank and the Asian Development Bank that emphasized the centrality of road construction for development (Gurung 1969; World Bank 2006), roads

---

4   This pro-development enthusiasm resonates strongly with the current frenzy and craze for highway development in India as well; see Rankin and Simpson, this volume.

are still positioned front and centre in Nepal's more recent plans for national infrastructural connectivity (MoPIT 2016; Lewison and Murton 2020). As a result of these ongoing trends, road development maintains a political and discursive power in Nepal that continues to reshape social relations between the state and its citizens as well as a range of corporate and business parties between the Kathmandu state centre and trans-Himalayan borderlands.

In many rural municipalities, for example, development budgets have been heavily weighted by road projects, and elected mayors and municipal chairs frequently acquire and mobilize bulldozers for the construction of roads that meet their own agendas. Critical political economists in Nepal like Dipak Gyawali and Dinesh Paudel call this form of nepotistic road development 'bulldozer terrorism'[5] (Poudel 2019). Seeing as local government performance is largely measured on the basis of percentages of capital expenditure in 'visible development', a vicious circle has observably formed whereby roads provide a conspicuous material form of spending that is positively embraced and promoted as 'development and change'. More simply (if not cynically), the more money that is spent, particularly on roads, the more likely politicians are to be re-elected and contractors are to be evaluated as good performers.

Ultimately, both road construction and transportation in Nepal are advanced by state and private actors working in different ways, yet in our view a majority of interventions are motivated by liberal and neoliberal logics. Seeing the evolution of roads in Nepal as ongoing spaces of neoliberal governmentality (Ferguson and Gupta 2002), we build on Duffield's post-structuralist critique (2008) in the sections below to argue that road development itself constitutes a liberal mode of governance. Specifically, this liberal mode of governance is evident as rural populations become participants in new, transportation-based political economies while they are at the same time enrolled in the bureaucratic practices of the state (Painter 2006). Moreover, as both Khan (this volume) and Sarma (this volume) illustrate with respect to south-eastern Pakistan and 'remote' regions of the Northeast India-Myanmar-China borderlands, rural road projects at once advance national priorities of modernization via mobility while at the same time bring historically peripheral populations under the gaze of central state authorities and into the powerful fold of capitalist entrepreneurs alike. Throughout such processes, citizens of Nepal are likewise repositioned as new consumers of rural and privatized transportation infrastructure while

5   Personal communication with Dipak Gyawali (3 May 2019, Kathmandu) and Dinesh Paudel (5 April 2018, Washington, DC).

also rendered more vulnerable to risk as a consequence of new dependencies on the very vehicles that ply the roads so eagerly anticipated.

Pathways of neoliberalism: Transport syndicates in Nepal

In order to analyse the challenges and problems with road development in Nepal, it is important to understand how open market neoliberal economic systems transformed the political economy of relationships central to Nepal's public transportation sector. During the Panchayat regime (1960-1990), an oligarchic Nepalese state controlled both political and economic systems before the adoption of more neoliberal reforms upon the restoration of multiparty democracy in 1990. Neoliberal practice and ideology (Harvey 2007), having evolved as an extending hand of global market capitalism, has been perceived as a driving force for Nepal's rapid economic growth and development (Gyawali et al. 2016). At the same time, neoliberal practices have also been linked and equated to the objectives of a more open society, politically democratic and decentralized (Mahat 2005).

In line with the driving principles of open market neoliberalism, in the 1990s the private sector in Nepal was quickly welcomed into the public sphere. Having expanded rapidly into numerous sectors previously controlled by the central state – such as the production and distribution of public goods and services like electricity, which led to rampant and systematic corruption at the hands of the Nepal Electricity Board (Shrestha 2016) – the historically public transportation sector was rapidly privatized into a new commercial industry. Reflecting the widespread privatization of public utilities and other national companies, Nepal's transportation industry, in concert with an ever-expanding private sector, subsequently weakened the regulatory capacity of the state. In Nepal, like elsewhere, this transition to privatization also included a wide range of previously public sectors including education, healthcare, telecommunications, and more.

Problematically, by reducing state power to the logics and ideology of neoliberal restructuring, Nepal concurrently failed to build a functional open society. Having largely ignored the need to build strong democratic structures, neoliberal restructuring has at once undermined the capacity of the Nepali state and allowed elite actors, building on long-established patronage networks, to capture power that was not previously within the grasp of the private realm. In the case of the transportation sector in particular, severe state weakness perversely enabled the wider mobilization and control of syndicate bodies. This is especially evident in the failure of the Government of Nepal (GON) to implement laws and regulate the private sector in public transportation. The case of the Kavre accident, outlined below, is but one tragic example of this pattern.

In August 2016, a bus en route from Kathmandu to Kattike Deurali in Kavrepalanchok district (hereafter Kavre) drove off the road and plummeted 300 metres downhill to the Khaharekhola River in central Nepal, killing 27 people and leaving dozens of other passengers injured. For a bus with a capacity of 30-35 passengers, it was estimated that upwards of 95 people were travelling inside and on top of the vehicle (Phuyal 2016). Both overloaded with people and in poor condition, the bus was, as Sigdel heard many say (including Mugu in 2017 and 2020 as well as Tanahun in 2019) an 'accident waiting to happen'. Gopal Gartaula, reporting on the dramatic increase in road deaths across Nepal in 2018-2019, presents a compelling statistical analysis of fatal road accidents with the data received from Nepal's Traffic Police, noting that it 'is no longer correct to call them accidents, this is slaughter' (Gartaula 2019).

Highlighting the ways in which the operations of transport syndicates pose a mortal threat to ordinary Nepali citizens, national media picked up the story and broadcast widespread criticism with sensational headlines such as 'Highways of Death' (Phuyal 2016) and 'Road Kill' (Magar 2016). At the time, local citizens in Kavre had been lobbying for additional, and newer, buses to serve the rural transport network. However, rather than opening the sector for more vehicles – as the chronically overcrowded buses demonstrated was in short supply and high demand – the transport syndicates instead colluded to block the entry of new companies' services and vehicles to the local and regional routes.

Making matters worse, government authorities and transport operators legally responsible for transport policy as well as road safety are routinely intertwined with the very transport syndicates they are required to regulate. In Kavre, the poorly maintained vehicle was owned by the Himalayan Transport Committee (HTC).[6] While the HTC neglected to maintain its own vehicles, it also blocked entry to other transport operators for the same route. With no other companies able to operate on this road, and facing typically high passenger demands, the HTC and its drivers overloaded the bus and allowed extra passengers to ride on the roof.[7] As Nepali media revealed after the accident, the HTC had been repeatedly fined by the Ministry of Physical

6　Pseudonym.
7　It is worth noting that riding on the roof of buses, despite being illegal, is common in Nepal and is not unique to HTC.

Infrastructure and Transport (Department of Transport Management) for violating a host of regulations, from passenger overcapacity to expired vehicle registrations to unlicensed drivers. Having paid numerous fines, the HTC was also found to have bribed government officials and other regulators to both maintain its exclusive operation along the route and also to keep other operators off the road (Magar 2016).

In light of the Kavre accident, local actors rightly claimed exploitation at the hands of the powerful transport cartels. Moreover, many also criticized the GON for failing to control, manage, or break the syndicate system. In response, the GON announced plans to scrap the transportation syndicate and its association of entrepreneurs (Kathmandu Post 2018; Tamang 2018). While the entrepreneurs were urged to register as private companies under new government regulations, the power of the syndicates – enabled largely by close relationships with government elites – in fact allowed them to undermine broader government efforts to implement legal reforms and advance safer and more responsible transportation and road policies. Reflecting the enduring power of patronage networks in the region and across Nepal (Rankin et al. 2019), transport entrepreneurs ultimately formed their own associations and the blocs came to control all regional transport services, at once in clear view of but also outside the hands of government regulation. As a result, local citizens and everyday passengers remain in a precarious position still, vulnerable to and yet dependent on the very transportation operators who often value profit over life.

As is evident in Kavre – but similarly the case in numerous other districts across Nepal – the proliferation and power of transportation syndicates reveals how private industry has leveraged open market-oriented, neoliberal reforms to circumvent (and usurp) state control, consolidate wealth, and remarginalize already precarious populations. According to the Motor Vehicles and Transport Management Act, 2049, and the Motor Vehicles and Transport Management Rules, 2054 (Government of Nepal 1993, 1997), any individual or firm can apply for vehicle registration and public vehicle operation. Under standard terms of due process and legal provision, an authorization agency, having reviewed a given firm's application, registers and grants permission for a vehicle's operation. However, this is no longer the way transport regulation works in Nepal. Instead, powerfully positioned individuals and groups organize as transport associations and committees, or blocs, and in so doing, capture near total control of the market, though illegally. While authorized agencies may ask applicants to produce a consent letter from existing committees for registration and the operation of new public vehicles, the committees themselves routinely obstruct the operation

of new vehicles despite the vehicles having received legal consent for operation. Imposing different quid pro quo systems – a form of cronyism called
'turn by turn' in Nepal – these committees effectively control the market
and, in so doing, rule the operations of so-called 'public transport'. The
case of Kavre is again instructive here and indicative of a broader trend
with respect to the private ownership and deregulation of public transport
services on a national scale.

The reach of transport syndicates such as the HTC goes all the way down
(and up) to police constables and high-ranking politicians. As former Chief
Secretary Leela Mani Poudyal stated, 'everyone benefits from the syndicate.
[...] The Chief District Officer and the district police chief get Rs. 100,000 and
Rs. 80,000 each, every month, and politicians and bureaucrats do not want
to stop them because they also receive money' (Phuyal 2016). Organized
under the National Federation of Transport Entrepreneurs Nepal, transport
companies like HTC also establish welfare funds to support drivers who face
legal trouble, and, using the same funds to protect the cartels, also pay both
fines and bribes to GON politicians, the police, and other legal authorities.
As activist Premlal Maharjan points out, '[t]he syndicate holds the license
to kill people on the road' (Phuyal 2016).

The network of syndicate operators and their access and influence to
the higher echelons of political power have been strongly established and
extended to many senior politicians and all levels of government. In a public
forum in Kathmandu held in summer 2016, former Chief Secretary Poudyal
also stated that numerous associations of transport entrepreneurs invest
huge amounts of money to directly and indirectly support the syndicates'
existence (Magar 2016). These actors accumulate money from their members
for both 'welfare funds' and in support of new entrants. As the associations
mobilize funds to influence political parties and leaders, they also relocate
regulating mechanisms of the state to local 'dons', who then recirculate this
capital (in the form of both of cash and social relationships) as and when
needed (Sigdel 2016).

The existence and practices of transportation syndicates in Nepal is
both a result of a weak state and a symbol of state failure. In reviewing the
intersections of liberal reforms and road development over the past three
decades in Nepal, we can see that the 'market' has provided neither quality
services nor set competitive pricing for such services themselves; instead,
the private sector has undermined competitiveness across the country. This
has happened because service providers, generally expected to provide
similar kinds of goods and services, have instead formed associations that
facilitate their capture of unnecessary benefits through the establishment

of cartels and the creation of syndicates. And because the Nepali state has failed to regulate and control the illegal activities that shape and control public transportation, a small number of elite actors now control not just an open market system, but what is perceived to be – though in fact is not – an open society and democratic process as a whole.

As described more than a century ago in Europe, what we see happening in Nepal is precisely what Robert Michels theorized as the 'iron law of oligarchy' (Michels 1911), where citizens suffer from both state and market failure. Importantly, the transport syndicates in Nepal not only enable the capture and accumulation of capital by oligarchic elites; they also reinforce positions of precarity for already marginalized populations that depend on a dubious 'public' transportation sector that has been syndicated, if not altogether privatized. This dynamic constitutes a vicious and pernicious cycle, as people are forced to pay more money for low-quality, and often dangerous, goods and services. As such, the Kavre accident is but one example of egregious state weakness and relative fragility, a predicament worsened by the ongoing privatization of power under liberal forms of development, ergo neoliberal governmentality. These very kinds of market-led imperatives not only motivate cartels to hit targets and capture outsized profits by overcrowding buses; they also generate and reproduce new systems of risk, routinely characterized by insurance protection for some but surely not for others.

Living uninsured

Exacerbated by an ideology of deregulated neoliberal reforms (Harvey 2007) and amplified by market-led imperatives for growth, speed, and efficiency, an asymmetrical imbalance of insurance protection is one of the most structurally and physically violent ways in which local communities have been rendered more vulnerable by the proliferation of poor-quality roads and unsafe vehicles in Nepal today. Both truck drivers and bus passengers express common sentiments and resignation about the routine risks one faces when travelling along rural roads. Ramesh,[8] a truck driver in Karnali Province whom Sigdel met in spring 2017, drew a stark contrast between the risks faced by labourers (such as himself) and the profits earned by owners with respect to cargo transport along the new roads in Mugu. 'Who understands the sorrows and hardship of the drivers who have been driving

8   All names are pseudonyms (March 2017).

trucks "to survive", putting their life at risk every-minute?' Allowing that investors also face some risk, he added, but 'they are rich people [Nep. *hunekhane*]. They have their own businesses and they earn profits. They have been educating their kids in Surkhet, Nepalgunj, and Kathmandu. If they experience losses [accidents], they get their losses reimbursed through insurance, but we lose our lives.' Sighing deeply, Ramesh's frustration – if not resignation – also echoes the sentiments of many other people employed in the transport sector whom we encountered, where lethal hazards are a daily reality for all, and yet safety and insurance mechanisms exist primarily to protect the elite (Sigdel 2016).

Taking a biopolitical analysis to development, Duffield (2007) argues that a definitive product of today's global development industry, and the security-development nexus in particular, is the powerful duality between insured and uninsured life. Duffield recognizes this distinction to be one increasingly produced and maintained not only by states, but by development agencies, NGOs, and private companies that themselves benefit from the power held over uninsured life. This power is gained particularly through capital, both financial and social, and generated via development and industrial modernization. Echoing Ramesh's sentiments, in March 2017 a traveller named Krishna grounded Duffield's theorization as well, stating that 'to travel by bus is like buying one's death ticket'. For Krishna, motorized transport in Mugu brings acute fear and mortal risk into everyday life. Not only did Krishna recognize that 'the road is very narrow and risky', but he also noted there are very few alternative transportation options for travellers like himself, his family, and his friends. Acknowledging that buses are hazardously overcrowded and jeeps rarely operate according to a set schedule, and are thus not very good options either, he continued to add that 'the local bus and jeep association do not allow the trucks to pick up passengers and the trucks do not give you a ride either from this bazaar'. As such, travellers must risk riding on dangerous buses, wait for indeterminate periods for equally overcrowded jeeps, or leave the bazaar to hitch a ride with cargo trucks out of the view and reach of the powerful syndicates. While passengers must pay for their travel, they ultimately have very little safety or security protection, exposed both physically and financially to the uncertainties of road travel, every single day.

In the case of road development in Nepal, collusion between syndicates, state officials, and private contractors configures a powerful and profit-driven motive that dictates where roads are (and are *not*) built, by whom, for whom, and what vehicles can travel them. Ravinder reflected on this asymmetry of power and access with respect to construction and transportation in Mugu in 2017. 'Powerful people influence rural road construction in the districts. These people have access to power [like] political leaders, and having close connections to political parties and leaders, they can influence them to allocate more budget for building roads that connect their villages.' This consideration also echoed Ramesh's view that the risks associated with low-quality road construction (and limited vehicle options) adversely and unevenly affects the poor, and far more severely than it does for the wealthy, elite, and powerful. Recognizing the corrupt practices that take place in road-building projects, Ramesh did not hide his anger and despair.

Control of road-building contracts by corrupt actors, known locally as *gundas*, is but one more egregious example of the way this social-political-financial process operates. In Mugu, Sigdel observed how construction projects are won and lost – or more precisely bought and sold – in an illegal but routine practice (Nep. *milemato*) through collusion between contractors and state officials (see Rankin et al. 2019). First, contractors sit together and make bids. The bid 'winner' must then make a payment to the other contractors. However, it bears emphasizing here that there is no free competition, as the bidding is typically carried out by the arrangement of those involved (Nep. *milemoto garera thekka haalne garchhan*). Contractors mobilize their political capital and connections to local politicians as well as youth groups in order to win such biddings (Nep. *thekka*), and the lead mobilizer is known as the *thekedar*. Having observed this process many times over, numerous informants stated that such corrupt practice was a fundamental characteristic of 'development culture' in Mugu. Like regional transportation syndicates, rural road building in Mugu and elsewhere throughout Karnali Province – as a well-known collusion between private contractors and state officials – is also a key indicator of how neoliberal governmentality operates, via development, throughout Nepal.

Particularly under new models of neoliberal development, public-private connections between state bureaucracy and the open market are further advanced by what happens on the *side of the road* with respect to new transportation infrastructure projects. For example, in areas within close proximity to the 'new road' zone in Gamgadi bazaar and around Bhulbhule, an active (and at times chaotic) market has emerged and expanded. In tandem with shifting political economies, police posts have also been established to monitor market activities and manage traffic. On the one hand, police installations and other forms of state bureaucracy – particularly as it relates to security and revenue generation such as tax offices and customs quarantine houses – may not in fact guarantee impressive new levels of safety and security. However, on the other hand, such bureaucratic structures nevertheless represent the predictable patterns by which state formation takes shape alongside market growth, and vice versa, in a dialectical relationship of mobility and containment (see Murton 2017). Of course, in few places is this process more apparent than along new road projects.

The analytic of neoliberal governmentality is again instructive for understanding how such an uneven, lucrative, and hazardous system has evolved in Nepal, and why. In addition to fundamental, profit-driven motives, it can be seen that state bureaucrats and private contractors – both the *thekedar* and more ethical business entrepreneurs alike, often with the support of NGO experts – effectively 'conduct the conduct' of populations through the implementation of new transportation networks. While a fairly universal phenomenon, in the specific context of Nepal this process of governmentality includes where new roads are built, what types of public or private vehicles operate there, with what kind of regularity, and how local travellers (or consumers) actually get around.

While ultimately intended as a classic development intervention of improvement to provide mobility and modernization to rural districts and their local communities, such projects in fact reinforce and reproduce conditions of marginality for populations already marginalized in both spatial and social contexts. Thus, while many development projects are visible and experienced as policy programmes and economic investments sponsored by a range of stakeholders, they also comprise a particular transport-oriented iteration of what Duffield identifies as a development-security nexus (2007; 2008) and we propose might be reformulated more specifically as an 'infrastructure-security nexus'. As such, while these interventions advance the perennial liberal project of progress and improvement in Nepal, they cannot be divorced from numerous unintended negative consequences, of which the heaviest burden is almost always borne by the poor.

Life on the margins of the roads and the state

In Mustang, local narratives also explain how roads are experienced as convenient and economical for some lucky residents, but alienating and marginalizing for many others. Jigme tersely expressed this reality to Murton during conversation outside his small shop in the historical trading centre of Kagbeni Mustang in August 2014: 'If you are poor, the road makes you poorer.' As a man without the means to own a private vehicle, and without the cash liquidity to charter a jeep to carry goods to his store from either the bazaars in southern Tibet or urban shops in central Nepal, Jigme has become increasingly dependent on public transportation networks that do not keep reliable schedules. In addition to creating new costs that he formerly avoided by walking with his goods loaded onto mules, Jigme described how new roads in fact make life harder in Mustang. While cargo costs are ultimately lower for truck transport than for mule caravans, the unpredictability of road travel adds additional hardship to what was previously a more dependable journey. 'Before [when we walked], you knew how long a trip to Beni or Pokhara would take, and you planned for that [ten to twelve days]. Today, it might take you two days, or it might take you two weeks. We never know.' Jigme emphasized the point that not only are transport schedules overwhelming unreliable, but that only the wealthy own vehicles and, when the rich travel by bus, they are also the ones to routinely secure seats (by paying more or leveraging their social connection).

The expansion of vehicle-dependent travel, coupled with transitions to more cash-based economic relations, has shifted the terms of engagement by which citizens in Mustang experience and struggle for access to roads, vehicles, and markets themselves. While talking about the social and economic impacts of new roads, another interlocutor named Dorje reminisced fondly for the days when the only choice of transport was mule or yak caravan.[9]

> It took longer, but it was easier to travel before the road came. We had our animals, and our *nyetsang* [fictive kin],[10] and we could plan for the journey. Now, it is harder to plan, and everything is more expensive. In some ways the roads have made things easier [for those with money], but in other ways the road made it more difficult [for people like me].

In previous years, Dorje could predictably plan for a trip from Kagbeni to Pokhara, knowing that it would be long and arduous, but that ten to twelve days was a reliable and dependable projected time frame for the trip. Today, in contrast, while it is quick (and costly) to reach Pokhara in just two days by jeep and bus, Dorje does not control his own movement. Reflecting and compounding a withering of *nyetsang* practice, if a vehicle does not come on time – or for that matter, doesn't come that day, or the next – Dorje is

---

9 Mustang, April 2015.
10 Historically, *nyetsang* ('fictive kin', Tib. *gnas tshang*) are fictive kin relationships maintained in the trans-Himalaya region that provide lodging, food and local security for travellers as well as fodder or grazing ground for their animals. The *nyetsang* network has nearly collapsed as a result of new road-based mobilities in Nepal and Tibet. See Murton 2018.

stuck, with a load that he can't carry alone, and subject to expenses that he must absorb himself or else go hungry and cold.

Jigme and Dorje's points are that motorized transport tests – and at times steals – one's agency. The impacts are asymmetrical and hierarchical, both tracing and reinforcing class distinctions, negatively affecting the poor while benefiting the wealthy. When a truck breaks down, and you have no other means of travel, nor *nyetsang* relations in a nearby village, you have little recourse than to pay for lodging until another vehicle comes by, and that may be in three hours or three days. Thus, if you are poor, road travel makes everything more difficult, and thereby can ultimately make you even poorer. Conversely, however, if you own a vehicle, or have the means to charter a private jeep, or at least sufficient disposable income to pay for lodging when necessary, motorized transport is perceived and lived very differently. That is, the roads are preferable and opportune for a privileged few and debilitating and frustrating for many others. Despite this distinction, however, elite members of Mustang society also complain about the roads.

Throughout Mustang, it is widely acknowledged that new roads have also negatively impacted foreign trekking tourism. Whereas Jigme and Dorje were open with their complaints about the effects of *road transport* on everyday life, Murton also heard far more grievances about the *road itself* – and its apparently negative impacts on business – from hotel owners such as Drolma, who stated, matter-of-factly, 'nobody stops and stays anymore'.[11] For entrepreneurs who have been running guesthouses and restaurants for nearly three decades, a widespread perception is that road travel is hurting business. Such critiques of the roads were widely voiced by those central to Mustang's tourism economy – the historically established and wealthier socioeconomic class of noble families and large land owners who had the savings and capital assets to invest in the new tourism industry in the 1990-2000s. However, such complaints are also somewhat ironic, as they are predominantly voiced by the very same people who own the vehicles, guest lodges, and cash reserves to invest in both tourism and transport systems, which in turn affords an accumulation and reinvestment of capital in new road-related political economies.

In addition to the collapse of fictive kin networks such as *nyetsang* (Murton 2018) and conflicting perspectives on the effects of roads on tourism, road-based travel has also transformed livelihood and consumption practices in the historically agro-pastoralist and trade-oriented spaces of both Gandaki and Karnali Provinces. Similar to import substitution – one

11   Mustang, August 2014.

of the hallmark effects of neoliberal restructuring policies in the developing world – road travel and the new access and mobility of goods and people has had a profound impact on what people grow, eat, and trade in both districts. In Karnali's Gamgadi, where there are now direct connections to the urban centres of Surket and Nepalganj, many such changes are apparent in everyday life. Though people regularly complain that the road is not good, mobility has increased, and some informants also said that it has generally made 'everyday life easier'.[12]

In Mugu, for example, where food insecurity has been an acute concern for decades, people no longer need to queue for days at the office of the Nepal Food Corporation. Instead, new provisions reach the open market by road and the foodstuffs are bought and sold with cash in the bazaar. Amidst a rapidly expanding marketplace that exists in both physical and social forms, many other modern facilities also proliferate, such as hotels, computer institutes, banks, NGOs, and new state bureaucracies. Unprecedented options exist to buy a range of rice varieties, dals, and oils, but the quality varies greatly. In fact, while quantity abounds, our interlocutors time and again emphasized that quality is overwhelmingly lacking. Much like in Mustang, many consumers in Mugu complain that expired rice (Nep. *samaya kateko*) – often imported from China – is often sold at discount on the market. And in regions with severe limitations on income generation, lower-quality Chinese rice is often the only viable purchase option, despite its limited nutritional value.

Moreover, in local economies historically dependent on agriculture as well as international and national welfare schemes such as rural food aid, access to cash in order to purchase foodstuffs, even expired goods, is not easy to come by in the first place. As land values along the roads escalate, many former farming families have sold land, but profits quickly vanish if not reinvested strategically and sustainably. As such, rather than growing one's own crops and trading surplus goods in exchange for other needs – a historical model of subsistence livelihoods in the trans-Himalaya – new dependencies on import and substitution have emerged. Importantly, it is key to note that this dependency exists across a range of class and demographic distinctions, including more elite district administrators of Mugu and Mustang as well as the historically agricultural, pastoralist, and trading families throughout the region.

Reflecting widespread grievances about the uneven impacts of new transportation systems on agriculture, tourism, and other political economies,

12   Mugu, September 2017.

it is evident that road travel – and concomitant paradoxical limitations on mobility – in fact reinforces rather than recalibrates social and economic hierarchies in Mustang and Mugu today. For those with more money, roads are expedient, and travel by vehicle is easy; but for those without sufficient cash to go by road, it is quite the opposite experience. Transportation requires money in cash or credit, and for communities historically dependent on subsistence agriculture and regional trade and whose livelihoods have been remarkably penetrated by liberal modes of governance and wider neoliberal logics predicated on capitalist relations, access to liquid cash or immediate credit can be uneven and tenuous. Enabling a few elites while excluding a majority of others, rural roads in Nepal truly function largely as vectors for commodity consumption, trans-local tourism, and out-migration rather than as the great social equalizers they are so often claimed to be (World Bank 2006; Gurung 2005; Blaikie et al. 1976; see also Heslop and Murton, this volume, as well as Rankin and Simpson, this volume).

Conclusion

In this chapter, we examine how new mobility systems are shaped by neoliberal structures and perpetuate the violence of social exclusion across several northern districts in Nepal. In so doing, we show that road infrastructures, transport syndicates, cash-based political economies, and bureaucratic institutions converge and transform everyday life, reinforce social hierarchies, and produce complex new configurations of state formation and private enterprise throughout the country. In other words, roads at once generate both change and stasis (Heslop and Murton, this volume), motility and hierarchy, or mobility and containment in both social and physical terms (Murton 2017). More importantly, experience with this dynamic is not limited to Nepal's northern and western districts of Mustang, Mugu, and Kavre; rather, the process has become nearly ubiquitous throughout Nepal and, of course, elsewhere in South Asia, too (see Gohain, this volume; Sarma, this volume). Alongside changes to socio-spatial and cultural practices, roads – not unlike disasters (Smith 2006) and other disruptive events – consistently deepen the ruts of social and spatial difference that they encounter. As shown elsewhere (Stewart 1996), rather than making new connections altogether, road access in fact shifts relations that reverberate with profound exclusions and disruptions. Thus, the problem – and paradox – is that while roads are often sold as great equalizers and vectors for capacity building (World Bank 2006; Taaffe et al. 1963), it is in fact just the opposite experience of social and physical exclusion as well as hierarchical reinscription that defines life by the road for many (Campbell 2010). That is, new mobilities reinforce old margins, in Nepal as almost everywhere else.

The expectation that roads will deliver social and economic development – or *bikas* in Nepal's national development imaginary (Shrestha 1995; Pigg 1992) – to the hills is ambitious but material progress and national modernization does not come so easily or evenly. As we analyse above, the social dynamics that roads set in motion via new political economies frequently trace old tracks of social division. This is not to say that the imagined benefits which undergird the development discourse – such as the material and ideological realization of growth, mobility, and modernization – do not reach a fortunate few. More often than not, however, roads instead serve to reinforce a certain socioeconomic status quo that continues to privilege the already privileged. Alongside these social reinscriptions, modern road systems also contribute to shifting livelihoods, the creation of new economic relationships, and the implementation of *dispositifs* of governmentality and techniques by which the Nepali state bureaucratizes and territorializes national space.

Reflecting on this reality and recognizing the very real desire, and need, for better transport connectivity in Nepal, we do *not* insist that roads are a bad thing for rural regions. To the contrary, there is good reason that rural roads have been dreamed and demanded for decades (Gurung 1969; see also Rankin and Simpson, this volume). However, to make the conditions for better lives on and alongside Nepal's new roads, what is necessary is a more responsible and critical engagement with road development from and for all constituents. This should and must include the state officials and regional bureaucrats who promote transportation networks, the contractors and developers who construct them, and the everyday people and national citizens who want them. Ultimately, it is a problem, and power, of will. As authors – one an academic (Murton) and another a professional instructor at the Government of Nepal Administrative Staff College (Sigdel), we feel it is imperative to speak not only to fellow academics but also to constituencies across Nepal's public sphere as well as government officials. In so doing, we hope to possibly help effect a more positive impact on development patterns and processes in Nepal. That is, without strong voices from civil society, in tandem with political will and commitment, strong policies will fail to function, and the vicious cycles where roads 'make one poorer' and are tantamount to 'buying one's death ticket' will perpetuate.

Yet the reproduction of marginality and mobility injustice (Cook and Butz 2016) is not a given or foregone conclusion, and change can and should happen.

In Karnali and Gandaki, like elsewhere, connectivity is, of course, a primary condition for the development of both the nation and its people – widely articulated as *bikas* or modernity in ideological, social, and structural forms. But development as a practice and an industry has failed the Nepali people for decades (Fujikura 2013). Rather than continuing to follow long-established but consistently problematic paradigms, the Government of Nepal, in concert with other stakeholders, must implement development projects that address and anticipate the underdevelopment and inequality that exist in society and that are reinforced via neoliberal policy and irresponsible investment. That is, 'real' change requires structural change, inclusive of social systems, welfare, standardizations, and planning; it is a different kind of development intervention that needs to be both procedural *and* substantive.

In the case of transportation systems as a preliminary point of change, it is necessary to mobilize effective state mechanisms that not only break down syndicate networks but that also dissolve and redistribute the density of power relations and capital accumulated in longstanding patronage networks. The future political economic relationships and development of Nepal's central and western districts, and all the provinces in the newly federated nation more widely, depends on how the government, local people, and other stakeholders can reimagine and operationalize the immense opportunities created by road networks. Effective participation, cooperation, and strong coordination is a smart and viable first step on the long path to correct the derailed course of liberalism in Nepal.

List of works cited

Blaikie, P., J. Cameron and D. Seddon (1977). *The Effects of Roads in West Central Nepal: A Summary.* Norwich: University of East Anglia.

Blaikie, P., J. Cameron and D. Seddon (1979). *The Struggle for Basic Needs in Nepal.* Paris: OECD Development Centre.

Blaikie, P., J. Cameron and D. Seddon (1980). *Nepal in Crisis.* Oxford: Oxford University Press.

Blaikie, P., J. Cameron, D. Feldman, A. Fournier and D. Seddon (1976). *The Effects of Roads in West Central Nepal.* 3 vols. Norwich: Overseas Development Group, University of East Anglia.

Campbell, B. (2010). 'Rhetorical Routes for Development: A Road Project in Nepal'. *Contemporary South Asia* 18(3): 267-279.

Campbell, B. (2013). 'From Remote Area to Thoroughfare of Globalisation: Shifting Territorialisations of Development and Border Peasantry in Nepal'. In *Territorial*

Changes and Territorial Restructurings in the Himalayas, ed. by J. Smadja. New Delhi: Adroit Publishers, 269-285.

Chambers, R. (1983). *Rural Development: Putting the Last First*. Essex: Longmans Scientific and Technical Publishers.

Chandler, D. (2007). The Security-Development Nexus and the Rise of 'Anti-Foreign Policy'. *Journal of International Relations and Development* 10(4): 362-386.

Cook, N., and D. Butz (2016). 'Mobility Justice in a Time of Disaster'. *Mobilities* 11(3): 400-419. DOI: 10.1080/17450101.2015.1047613.

Corbridge, S., G. Williams, M. Srivastava and R. Véron (2005). *Seeing the State: Governance and Governmentality in India*. Cambridge: Cambridge University Press.

Department of Roads (2019). *Strategic Road Network 2017-18*. Kathmandu: Government of Nepal.

Duffield, M. (2007). 'Development, Territories, and People: Consolidating the External Sovereign Frontier'. *Alternatives: Global, Local, Political* 32(2): 225-246.

Duffield, M. (2008). *Development, Security, and Unending War*. Cambridge: Polity Press.

Duffield, M. (2010). 'The Liberal Way of Development and the Development-Security Impasse: Exploring the Global Life-Chance Divide'. *Security Dialogue* 41(1): 53-76.

Ferguson, J., and A. Gupta (2002). 'Spatializing States: Toward an Ethnography of Neoliberal Governmentality'. *American Ethnologist* 29(4): 981-1002.

Flower, J.M. (2004). 'A Road Is Made: Roads, Temples, and Historical Memory in Ya'an County, Sichuan'. *Journal of Asian Studies* 63(3): 649-685.

Fluri, J. (2011). 'Bodies, Bombs, and Barricades: Gendered Geographies of In(security)'. *Transactions of the Institute of British Geographers* 36(3): 280-296.

Foucault, M. (1991). 'Governmentality'. In *The Foucault Effect: Studies in Governmentality*, ed. by G. Burchell, C. Gordon and P. Miller. Chicago: University of Chicago Press, 87-104.

Fujikura, T. (2013). *Discourses of Awareness*. Kathmandu: Martin Chautari.

Gartaula, G. (2019). 'Nepal's Deadly Roads Take Their Toll'. *Nepali Times*, 18 January. https://www.nepalitimes.com/banner/nepals-deadly-roads-take-their-toll/ (accessed 1 October 2020).

Government of Nepal (1993). *Motor Vehicles and Transport Management Act, 2049*. https://www.lawcommission.gov.np/en/archives/category/documents/prevailing-law/statutes-acts/motor-vehicles-and-transport-management-act-2049-1993 (accessed 10 April 2021).

Government of Nepal (1997). *Motor Vehicles and Transport Management Rules, 2054*. https://www.lawcommission.gov.np/en/wp-content/uploads/2018/09/motor-vehicles-and-transport-management-rules-2054-1997.pdf (accessed 10 April 2021).

Gupta, A. (2012). *Red Tape: Bureaucracy, Structural Violence, and Poverty in India*. Durham, NC: Duke University Press.

Gupta, A., and J. Ferguson (1997). *Culture, Power, Place*. Durham, NC: Duke University Press.

Gurung, H. (1969). *Regional Development Planning for Nepal*. No. 1. Kathmandu: National Planning Commission, His Majesty's Government of Nepal.

Gurung, H. (2005). 'Nepal Regional Strategy for Development'. Working Paper Series No. 3, Nepal Resident Mission, June. Asian Development Bank. http://hdl.handle.net/11540/3289 (accessed 10 April 2021).

Gyawali, D., M. Thompson and M. Verweij (2016). *Aid, Technology, and Development: The Lessons from Nepal*. London: Routledge.

Hagen, T. (1994). *Building Bridges to the Third World*. Delhi: Book Faith India.

Hagen, T. (2012). *Decentralization and Development*. Kathmandu: Ratna Pustak Bhandar.

Harvey, D. (2007). *A Brief History of Neoliberalism*. Oxford: Oxford University Press.

Harvey, P. (2016). 'Introduction'. In 'Attention to Infrastructure Offers a Welcome Reconfiguration of Anthropological Approaches to the Political', ed. by S. Venkatesan, L. Bear, P. Harvey, S. Lazar, L. Rival and A. Simone, *Critique of Anthropology* 38(1): 1-50.

Harvey, P., and H. Knox (2012). 'The Enchantments of Infrastructure'. *Mobilities* 7(4): 521-536.

Harvey, P., and H. Knox (2015). *Roads: An Anthropology of Infrastructure and Expertise*. Ithaca, NY: Cornell University Press.

HMG (2020). His Majesty's Government vs Pūrva-Paśim Rājmārga ra Hāmro Kartavya. Kathmandu: Ministry of Panchayat, His Majesty's Government of Nepal.

IBRD 1965. *A National Transport System for Nepal: Including an Investment Program for the Third Plan 1965/66-1969/70*. Washington, DC: International Bank for Reconstruction and Development and Government of Nepal.

Kathmandu Post (2018). 'Govt, Transport Entrepreneurs Agree to End Syndicate'. *Kathmandu Post*, 7 May. https://kathmandupost.com/national/2018/05/07/transport-ministry-transport-entrepreneurs agree-to-end-syndicate (accessed 1 October 2020).

Klare, M. (2001). *Resource Wars: The New Landscape of Global Conflict*. New York: Henry Holt.

Lewison, E., and G. Murton (2020). 'Geographical Scholarship in Nepal: Sustainability, Infrastructure, Disaster and Power'. *Studies in Nepali History and Society (SINHAS)* 25(1): 15-58.

Li, T.M. (2007). *The Will to Improve: Governmentality, Development, and the Practice of Politics*. Durham, NC: Duke University Press.

Liechty, M. (1997). 'Selective Exclusion: Foreigners, Foreign Goods, and Foreignness in Modern Nepali History'. *Studies in Nepali History and Society (SINHAS)* 2(1): 5-68.

Magar, S.G. (2016). 'Highways of Death'. *Nepali Times* #823, 26 August-1 September. http://himalaya.socanth.cam.ac.uk/collections/journals/nepalitimes/pdf/Nepali_Times_823.pdf (accessed 10 April 2021).

Mahat, R.S. (2005). *In Defense of Democracy: Dynamics and Fault Lines of Nepal's Political Economy.* New Delhi: Adroit.

Michels, R. (1911). *Zur Soziologie des Parteiwesens in der modernen Demokratie* [On the sociology of the party system in modern democracy]. Leipzig: Klinkhardt.

MoPIT (2016). *5 Year Plan for Transportation Infrastructure Development.* Kathmandu: Ministry of Physical Infrastructure and Transport, Government of Nepal.

Mostowlansky, T. (2017). *Azan on the Moon: Entangling Modernity along Tajikistan's Pamir Highway.* Pittsburgh: University of Pittsburgh Press.

Murton, G. (2017). 'Making Mountain Places into State Spaces: Infrastructure, Consumption, and Territorial Practice in a Himalayan Borderland'. *Annals of the American Association of Geographers* 107(2): 536-545. DOI: 10.1080/24694452.2016.1232616.

Murton, G. (2018). 'Nobody Stops and Stays Anymore: Motor Roads, Uneven Mobilities, and Conceptualizing Borderland Modernity in Highland Nepal'. In *The Routledge Handbook of Asian Borderlands*, ed. by A. Horstmann, M. Saxer and A. Rippa. London: Routledge, 315-324.

Murton, G. (2019). 'Facing the Fence: The Production and Performance of a Himalayan Border in Global Contexts'. *Political Geography* 72: 31-42. DOI: https://doi.org/10.1016/j.polgeo.2019.03.001.

Painter, J. (2006). 'Prosaic Geographies of Stateness'. *Political Geography* 25(7): 752-774.

Paudel, D. (2018). 'Bulldozing Democracy'. *Nepali Times*, 6 July. https://www.nepalitimes.com/editorial/bulldozing-democracy-2/ (accessed 23 February 2019).

Paudel, D., and P. Le Billon (2018). 'Geo-logics of Power: Disaster Capitalism, Himalayan Materialities, and the Geopolitical Economy of Reconstruction in Post-Earthquake Nepal'. *Geopolitics* 25(4): 838-866. https://doi.org/10.1080/14650045.2018.1533818.

Peet, R., and E. Hartwick (2015). *Theories of Development: Contentions, Arguments, Alternatives.* New York: Guilford Press.

Phuyal, S. (2016). 'Road Kill'. *Nepali Times* #790, 8-14 January. https://archive.nepalitimes.com/article/nation/traffic-accidents-continue-to-increase-worryingly-in-Nepal,2799 (accessed 11 February 2019).

Pigg, S.L. (1992). 'Inventing Social Categories through Place: Social Representations and Development in Nepal'. *Comparative Studies in Society and History* 34: 491-513.

Poudel, U. (2019). 'Nepal's Development Model Has Increased Our Dependency'. *Himalayan Times*, 16 July. https://thehimalayantimes.com/business/nepals-development-model-has-increased-our-dependency/ (accessed 1 October 2020).

Rankin, K.N., P. Hamal, E. Lewison and T.S. Sigdel (2019). 'Corruption as a Diagnostic of Power: Navigating the Blurred Boundaries of the Relational State'. *South Asia: Journal of South Asian Studies* 42(5): 920-936. https://doi.org/10.1080/008 56401.2019.1644470.

Rankin, K.N., T.S. Sigdel, L. Rai, S. Kunwar and P. Hamal (2017). 'Political Economies and Political Rationalities of Road Building in Nepal'. *Studies in Nepali History and Society (SINHAS)* 22(1): 43-84.

Reid, J. (2012). 'The Disastrous and Politically Debased Subject of Resilience'. *Development Dialogue* 58: 67-79.

Roberts, S., A. Secor and M. Sparke (2003). 'Neoliberal Geopolitics'. *Antipode* 35(3): 886-897.

Rose, L. (1971). *Nepal: Strategy for Survival*. Berkeley: University of California Press.

Scott, J.C. (1998). *Seeing Like a State: How Certain Schemes to Improve the Human Condition Have Failed*. New Haven, CT: Yale University Press.

Shrestha, N. (1995). 'Becoming a Development Category'. In *Power of Development*, ed. by J. Crush. London: Routledge, 276-287.

Shrestha, S. (2016). 'Speaking Truth to Power'. *Nepali Times* #836, 9-15 December. https://archive.nepalitimes.com/article/nation/corruption-in-electricity-industry-of-Nepal,3408 (accessed 1 October 2020).

Sigdel, T.S. (2016a). 'Kamjor Rajya Ra Baliyo Syndicate' ['Weak state and strong syndicate']. *Baarhakhari*. http://baahrakhari.com/news-details/4131/12khari (accessed 26 August 2019).

Sigdel, T.S. (2016b). 'Karnaalima Sadak: Artha-Raajnitik Sambandha Ra Bikaas' ['The road in Karnali: Politico-economic relations and development?']. *Baarhakhari*. http://baahrakhari.com/news-details/492/12khari (accessed 6 July 2019).

Smith, N. (2006). 'There's No Such Thing as a Natural Disaster'. *Items*, 11 June. https://items.ssrc.org/understanding-katrina/theres-no-such-thing-as-a-natural-disaster/ (accessed 10 April 2021).

Smith, N. (2008). *Uneven Development: Nature, Capital and the Production of Space*. Athens: University of Georgia Press.

Stewart, K. (1996). *A Space on the Side of the Road: Cultural Poetics in an 'Other' America*. Princeton, NJ: Princeton University Press.

Taaffe, E.J., R. Morrill and P. Gould (1963). 'Transport Expansion in Underdeveloped Countries: A Comparative Analysis'. *Geographical Review* 53 (4): 503-529.

Tamang, R.S. (2018). 'Govt Promises Tough Measures to End Transport Syndicate'. *My Republica*, 2 April. https://myrepublica.nagariknetwork.com/news/govt-promises-tough-measures-to-end-transport-syndicate/ (accessed 1 October 2020).

Wilson, F. (2004). 'Towards a Political Economy of Roads: Experiences from Peru'. *Development and Change* 35(3): 525-546.

World Bank (2006). *Infrastructure at the Crossroads: Lessons From 20 Years of World Bank Experience*. Washington, DC: World Bank Group (The International Bank for Reconstruction and Development).

World Bank and International Development Association (1968). *Annual Report 1968*. Washington, DC: World Bank Group. http://documents.worldbank.org/curated/en/899001468142184968/World-Bank-International-Development-Association-annual-report-1968 (accessed 1 October 2020).

About the authors

GALEN MURTON is Assistant Professor of Geographic Science at James Madison University in Harrisonburg, Virginia, US. His work is primarily concerned with the politics of large-scale infrastructure development throughout the Himalayas and especially in the borderlands of Nepal, India, and the Tibetan regions of China.

TULASI SIGDEL is Senior Director of Studies at Nepal Administrative Staff College. He is also associated with research project entitled 'Infrastructures of Democracy: State Building as Everyday Practice in Nepal's Agrarian Districts'. His areas of research interest are cultural politics, democracy, governance and administration in Nepal.

3 A road to the 'hidden place'

Road building and state formation in Medog, Tibet

Yi Huang

Abstract

Medog County, located in the southeast of Tibet, was the last county inaccessible by road in China and was widely described as 'a lotus in the hidden place'. The Medog Highway, linking Medog with the rest of the country, was constructed first in 1994 and, following years of landslides and natural disasters, completed for the second time in 2013. Utilizing ethnographic insights into the usage and non-usage of the Medog Highway, this chapter reveals how the road was constructed and used in specific political, social and cultural contexts. In terms of state formation, the road was not only used as a material infrastructure to integrate the Medog people and a strategic investment of international politics, but also as a discursive symbol to enhance the state's legitimacy to the whole nation. This chapter argues that, besides connection and integration, two other techniques – channelling and filtering – are also constitutive of state formation via road construction. With this road, goods and ideas connected to broader processes of globalization were also channelled into the area, producing both asymmetric connectivity and one-way integration. Furthermore, control and surveillance have also increased after the completion of the road, resulting in both proactive and reactive state efforts to evict unwelcome activities. Producing not only connectivity but also new disconnectivity and social exclusion, I therefore describe the Medog Highway as 'a punctuated road'.

Keywords: Tibet, China, state formation, connectivity, integration

Introduction

Medog County was the last county inaccessible by road in China. The completion of the Medog Highway ends Medog County's history of

Heslop, Luke, and Galen Murton (eds), *Highways and Hierarchies: Ethnographies of Mobility from the Himalaya to the Indian Ocean*. Amsterdam, Amsterdam University Press 2021
DOI: 10.5117/9789463723046_CH03

inaccessibility. With the concerns of the central government, a motorway
began to be built in 1975, however, the construction project was suspended
until 1988. With the approval in 1988 and 1990, the road was extended and
is completed today. The road has great political and economic significance.
The starting point of the Medog Highway is Zhamu Township in Bomi
County, and the 142-kilometre-long route ends in the county seat of Medog
County. This road climbs over the Galongla Snow Mountain, and crosses
the geologically complex regions of the Galongla Zangbu River Valley and
the Jinzhu Zangbu River Valley. The mountains are very high and the
valleys are deep along the route, with an average annual rainfall of over
2500 mm in this region as well as many extraordinarily serious natural
disasters, such as mudflows, torrents, landslides, avalanches and so on.
Governments at all levels and relevant units attached great importance
and offered strong support to the extension project of the Medog Highway
in 1990. The commanding officers, construction workers, engineers and
technicians were fearless of dangers and difficulties, and worked hard
for the construction of this road. The Medog masses said gratefully: 'Only
the Chinese Communist Party has the ability to build a road to Medog!'
The completion of the Medog Highway is the second liberation of all
ethnic groups in Medog. The completion of the road marks a new era in
the development of Medog's productivity.
– Text on a monument erected by the Department of Transportation of
Nyingchi Prefecture, Tibet Autonomous Region, 1 January 1994

The opening piece of text is from a monument built at the starting point
of the Medog Highway and translated from Chinese.[1] The monument was
erected by the Department of Transportation of Nyingchi Prefecture in 1994
to celebrate the first-time completion of the Medog Highway and describes
part of the road-building history into Medog.

Medog (in Mandarin Chinese, *Motuo*) County is located in the southeast of
Tibet, and is one of the six counties of Nyingchi (in Mandarin Chinese, *Linzhi*,
a prefecture-level city in Tibet that governs Medog County). As is evident
from the monument text, Medog County was the last county inaccessible by
road in China. Due to its long-time inaccessibility by road, Medog is widely

---

1   Throughout this chapter, the author has closely translated the unique political and bureaucratic language used by the Chinese Communist Party into English. Therefore, some sentences
of the translation may look strange for those readers unfamiliar with the conventions of literal
translation of Mandarin into the English language.

described as 'the lotus in the hidden place' (*mijing lianhua*),[2] imagined as a virgin land that has not yet been polluted by modern civilization. Medog is also popularly identified as 'an isolated island in the plateau' (*gaoyuan gudao*), referring to the hardship of isolation during the long period without road connections. An editorial published in *Zhongguo Gonglu* (Highway of China, a magazine sponsored by the Ministry of Transport of China) in October 2013 describes the lives of the Medog people before the completion of the Medog Highway as follows:

> Before the completion of the road, for the Medog people, this 100-kilo-metre-long route represents the isolation from the world and the endless dangers. Every year the god of death came to those who brought supplies and goods on their backs from outside – those porters who carried the hopes of Medog staggered in the snow and heavy rain. However, the prices of goods were still very high in Medog, life was extremely inconvenient, and the social development had stagnated. [...] To build a highway into Medog has been the dream of the Medog people for generations.

Medog County had a population of over 11,000 in 2012. Menba and Luoba (rather than Tibetan) people comprise the largest ethnic groups (together totalling about 80 percent of the population) in Medog (MTXWXCB 2012). Menba and Luoba are two of the 55 officially identified ethnic minorities in China, and Luoba has the smallest population (2965) among the 56 ethnic groups in China (SEACoPRC 2014a), while according to the Sixth National Population Census of the People's Republic of China, in 2000 Menba has a population of 8923 (SEACoPRC 2014b).

Menba and Luoba people in Medog have their own languages, but they also start to learn Mandarin Chinese and Tibetan in primary school from first grade, and study English in class from third grade (see also Wang 2011: 101). According to the author's and informants' mutual language abilities and popular conventions in the region, the author conducted his fieldwork primarily in Mandarin Chinese in Medog, and informants provided their Mandarin Chinese names throughout daily dialogues in Medog. Therefore, in this chapter, Mandarin Chinese Pinyin pseudo-names are given to all the informants (including Menba, Luoba, and Han Chinese).

The average elevation of Medog County is only 1200 metres and the average annual temperature is 16°C. (For relative comparison, the average elevation

---

2   In Tibetan, *medog* means 'flower' or 'bloom'. The lotus is a flower commonly associated with Buddhism, and the Medog region was also formerly known as Pemako ('Lotus Array').

of the Tibet Autonomous Region – or TAR – is more than 4000 metres with significantly colder temperatures throughout the TAR.) Unlike other parts of the Qinghai-Tibet Plateau, Medog has a typical subtropical monsoon climate, which includes heavy rainfall across the region. In Medog, rainfall accumulation reaches over 4000 mm annually, compared to just 600 mm in Beijing.

Landslides and mudflows caused by the huge rainfall brought by the Indian Ocean monsoon were key components of the huge obstacles that long complicated building a road into Medog. As the monument erected by the Department of Transportation of Nyingchi notes, construction of the Medog Highway began in 1975 and was completed for the first time in 1994. However, the road was soon destroyed by mudflows and landslides. After the announcement of the road's completion, it was often referred to as 'being open to traffic for only one day', such was the severity of the landslides.

In October 2008, the State Council of China approved a new construction project for the Medog Highway with the investment of 950 million yuan. This new construction project was initiated in April 2009 and the project finally cost 1.6 billion yuan (the Nyingchi Prefecture's GDP in 2013 was 8.36 billion yuan). On 17 October 2013, the government announced the completion of the Medog Highway for the second time. This time, a key tunnel was built to allow the road to go through the 4800-metre-tall Galongla Mountain instead of climbing over it, guaranteeing nearly year-round connectivity of the road.

Medog borders Arunachal Pradesh, India. The Chinese government has had a border dispute in this area with India for nearly 60 years, and over two-thirds of the territory of Medog County claimed by China are under the control of India (and part of the area controlled by China is also claimed by the Indian government) (for a thorough account of this dispute, see Gohain 2019; 2020). This particular border contestation is part of the dubious legacy of the McMahon Line, a disputed Sino-Indian (Tibetan-India) border line proposed by British colonial administrator Henry McMahon in 1914, which also further links the area to complicated colonial and post-colonial histories across Highland Asia and trans-Himalayan spaces in Tibet, China, India, and Nepal (Plachta and Murton forthcoming).

In the summer of 2014, I conducted field research in Medog County, mainly focusing on people's everyday use (and non-use) of the Medog Highway. In this chapter, I provide ethnographic insights into the physical and social, daily and ritual use (and non-use) of the Medog Highway to reveal how this road was constructed and used in a specific social, cultural, and political context. The Medog Highway has been used not only as a material infrastructure to integrate the Medog people and as a strategic international political investment by the central authorities (considering the territorial disputes between China and India in the region), but also as a discursive symbol to enhance the state's legitimacy to the whole nation. As such, the Medog Highway is a production of both technologies and political ambitions. With this road, Medog was not only further integrated into the national political system, but also further integrated into the global market, producing dynamics of asymmetric connectivity via the road.

Furthermore, as I show in this chapter and in conversation with other papers comprising *Highways and Hierarchies* (see also, for example, Murton and Sigdel, this volume; Sarma, this volume), the road produces not only connectivity but also new disconnectivity and social exclusion. As discussed in more detail below, Medog has continued to be maintained as a 'hidden place' in the Chinese cultural imagination, and this despite political and economic exclusion that has been generated even after the completion of the road. It is for this reason that I call the Medog Highway a 'punctuated road'. My conceptualization of a punctuated road builds upon Smart and Smart's (2008) idea of 'time-space punctuation', which they use to describe 'the complex forms of discrimination and differentiation' (2008: 192) of the Shenzhen-Hong Kong border. In the final section of the chapter, I further discuss how road-building projects can contribute to the state-formation efforts of central authorities.

Getting into Medog along the road

Although completion of the Medog Highway was announced years ago, getting into[3] Medog is still not easy, as the condition of the road is generally poor. This is especially true with respect to road sections on the south side of the Galongla tunnel, comprising about two-thirds of the overall route. The part of the Medog Highway on the north side of Galongla Mountain is flat and laid with asphalt, whereas the part on the south side is still unsurfaced and has bumps and hollows. The 4800-metre-tall Galongla Mountain obstructs the Indian Ocean monsoon from the south and causes far more rainfall on the south side than the north side. This geographical

---

3   From my personal perspective, as an 'outsider' of Medog, I use the word 'into' to describe my experience of using the Medog Highway, assuming Medog as a place to be revealed. However, this may not reflect the common feeling and imagination of using the Medog Highway for other people, especially the local inhabitants.

effect turns the landscape on the south side into rainforest, making road construction and maintenance much more difficult.

The Medog Highway is mainly built along the Galong Zangbu River and the Yalu Zangbu River (known in Tibetan as the Yarlung Tsangpo and in India as the Brahmaputra), hence one side of the road is mountain slope, and the other side is a river valley. The south part of the road is wet and slippery with frequently occurring landslips, especially during the rainy season. Therefore, drivers must be very sensitive to the dynamic road conditions and make proper driving adjustments to avoid potential dangers; this includes, for example, avoiding rocks lying on the road, or avoiding driving into the river valley on a sharp bend. Thus, to travel to Medog more safely and efficiently, it is important to find a professional and experienced driver who frequently drives on the Medog Highway and is familiar with the latest conditions of the terrain.

In fact, professional drivers are routinely waiting for passengers at both ends of the Medog Highway (i.e. Zhamu Township and Medog County seat). These professional drivers run taxi-like business with their SUVs. Travellers can hire a private SUV to take one's party into or out of Medog, or go with other passengers for a cheaper cost. For example, the first time I entered Medog, I went with five other passengers (four Han Chinese and a Luoba youth) in a Mitsubishi Pajero SUV driven by a professional Tibetan driver.

Having a professional driver, however, does not mean that the passengers are completely at ease during the road trip. The passengers as well as the driver are often required to pay close attention to the dangerous environment surrounding the road. When the car drives over the massive bumps and hollows in the road, it sways and shakes. 'The vehicle dances on the Medog Highway', as a Menba woman said to me in the summer of 2014. Therefore, as a passenger, one should always be aware of their surroundings, keep their muscles tense, and tightly grasp the handles inside the car in order to avoid hitting their head (or other body parts) in the 'dancing' car.

By paying attention to the surrounding environment, people are also reminded of tales on the road, especially stories about the deaths and accidents which have occurred there over time. In 2014, a woman from Sichuan Province who worked for years in Medog sat beside me during my first drive into Medog. When she saw the surging river outside the car window, she told me a story about a couple who were swept away by the river one year previously:

> It was raining heavily those days, and the local people told them that they should wait until the rain had completely stopped. However, they

Figure 3.1   A crashed vehicle lying in the river valley

Photo by author

> were tourists and were anxious to go out of Medog to go back to work as
> soon as possible, hence they neglected the warnings from the locals. They
> drove their car along the road. Finally, the tragedy happened. (Author's
> field notes, 10 July 2014, Medog)

After hearing this story, the Luoba youth travelling with us told another
story about his uncle's family:

> It was a hard, rainy day as well. My uncle rode a motorcycle on the road,
> carrying his wife and his child. You know, it was a hard, rainy day, the
> road was slippery, and he rode so fast that they rushed into the river on
> a sharp bend. [...] We could not even find their bodies. (Author's field
> notes, 10 July 2014, Medog)

Driving along the Medog Highway also involves the development of various
social relations with others. For example, the first time I entered Medog, when
the car was approaching the 105 km point on the Medog Highway, our Tibetan
driver got a mobile phone call from his friend, who is also a professional
Tibetan driver. Our driver's friend told him that near the 113 km point there
was a serious landslip and the traffic was backed up. Our driver then decided
to stop the car in a lay-by and wait for further information. Fortunately,

Figure 3.2   Yellow prayer flags standing on the Medog Highway

Photo by author

after about 20 minutes' waiting, our driver's friend called him again and told him that the road had been cleared by a highway maintenance team and the traffic restored. The communications and the person-to-person social relations with others are very important ways for a driver to get information about the traffic dynamic when driving on the Medog Highway.

The Medog Highway entwines and refracts the local culture. For instance, on a sharp bend near the 125 km point fly many colourful prayer flags (in Tibetan, *rlung rta*, or in Mandarin Chinese, *jingfan*). Some people told me that a serious traffic accident had happened at this site just a few months before, and that those prayer flags were erected by the family of the dead. Without adequate traffic signs and protection facilities on the Medog Highway, these prayer flags not only spread good will (according to the local people's religious beliefs) but also functioned to remind other drivers that this was an accident black spot.

Driving and travelling on the Medog Highway is by no means a distracted and separate state, as some studies of the driving experience and car space have suggested (Relph 1976; Morse 1998). As described in this chapter and throughout the volume (see, for example, Gohain, this volume, and Khan, this volume), the drivers and passengers have various embodied, emotional and narrative connections and interactions; this is especially true with respect to the surrounding environment and landscapes of the Medog Highway.

During travels along this particular road, a state of coexisting emerged: the landscape, the car, and, of course, the driver co-perform the 'dance'; the dead and the living coexist in the same world, and the dead guide the living along the road through both the stories created by their fatalities and then retold by the living. To enhance safety and reduce risks, drivers build up a cooperative mutual aid network, and the decorative prayer flags serve multiple functions to disseminate good luck and generate good karma.

Ultimately, the failure to implement safety standards along the Medog Highway has created a space for the emergence of this state of coexisting. It is possible that the stories of the dead will stop circulating and the dead will be evicted from the road with the central government's 'great efforts' to complete the standardized flat road; this includes the future installation of uniform road signs and protection facilities. With the progress of road building and the seemingly inevitable standardization, my experience of getting into Medog may become a snapshot in time. I return to this picture in the final section of the chapter, specifically to consider how it contributes to one's understanding of the state-building process in both China and broader global contexts.

A road for whom?

Roads are often publicly proposed to be built for the local people and as infrastructure that has great impact at a regional scale. Whilst the efficacy and outcomes of this connectivity has been critically analysed by contributors to this volume (see, for example, Sarma; Heslop and Jeffery), this is a notion which is maintained in mainstream development discourse, and the orthodox notion that roads are important for local economic development makes road construction a priority within development projects (see also Murton and Sigdel, this volume). Such statements have been made about the Medog Highway specifically in the Chinese media; for example, a 2014 news report (ZGXZXWW 2014) describes how Medog's economy rapidly developed after the completion of the highway:

> After the completion of the Medog Highway, Medog's various economic indicators improved significantly. The county's GDP rose to 350 million yuan in 2013 from 266 million yuan in 2012, seeing year-on-year rises of 31.6%. [...] 'I have to say, the completion of the Medog Highway brings a great historic opportunity to Medog's economic and social development,' Zhaxi, the magistrate of Medog County, said excitedly.

In addition to social and economic benefits – and as other chapters in this volume also show in Northeast India (Sarma, this volume) and rural Nepal (Murton and Sigdel, this volume) – roads also imply the promise of political freedom for local people (Harvey and Knox 2012), and at the same time enhance one's feeling that they are 'incorporated as citizens in national life' (Wilson 2004: 525). This is reflected in a news report (XHW 2012) about Xirao Cuomu, a member of the Chinese People's Political Consultative Conference (CPPCC) of the Tibet Autonomous Region who is a Menba from Medog. According to this news report, it took more than ten days for Xirao Cuomu to travel from Medog to Lhasa to attend the CPPCC before the completion of the road. However, with the opening of the Galongla tunnel in 2011, she no longer had to climb over the Galongla Mountain. It just took her two days to travel to Lhasa to attend the CPPCC in 2012. 'This year, she attended the CPPCC as scheduled, carrying the hopes and entrustment from over 10,000 people of all ethnic groups in Medog,' the news report states (XHW 2012).

With respect to the popular imaginaries and political promises of roads, Harvey and Knox point out that 'their appearance also requires a force of social and political will which is able to generate and foster the belief that these technologies have a capacity to transform the spaces through which they will pass' (2012: 523). Although road building is usually depicted as meeting the needs of local society, it is well established that local demands are not always the major driving forces in building a road. In the case of road-construction projects in general but especially the Medog Highway, it is worth reconsidering two important questions raised by Wilson (2004: 526): Who decides how/where connections are made and how/where is movement channelled? Answering these two questions allows me to trace and reveal what kind of 'social and political will' has transformed Medog via road building.

By reviewing the history of the construction of the Medog Highway, it becomes apparent that the state (especially the central authorities) has played the most important role in building the road. According to state records, the central government made attempts to build a road into Medog five times; in 1965, 1975, 1980, 1990, and 2009, respectively. Considering the condition and legacy of this road, it is also extraordinary that, according to the National Highway Network Plan (2013-2030) published by the National Development and Reform Commission of China in 2013, the Medog Highway was renamed as the G559 National Highway (*guodao*) and became one of the 200 national highways in China. Moreover, it is also critical to note that a marker signifying the 'zero kilometre marker of China's highways' (*zhongguo gonglu ling gongli biaozhi*) is located at Tiananmen Square (the symbol of China's central authorities), which stands for the symbolic starting point for all of the national highways in China. And as Harvey and Knox have further noted, 'roads hold a central place in the imagination of state space' (2012: 522).

According to this logic, the G559 National Highway, or the Medog Highway – whose symbolic starting point is Tiananmen Square – plays a major role in reinforcing the effective imaginary of Beijing as the central nucleus and Medog as a peripheral node. As a corollary, this thinking also includes the asymmetrical, material and ideological movement of people, goods, and ideas from Beijing to Medog. Belying this state thinking, however, is the fact that Medog is by no means a 'hidden place' to its local people, but in a sense was rather considered a 'hidden place' to Beijing before the road-building project.

In fact, according to records (for example, Yang 2013), before the 1950s[4] the Medog people could gain salt, iron and other resources from India. In India, the total population of Menba and Luoba people was 55,876 and 198,462, respectively, in 2001 (Haokip 2011), compared with only 8923 Menba and 2965 Luoba in China in 2000 (SEACoPRC 2014a and 2014b). One of my main informants, Duoji, graduated from university in 2010 and is now a local government official in Medog. In 2014, he told me that some of his friends crossed the border surreptitiously when they decided to have a picnic on the mountain:

> They saw there was a playground beneath the mountain on the Indian side, and some children played football in the playground, and what is amazing is that they found those children also spoke the same Menba language as us! (Author's field notes, 13 July 2014, Medog)

I also asked Mr. Li, who is from Chongqing and has been a driver and an auto mechanic for the Medog County government since 2009, whether it would be much easier to build a road to Medog from the Indian side. Master Li responded instantly:

> Of course! If you climb to the top of the mountain near the border, you will see clearly that there is the boundless plain on the Indian side. If you build a road from India, the road needs to climb just a few lower

---

4   The People's Liberation Army entered Medog for the first time in 1952, according to the official record.

mountains instead of the very high Galongla Mountain. (Author's field
notes, 1 August 2014, Medog)

Therefore, the making of the 'hidden place' of Medog not only accounts for
the harsh natural conditions but also for contemporary political conditions.
Before the 1950s, Medog and its inhabitants had close ties with what are
today the Indian-controlled areas of Arunachal Pradesh and its local people
(Gohain 2020). However, due to contemporary geopolitical conditions, a
road can only be built to connect Medog with Beijing but not with cities
or towns in India. As a result of this geopolitical and social reality, Medog
has been constructed as a 'remote' and 'hidden' place specifically to Beijing.
Subsequently, this kind of thinking combined with the region's physical
environmental challenges continues to render Medog as 'an isolated island
in the plateau' in wider Chinese national spatial imaginaries.

Since roads are 'emblematic of a state's ability to infiltrate and dominate
geographical space and impose itself on the people inhabiting that space'
(Rigg 2002: 619), the construction of the Medog Highway is also a way
to show off the ability of the state. Xianzhi He, the general secretary of
the CCP committee of a state-owned highway construction consulting
company responsible for the design of the Medog Highway, told the media:
'for the construction engineers like us, the inaccessibility of Medog by
road is just like a thorn in our minds' (Li and Liu 2013). Actually, the
inaccessibility of Medog by road was not only 'a thorn' in Xianzhi He's
mind but also a thorn in the state body, just as the famous analogy made
by Hobbes suggests: the state is 'an artificial man' (Hobbes 1998; see also
Billé 2014). The failure to build a road into Medog implied an inability and
impotence of the state body – the disconnection was a potential threat
to its health. Reviewing the genealogy of the nation-as-body analogy
while also examining the case of Sino-Russia territorial disputes in the
Manchuria area, Billé has noted that, '[l]ost territories, no longer included
within the national body, remain part of a previous national incarnation
and as such continue to elicit affect, producing something akin to the
phenomenon known as "phantom pains"' (2004: 164). The sense of a frontier
county, Medog, without a road connection also captures the sense of 'lost
territories', which, I suggest, also elicits Xianzhi's 'phantom pains' (or what
he called 'a thorn' in his mind). The completion of the Medog Highway thus
offers an opportunity for the central authority to affirm its health (or, its
legitimacy) and assert its potency, removing the thorns in Xianzhi He's
mind and healing the state's pains by '(re)gaining the territories' through
the road-building project.

The completion of this particular road also showcases the state's potency not only to the Medog people, who have daily interactions with the road (those who are 'inhabiting that space', as Rigg [2002] suggests), but also to people across the country, the vast majority of whom will not have an opportunity to travel to Medog during their lifetime. At the 2014 annual meeting of the National People's Congress of China, one of the most important political events in China, Baima Quzhen, a Menba representative from Medog, told the Xinhua News Agency that '[t]he completion of the Medog Highway showed that the Chinese Dream has never forgotten any corner of our mother country. Although the conditions are very harsh, the central government has always helped us' (XHNA 2014). By letting the Medog representative talk about the Medog Highway in this way at a national political event, the construction of the Medog Highway became a national political performance to the people of the whole nation. As the 'materiality of state-effects' (Harvey 2005), roads can be used to integrate local people into the state; the Medog Highway is also used by the central authorities as a discursive form to enhance both their legitimacy and political integration of the whole nation.[5]

In addition, as Norbu (2008) points out, road building has also played an important role in China's strategic plans for Tibet and the Himalayan region. The completion of the Medog Highway is also widely represented by the Indian media as a security threat to the strategic border of Arunachal Pradesh (see, for example, Krishnan 2013; India Times 2013). Although the Chinese refute this opinion (see, for example, ZXW 2010), one of my informants in Medog made an interesting comment to me about how the Medog Highway will influence India:

After the completion of the Medog Highway, it is much easier to transport the large machines and construction materials into Medog. Therefore, hydro power stations can be built along the Yalu Zangbu River[6] in the near future, which will become a large threat to India. Once the hydro power stations are built, China can control the flow of the Yalu Zangbu

5   Of course, the Medog Highway is not the only infrastructure construction project in China that functioned in this way. The Hong Kong-Zhuhai-Macao Bridge and a proposed bridge between Xiamen and Taiwan's Kinmen are also imagined as important symbols of 'national unity' as was the spectacular construction of the Qinghai-Tibet Railroad in the early 2000s.
6   The Yalu Zangbu River is called the Brahmaputra River in India. It is a very important river for India.

Figure 3.3   Medog County seat and the Yalu Zangbu River

Photo by author

River by dams, and if India provokes China then China will be able to shut the river flows to India.[7] (Author's field notes, 6 August 2014, Medog)

Numerous observers of international politics hold opinions similar to those of my informant, noting that the completion of the Medog Highway will boost further infrastructure development projects in the area, and 'any gigantic project near the Great Bend of the river is sufficient cause for concern for the people of Northeastern India and the Assam plains in particular' (Mukherjee 2014). A news report about the connections between road construction and military conflict between China and India at the time of the opening of the Medog Highway published in *The Hindu* (Krishnan 2013) also cited an interview with Han Hua, a South Asia scholar at Peking University, who suggested that 'the "basic reason" for the incident[8] was "too much construction" along the border'.

7   In fact, during my fieldwork I saw that three major Chinese state-owned hydropower companies had established their branch offices in Medog and, according to some local informants, the companies had started to conduct geo-surveying and mapping for the design of the hydropower station(s).

8   A three-week-long Indo-China stand-off in Depsang in eastern Ladakh (known as Tiannan River Valley in China) occurred in April 2013. Also, in June 2017, another Indo-China stand-off occurred in Donglang, Yadong County (known as Doklam in Bhutan and India, located about

Asymmetric connectivity of the Medog Highway

As Harvey and Knox (2012) point out, road-building projects make at least three promises: physical speed, political integration, and economic connection (for a similar discussion, please also see Khan, this volume). Rigg (2002) and Dalakoglou (2010) further argue that, in addition to political integration, integrating into the web of a neoliberal globalized market has also become a primary rationale for building roads. Flower's (2004) case study of a road in Ya'an County, Sichuan, China, also shows that road building in China came together with the state's modernization project, and that market reforms and integration with global capitalism were also legitimatized in the name of modernization. Zhou (2013: 248) notes that road building in China is 'related to a particular understanding of economic globalisation': local, provincial, and national economic development can be driven by a fuller integration with the global economy, and road building plays a centrally important role in this broader process across a range of scales.

The economic indicators discussed above in the previous section indicate huge changes to and development of Medog's economy after the completion of the Medog Highway. However, the impacts brought by the Medog Highway to Medog's local inhabitants are far more nuanced than quantitative metrics reveal. A 20-year-old Luoba from Medog named Suolang accompanied me when I travelled to Medog for the first time. Soulang has been a lorry driver since he was eighteen and during the journey, he told me much about the opportunities and challenges of his job. This included how his lorry broke down on the mountain during his first time driving, and how he cried desperately when he found that it was impossible to get help from others on the mountain. He also told me that during the past year he had transported goods from 'outside' into Medog over 20 times. I asked him how many times he had transported goods from Medog to outside this year? He thought for a few seconds and answered: 'None. I always went out of Medog with an empty lorry' (author's field notes, 10 July 2014, Medog). Although I do not mean to imply that a full lorry coming in in exchange for a full lorry going out constitutes fair trade, Suolang's answer did astonish me and gave me the first impression of the asymmetric connectivity of the Medog Highway.

In a later conversation I had with Duoji, the local Menba youth mentioned above, Duoji also told me that nowadays Menba people in Medog no longer make traditional Menba rice wine by themselves: '"We have got Lhasa Beer,"

600 kilometres south-west of Medog County), triggered by a Chinese construction team with earth-moving equipment entering that area to build a new road.

Duoji said, "and if you want something better, you can choose Tsing Tao or Budweiser"' (author's field notes, 13 July 2014, Medog). Duoji also told me:

> You should not expect that you can have the authentic Menba cuisine in Medog's restaurants. Even we as Menba no longer cook in the Menba way. Nowadays we buy the flavourings from stores, and those flavourings are all from the outside. Therefore we all cook the food in the same style as Han Chinese, the Sichuanese cuisine.

Besides the massive amount of goods from outside, a lot of *waidi ren* (non-local residents or 'outsiders', including migrant workers, businessmen, tourists, etc., especially non-Menba/Luoba people) also came to Medog after the completion of the Medog Highway. In Medog, almost all the restaurants and shops are run by *waidi ren*, most of whom are Han Chinese from Sichuan Province or Chongqing Municipality. Lamu, a Menba girl from a single-parent family who recently graduated from university, once told me:

> My mother runs a store to earn a living and raise my younger brother and me. However, you Han Chinese [*hanren*] are so good at doing business and making money. After the completion of the highway, so many Han Chinese came to Medog to run stores, and then the business of my mother's store went downhill. Fortunately, this year my mother got a new part-time job as a street cleaner and can earn a salary from it. (Author's field notes, 6 July 2014, Nyingchi)

Although the economic connections brought by the highway have made this region richer, it does not follow that the local inhabitants have also become rich and enjoyed the benefits of such connections. All of my informants told me that even after the completion of the Medog Highway, very few local Menba or Luoba people went outside to find a job, and most of the local Menba or Luoba people are still farming, or working as waiters in restaurants or as construction workers in building projects within Medog under the supervision of Han Chinese bosses.

The following story illustrates what the connectivity of the Medog Highway means for Medog's local inhabitants. It is a story about Yangjin, a Menba girl and an employee of the Medog business office of China Unicom (a Chinese state-owned telecommunications operator). The story was told by Shufang, the Sichuanese director of the Medog office of China Unicom, as we climbed a hill to a mountain village where she planned to promote the China Unicom mobile telecommunications service. The Nyingchi Prefectural office of China Unicom sent Shufang to Medog to set up the Medog office after the completion of the Medog Highway, and Yangjin was recruited as an employee of the office. Shufang told me:

> Once our office ran a promotion offering a 200 yuan reduction on an iPhone. But I still sold an iPhone to a customer at its original price, because that customer asked me to give him an iPhone case and a portable power bank as gifts for free. I gave these to him and sold the iPhone at its original price, because the gifts were valued at over 200 yuan. However, Yangjin thought I was dishonest for not selling the iPhone at its promotional price. She thought I did the wrong thing. At her insistence, I finally topped up 200 yuan to that customer's mobile phone account.
>
> In fact, Yangjin is a kind-hearted girl. For example, we climbed the mountain together and went to Rinchenpung Temple [an important Tibetan Buddhist temple in Medog] two months ago on a festival day. She shared her food and drink with strangers along the route. According to their religious beliefs, they will gain a hundred times more good fortune by doing good [*zuo shanshi*] during the festival. Yangjin is sincerely concerned about the customers, but she is also rigid and dull [*si'naojing*], and cannot understand so many things. Previously I thought that if she is able to learn how to run the business, once I leave Medog in the future she could succeed me as the director. But up until now I do not think she can achieve that. And I also heard that she planned to move back to her home village on a remote mountain with her boyfriend. She may think the life in the county seat is too complex, and the village life is more suitable to her. (Author's field notes, 21 July 2014, Medog)

Both the stories told by Lamu and Shufang are stories about doing business (*zuo shengyi*), and how the performances of doing business differ between the *waidi ren* and the locals. According to both of the stories, it seems that Medog's local inhabitants fail to engage in competitive business practices and are less familiar with the enterprising and profit-oriented strategies of the global market economy. Reflecting on Lamu and Yangjin's experiences, these two stories imply that the *waidi ren* are the winners, while the local inhabitants are the outsiders and left behind upon the recent arrival, via the road, of the powerful forces of global capitalism and market competition.

However, the story told by Shufang actually indicates that the most important things introduced by the connectivity of the Medog Highway to Medog's local inhabitants may not be goods from the outside but the mainstream market ideology, rules and ethics. In the story told by Shufang,

Yangjin criticized Shufang for being dishonest in not selling the iPhone at its promotional price, referring to the transgression of a moral order of entangled relationships between people. However, Shufang's concerns centred on the price calculation, which is more abstract and disembedded and speaks to a failure to 'do business'. According to Shufang, Yangjin was treated as 'rigid and dull', and not able to learn how to do business from Shufang; in other words, she viewed Yangjin's ineptitude not as an inability to calculate but rather as an effect of her local moral consciousness (that in Shufang's opinion was drawn from Yangjin's Buddhist beliefs), all of which contradicts the market ethics introduced by Shufang. This way of thinking is evident in the comparison Shufang made between the price dispute in selling the iPhone and Yangjin's actions in sharing her food with strangers during the Buddhist festival. The structural transition of new economic ethics even led Yangjin to struggle (and perhaps fail) with re-organizing her life in the county seat, as she instead planned to move back to her home village in a remote mountain.

Moreover, from Shufang's narrative, Shufang (as a *waidi ren*) assumed a tutor-student relationship with Yangjin: she tried to teach Yangjin how to do business in the market, but was not successful. This unequal power relationship (tutor-student) can also be further be mapped on to the unequal and asymmetric connectivity of the Medog Highway: the locals were forced to be involved in and subjected to the newly introduced and more powerful market ethics by the connectivity of the road. Alternatively, if they did not participate in this new way of operating, just like Yangjin, they could otherwise only choose to escape from it by moving to a more 'remote' area.

However, with respect to 'asymmetric connectivity', it does not follow that outsiders do not 'transport' anything from Medog. A Hui Chinese medicine dealer told me how he purchased exotic and illegal wildlife parts used in traditional Chinese medicine such as caterpillar fungus (*Cordyceps sinensis*), bear paws, bear gall bladders, musk, and even tiger bones in Medog and transported them in disguise to sell to the Han Chinese travellers. Informants also told me that, in recent years, many Menba or Luoba girls got married to Han Chinese; the reason often given for this was that Han Chinese are better at doing business and making money. As a result, it became harder for young Menba or Luoba men to find a girlfriend or a wife. A Menba woman, who also got married to a Han Chinese and now lives in the Medog County seat, once told me that in her home village, over two-thirds of male Menba youth remain single. Revealed through the 'takings' of and by the outsiders (women and medicinal products), asymmetric connectivity thus also happens throughout Medog in invisible and subtle ways.

Another story widely circulated in Medog merits final attention: one day in years past, someone tried to ride a BMW motorcycle into Medog. But the motorcycle had engine trouble due to the poor condition of the road, and the owner could not find a replacement part to fix the motorcycle, and this put him in a very difficult and embarrassed condition. In response, local people joked that in Medog, a Chinese-made motorcycle is far better than a BMW motorcycle. In a similar vein, a Menba in Medog once also told me that when one gets stuck in a traffic jam caused by a landslip on the Medog Highway, 'even though you are a central government official, you can do nothing to pass the lorries but to follow them'. Like the BMW motorcycle debacle, this story also shows that the privilege and priority usually exercised by elite individuals is all but dismissed during a landslip when they come to Medog.

In these two stories, the power relationship was totally reversed by the disconnectivity generated by the poor condition of the road. A BMW motorcycle rider and a central government official, both with considerable economic and political power *outside* of Medog, became helpless on the road *inside* Medog. And ironically, as both stories imply, it is in fact the landscapes of disconnectivity that in some particular instances enable local people to maintain a relatively equal or more knowledgably situated status, and thereby exercise their agency and defend themselves from the feeling of losing out.

A punctuated road and a flying motorcycle

Road building and the motor mobility on roads decrease travel time and distance, concretizing the sense of time-space compression which characterizes 'modernity' (Harvey 1989). However, Penny Harvey's (2005) case study of a Peruvian road shows that such time-space compression is discontinuous and uneven. Similarly, travelling on the Medog Highway is not always continuous and even. People's use (and non-use) of the Medog Highway is also embedded in specific socio-economic structures, which produce not only connectivity and inclusion, but also new disconnectivity and exclusion.

Travel along the Medog Highway is punctuated by landslips due to the particular climate and natural condition of the region. Both drivers and passengers who travel along the road do not know whether, when, or where a landslip might occur before their departure. Encounters with landslips usually cost travellers between 30 minutes and 3 hours (and sometimes even longer), while they wait for the clearance of the road by the highway maintenance team. In the case of large-scale landslides, it can take two to three days to clear the mud and rocks from the road.

However, the environmental conditions are not the most common reason for journeys along the Medog Highway to be punctuated. Although landslips and other natural disasters occur frequently, they do not occur every day or on every journey. The most common reason for delays in journeys is the two police checkpoints on the Medog Highway: all traffic that passes on the highway, other than governmental vehicles, must stop and wait for about 20 minutes for a police inspection.

One day when I was in a motorcycle repair shop in Medog, Shandong – a Han Chinese man – came to have his motorcycle repaired by the mechanic. Shandong is called 'Shandong' by others because he was born in Shandong Province, and nobody knows his real name. While Shandong was waiting for his motorcycle to be repaired, he began to boast:

> I have thought about inventing a flying motorcycle for a long time. It is not necessary for it to fly for a long distance. To fly for 100 or 200 metres is enough. When I encounter a collapsed bridge or a landslip, then I will twist the throttle, and the motorcycle will fly over the collapsed bridge or the landslip site. [...] And with this flying motorcycle, I will also be able to fly over the police checkpoint. When I see the checkpoint ahead, I twist the throttle and fly up. After passing the checkpoint, the motorcycle will beat its wings and land quietly, and the policemen will by no means notice me! Just let them make their holy inspection! (Author's field notes, 14 July 2014, Medog)

In Shandong's imagination, a flying motorcycle can be used not only for passing obstructions caused by the natural conditions on the mountain, but also for passing the police checkpoints. Shandong moved to Medog in the 1990s and has never been back to his hometown since then, and nobody seems to know the reason why he came to Medog in the first place. At this point, it is virtually impossible for Shandong to get an ID card after a 20-year disappearance from his hometown (which was his legal household [*hukou*] registration place). Without an ID card, it is also not possible for Shandong to pass the checkpoint. Other informants told me that before the completion of the Medog Highway, there was no checkpoint on the route. With the completion of the highway, mobility has increased, but so too have control and surveillance of the road.

In addition to Shandong, other individuals have lost their right to use the Medog Highway. According to a professional Tibetan driver, the

Tibetans from A'ba Prefecture, Ganzi Prefecture and Changdu Prefecture are not allowed to pass the checkpoint either, due to the restive activities of Tibetan independence movements in those areas. Those who come from the Xinjiang Uyghur Autonomous Region (both Han and non-Han Chinese) must undergo an even stricter inspection than the ethnic Tibetans, since the 'Xinjiang independence movement' (in the Chinese government's term) is also a very sensitive issue. Recently, a nationwide and uniform political surveillance system and standard were imposed on the road in this area by the central authorities. In processes similar to what I encountered in Medog, Joniak-Lüthi's study on roads in Xinjiang Uyghur Autonomous Region notes that, '[b]ecause tarmac roads and roadside checkpoints are popularly linked with "the state", the presence of the state is reproduced through mundane practices of mobility, even if this presence is fraught with ambiguity' (Joniak-Lüthi 2016: 120).

Besides the police checkpoint, there is also another checkpoint on the Medog Highway, set up by the Tourism Bureau of Medog. From 20 June 2014, 'outside' travellers (people who do not hold a residence permit for Medog) are required to pay 160 yuan per person to buy an entrance ticket (called a 'garbage disposal fee') to enter Medog.[9] At the time of writing, Medog is evidently the only county in China where Chinese citizen 'outsiders' must pay an entrance fee to access most of its county territory (including its county seat). Although it is very common to pay for a ticket to enter a tourist attraction (*jingqu*) in China – and foreigners are required to obtain alien travel permits in order to visit restricted areas such as the Tibet Autonomous Region – it is unprecedented for Chinese nationals to pay for a ticket to enter an entire county. In many ways, the whole county (and the social life of its people) have been converted into and enclosed as a huge tourist attraction as a result of this policy.

Many travellers in Medog talked to me about the entrance ticket. Most of the self-driving tourists thought that the 160 yuan entrance ticket is acceptable.[10] But other travellers, especially backpackers and students, thought that the ticket is too expensive. A hotel owner in Medog also told me that some travellers even cancelled their bookings and backtracked when they found that they were required to pay for the entrance ticket to

9   As of 2020, the ticket price has been raised to 210 yuan per person during the peak season (May to October) and was sold/collected by a state-owned tourist service company called Tibet Nyinchi Medog Lotus Holy Land Tourism Development Co., Ltd., replacing the 'garbage disposal fee' that was being collected in 2014 with a 'Medog tourist attraction ticket'.
10   In 2014, the per capita disposable income of China was 20,167 yuan, averaging 1,680 yuan a month.

Medog. Some informants, including hotel owners and professional drivers, told me that their business reduced by about half after the collection of entrance fees by the Tourism Bureau.

However, Zhaxi, the magistrate of Medog County, said to the media that, '[i]n the future, we will strive to make Medog County a high-end and premium travel destination, adopting the high-end tourism development mode' (XHW 2014). To some extent, by collecting entrance fees, the Medog government maintains Medog as a 'hidden place', particularly to those economically 'hidden' people (that is, those who cannot afford more 'high-end' tourism), even after the completion of the Medog Highway. As such, travelling to Medog is related not only the matter of physical connection by the road, but also a matter of economic accessibility. Moreover, Medog's pristine and preserved 'isolation' is now also a commercial interest.

The backpacker industry in Medog has been bolstered by its popular representation in novels and news reports. These have contributed to the romanticization and mythology of the adventure of trekking into Medog – in particular, An'ni Baobei's novel *The Lotus* (*Lianhua*) – a love and self-redemption story about trekking into Medog – which was first published in 2006 and has over 1 million copies in print. Even after the completion of the Medog Highway, a large number of travellers choose to trek into Medog by avoiding the highway and following another mountain and forest route. In fact, the number of trekking travellers even increased after the completion of the Medog Highway, possibly because the trekking travellers were afraid that the government would build another highway into Medog along the trekking route after the completion of the Medog Highway. If this happens, they reason, trekking travellers will no longer have the opportunity to experience such an adventure.

Although Medog is already connected with a highway, those trekking travellers reproduce Medog as a mythical place through their experience of trekking. This situation resonates strongly with the similar case of Zhongdian, a county in north-west Yunnan Province which renamed itself as Shangri-la in 2001 to construct itself as a legendary paradise and generate a popular geographical imaginary and powerful tourist economy (Hillman 2003).

Conclusion: How road building contributes to state formation

The relationship between road building and state formation has been taken up in many studies, and it is well established that road building is routinely associated with the aspiration of connecting and integrating marginal regions as part of a broader state-building exercise (see, for example, Rigg 2002; Harvey 2005; Harvey and Knox 2012; Joniak-Lüthi 2016; Murton 2017). However, sometimes the achievement of such an aspiration is far from absolute (Harvey 2005). In the case of the Medog Highway, as I have shown, the road reflects statecraft, and specifically embodies and operationalizes the political ambition to connect and integrate Medog into China as a whole. However, my suggestion is that the state-formation process does not only involve connection and integration, especially in light of the new forms of disconnectivity and exclusion generated by the road. In the process of state formation, that is, connection and integration incorporate two other techniques: channelling and filtering.

In the case of the Medog Highway, it is apparent that connectivity and flows of movement are not symmetrical or mutually directional (but this is not to say that they are unidirectional either). The flows of movement are channelled from Beijing as the centre to Medog as the periphery, embodying the imagination of Beijing as the capital of the state. In addition, as Rigg notes with respect to the uneven material and ideological linkages between modernization projects and road construction: '[M]odernity involves changing mindsets and world views, not just providing people with the material components of development' (2002: 620). Roads, thus, are the conduit by which the market and the state introduce new ideas and belief systems. Very much like the story of Shufang and Yangjin discussed in this chapter, the introduction of new ideas and belief systems also imposes a new hierarchy of values which places the national mainstream market ideas at an elevated position and the local beliefs at a lower status. Theoretically, the connection of a road should allow not only outsiders to get in but also local ideas and people to get out. And yet, the hierarchical relationship of ideas in fact asymmetrically channels the direction of the movement, allowing mostly one-way integration to occur.

As the narratives and vignettes of the Medog Highway also show, with improved connectivity after the completion of the road, control and surveillance on the road (as well as throughout the wider area) also increase. Any politically and economically unwelcome people can be filtered by the surveillance system. Without filtering, the connection and integration brought by road building could potentially harm the so-called state-formation process by enabling the mobility of less-desired populations, as 'nomads and pastoralists [...] hunter-gatherers, Gypsies, vagrants, homeless people, itinerants, runaway slaves, and serfs have always been a thorn in the side of states' (Scott 1998: 1). In the case of Medog County, the potentially politically dangerous people from the state's perspective – for example, the unidentified Shandong, or ethnic Tibetans or Uyghurs or other the people from sensitive areas participating in 'independence activities' – are limited to (if not prohibited from) the use of the road as well as the access of/mobility in the region.

Moreover, filtering is also a process of purification and standardization: with the constant efforts from the government to build a flat, safe, and standardized road,[11] the co-performed 'dance' that intensively links the driver and passenger with the landscapes will vanish. For example, under such standardized 'improvements', uniform road signs and protection facilities are expected to replace the prayer flags which serve as black spot signs, and the stories of those deaths might cease to be told, and the drivers' mutual-aid network will be no longer indispensable. Giersch (2001) describes the frontier areas on south-west China in 1700-1880 (that is, before the formation of the modern nation-state) as a 'middle ground' crowded with 'a motley throng' and without clear state boundaries: 'the destructively creative formulation of "something new" in lands where alien cultural and political institution meet' (Giersch 2001: 88-89). The concept of 'middle ground', I would like to suggest, is similar to the 'state of coexisting' discussed above in the second section of this chapter. However, the filtering process, with its purification and standardization, allows both human and environmental factors to be classified and controlled: boundaries to be set up for separation, unwelcome elements from the state's perspective to be evicted, and local multi-relations to be rearranged by the newly introduced dominant power. Likewise, with the standardization of the road in the future, I anticipate that the 'state of coexisting' at this stage will end.

To conclude, road building facilitates news forms of channelling and filtering. Ideas from the state as well as goods for the market and populations of the nation can be mobilized and controlled through connection and integration. And from the state's perspective, this makes state formation possible, in both material and ideological ways. And yet, a punctuated road and the asymmetric connectivity it engenders are not the contradictions of connection and integration. Rather, they are allies in reintroducing and reshaping the rhythms and forms of everyday lives, defining (though in a constant and iterative struggle) who the subjects of the state are, and how they will be treated.

11   The Medog Highway Renovation and Reconstruction Project (*Motuo gonglu zhengzhi gaijian gongcheng*), with a national investment (*guojia touzi*) of 1.2015 billion yuan, started construction in October 2017 in order to improve the Medog Highway to a Grade 4 (and partly Grade 3) highway (MTXJYJ 2019). In China, highways are divided into five grades, from Grade 4 (the lowest grade) to Grade 1, with the designation 'expressway' indicating the highest-grade type of highway.

Epilogue

A few days before the end of my fieldwork, I climbed to a place on a mountain where I could have a bird's-eye view of the Medog County seat. There I met three local youth, and we travelled back down the mountain together. On the way, we spoke about the Medog Highway. One of these youths, a Menba university student studying in Guangzhou, a south-eastern coastal city, told me that in the time before the highway, when he was in middle school, he used to carry goods by foot over the mountain into Medog with his father and cousins to earn some money for the family. They needed to set up camp and stay overnight at the halfway point, and his father always told him that they should never approach certain places around them at night, due to potential attacks by the ghosts hidden there. I wondered whether there were any ghosts on the road after the completion of the highway. 'No,' the Menba youth responded. 'I think the ghosts were all scared away by the peals of bulldozers from the road construction.'

List of works cited

Bebbington, A. (1999). 'Capitals and Capabilities: A Framework for Analyzing Peasant Viability, Rural Livelihoods and Poverty'. *World Development* 27(12): 2021-2044.

Billé, F. (2014). 'Territorial Phantom Pains (and Other Cartographic Anxieties)'. *Environment and Planning D: Society and Space* 32(1): 163-178.

Dalakoglou, D. (2010). 'The Road: An Ethnography of the Albanian-Greek Cross-Border Motorway'. *American Ethnologist* 37(1): 132-149.

Fan, S., and C. Chan-Kang (2005). 'Road Development, Economic Growth, and Poverty Reduction in China'. Research Report 138. International Food Policy Research Institute.

Flower, J.M. (2004). 'A Road Is Made: Roads, Temples, and Historical Memory in Ya'an County, Sichuan'. *Journal of Asian Studies* 63(3): 649-685.

Giersch, C.P. (2001). '"A Motley Throng": Social Change on Southwest China's Early Modern Frontier, 1700-1880'. *Journal of Asian Studies* 60(1): 67-94.

Gohain, S. (2019). 'Selective Access; or, How States Make Remoteness'. *Social Anthropology* 27(2): 204-220.

Gohain, S. (2020). *Imagined Geographies in the Indo-Tibetan Borderlands*. Amsterdam: Amsterdam University Press.

Haokip, P. (2011). *Socio-Linguistic Situation in North-east India*. New Delhi: Concept Publishing Company.

Harvey, D. (1989). *The Condition of Postmodernity*. Oxford: Blackwell.

Harvey, P. (2005). 'The Materiality of State Effects: An Ethnography of a Road in the Peruvian Andes'. In *State Formation: Anthropological Perspectives*, ed. by C. Krohn-Hansen and K.G. Nustad. Ann Arbor, MI: Pluto Press, 123-141.

Harvey, P., and H. Knox (2012). 'The Enchantments of Infrastructure'. *Mobilities* 7(4): 521-536.

Hillman, B. (2003). 'Paradise under Construction: Minorities, Myths and Modernity in Northwest Yunnan'. *Asian Ethnicity* 4(2): 175-188.

Hobbes, T. (1998). *Leviathan*. Oxford: Oxford University Press.

Howe, J., and P. Richards (1984). *Rural Roads and Poverty Alleviation*. London: Intermediate Technology Publications.

India Times (2013). 'China to Restrict Tourists Near Arunachal Pradesh'. 13 November. http://timesofindia.indiatimes.com/india/China-to-restrict-tourists-near-Arunachal-Pradesh/ar ticleshow/25714756.cms (accessed 5 September 2014).

Joniak-Lüthi, A. (2016). 'Roads in China's Borderlands: Interfaces of Spatial Representations, Perceptions, Practices, and Knowledges'. *Modern Asian Studies* 50(1): 118-140.

Krishnan, A. (2013). 'China Opens New Highway Near Arunachal Pradesh Border'. *The Hindu*, 1 November. http://www.thehindu.com/news/international/world/china-opens-new-highway-near-arunach al-pradesh-border/article5302068.ece (accessed 5 September 2014).

Morse, M. (1998). *Virtualities*. Bloomington: Indiana University Press.

Mukherjee, A. (2014). 'China and India: River Wars in the Himalayas'. *Geopolitical Monitor*, 1 April. http://www.geopoliticalmonitor.com/china-and-india-river-wars-in-the-himalayas-4954/ (accessed 5 September 2014).

Murton, G. (2017). 'Making Mountain Places into State Spaces: Infrastructure, Consumption, and Territorial Practice in a Himalayan Borderland'. *Annals of the American Association of Geographers* 107(2): 536-545. DOI: 10.1080/24694452.2016.1232616.

Norbu, D. (2008). 'Chinese Strategic Thinking on Tibet and the Himalayan Region'. *Strategic Analysis* 32(4): 685-702.

Plachta, N., and G. Murton (forthcoming 2021). 'The Tibetan Frontier: From Regional Boundaries to Disputed Borders'. In *The Routledge Handbook of Contemporary Highland Asia*, ed. by M. Heineise and J. Wouters. London: Routledge.

Relph, E. (1976). *Place and Placelessness*. London: Pion.

Rigg, J. (2002). 'Roads, Marketization and Social Exclusion in Southeast Asia: What Do Roads Do to People?' *Bijdragen tot de Taal- Land-en Volkenkunde* 158(4): 619-636.

Scott, J.C. (1998). *Seeing Like a State: How Certain Schemes to Improve the Human Condition Have Failed*. New Haven, CT: Yale University Press.

Smart, A., and J. Smart (2008). 'Time-Space Punctuation: Hong Kong's Border Regime and Limits on Mobility'. *Pacific Affairs* 81(2): 175-193.

Wilson, F. (2004). 'Towards a Political Economy of Roads: Experiences from Peru'. *Development and Change* 35(3): 525-546.

Zhou, Y. (2013). 'Branding Tengchong: Globalization, Road Building and Spatial Reconfigurations in Yunnan, Southwest China'. In *Heritage Politics in China*, ed. by T. Blumenfield and H. Silverman. New York: Springer, 247-259.

Chinese-language sources

Li, W., and M. Liu (2013). 'Motuo zhulu ji'. *Sanlian shenghuo zhoukan* 2013(47): 72-79.

[MTXJYJ] Motuo jiaoyun ju (2019). 'Guodao 559 xian bomi zhi motuo gonglu zhengzhi gaijian gongcheng wancheng zongtouzi de 42.6%'. http://www.linzhi.gov.cn/mtx/c101880/201902/0c3b02c55adb4e48ad81eb639dedaf5b.shtml (accessed 5 August 2020).

[MTXWXCB] Motuo xianwei xuanchuanbu (2012). 'Motuo xian jiben qingkuang'. http://www.motuo.gov.cn/Info_3021_163.html (accessed 5 September 2014).

National Development and Reform Commission of China (2013). 'Guojia gongluwang guihua (2013 nian-2030 nian)'. http://www.sdpc.gov.cn/zcfb/zcfbghwb/201402/P020140221361534132568.pdf (accessed 5 September 2014).

[SEACoPRC] State Ethnic Affairs Commission of the People's Republic of China (2014a). 'Luoba zu'. http://www.seac.gov.cn/col/col451/index.html (accessed 5 September 2014).

[SEACoPRC] State Ethnic Affairs Commission of the People's Republic of China (2014b). 'Menba zu'. http://www.seac.gov.cn/col/col451/index.html (accessed 5 September 2014).

[XHNA] Xinhua News Agency (2014). 'Baima Quzhen daibiao: wode zhongguomeng shi jiaxiang motuo gonglu xiangxiangtong'. http://www.gov.cn/xinwen/2014-03/07/content_26326 87.htm (accessed 5 September 2014).

[XHW] Xinhua wang (2012). 'Xizang lianghui daibiao weiyuan: zheci cong Motuo dao Lasa zhi yongle liangtianban shijian'. http://news.xinhuanet.com/politics/2012-01/13/c_111433839.htm (accessed 5 September 2014).

[XHW] Xinhua wang (2014). 'Xizang Motuo xian dazao "gaoduan jingpin lvyou"'. http://news.xinhuanet.com/local/2014-05/19/c_1110759891.htm (accessed 5 September 2014).

Wang, L. (2011). *Motuo cun diaocha*. Zhongguo jingji chubanshe. China: China Economic Publishing House.

Yang, L. (2013). 'Shoufu Jidu: mapi, cheliang yu daolu'. *Sanlian shenghuo zhoukan* 2013(47): 88-90.

[ZGXZXWW] Zhongguo Xizang xinwen wang (2014). 'Motuo xianzhang zhaxi: xiri "gudao" bianshen "baodao"'. http://www.chinatibetnews.com/2014/0111/1316003. shtml (accessed 5 September 2014).

[ZXW] Zhongxin wang (2010). 'Gangmei: Xizang Motuo gonglu anquan yiyi wuxu fangda jiedu'. http://www.chinanews.com/hb/2010/12-20/2732878.shtml (accessed 5 September 2014).

About the author

Yi Huang is an independent scholar. He graduated with a BA from Fudan University and an MA in Social Anthropology from SOAS, University of London. He works in the NGO sector teaching anthropology and ethnographic research methods to development workers in China and as a consultant on Chinese development projects.

4   *Dhabas*, highways, and exclusion

Swargajyoti Gohain

Abstract

This chapter is an ethnographic study of 'hybrid *dhabas*' or inns that have emerged in the wake of massive highway construction all over India. Focusing especially on the *dhabas* on National Highways NH 1 and NH 37 passing through Murthal, Haryana, and Nagaon, Assam, this chapter argues that these hybrid *dhabas*, which combine features of traditional *dhabas* and city-based restaurants, reveal a particular social character of highways. These *dhabas* cater to a mostly middle-class clientele, while remaining inaccessible to less privileged classes and former users of highway inns, such as truck drivers. While scholars of urban studies have shown how material constructions such as shopping malls, theme parks, or gated communities give the city a middle-class character, this chapter shows how *dhabas* play a similar role in peri-urban areas by constructing the highways as middle-class spaces and sites of neoliberal exclusion.

Keywords: India, *dhabas*, class, exclusion, consumption

Introduction

A brightly lit two-storied building, signboard glowing in the dusk, and fairy lights hanging on the walls, Anurag *dhaba* is one of the swankier *dhabas* or highway inns that have come up on national highway NH 37 at the Nagaon bypass road in Assam since this highway stretch was upgraded.[1] Owned by Mahendra Borah – a local from the Puronigudam village of Nagaon – and managed by his relative Rip Hazarika, the *dhaba* is segregated

1   This road is locally known as a bypass because it bypasses Nagaon town. In India, till recently, highways have typically cut through human settlements – although, the newer highways are now increasingly being constructed away from villages and towns – hence, 'bypass' remains both the official and popular term for the diverted highways stretches.

Heslop, Luke, and Galen Murton (eds), *Highways and Hierarchies: Ethnographies of Mobility from the Himalaya to the Indian Ocean*. Amsterdam, Amsterdam University Press 2021
DOI: 10.5117/9789463723046_CH04

into two spacious compartments, one air-conditioned and the other with open windows ('because not everybody likes AC, and closed rooms'), each with around six tables seating four, and a giant television at one end. The manager told me that around 60 staff work in this *dhaba* and claimed that its unique selling proposition (USP) is the authentic Assamese fare served by young women in traditional attire. With numerous such *dhabas* that have proliferated in recent years – six to seven *dhabas* at distances of 300 to 400 feet – the Nagaon bypass in this north-eastern state has entered the highway food map of India.

More than 2000 km away in Sonepat, Haryana, in the northern part of India, where my workplace is located, another highly popular eating spot is Murthal on NH 1 or the Grand Trunk Road, which has over 40 *dhabas* within a three-to-four-kilometre stretch. Amrik Sukhdev *dhaba*, an old favourite owned by Amrik Singh, is located in a glittering U-shaped plaza, resplendent with designer fountains, mini-amusement rides, and compact stores selling branded stuff, cigarettes, and daily necessities. The *dhaba* has two large seating areas, one outdoors and the other indoors, labelled AC hall. With plush interiors, luxurious washrooms, foot massage chairs, and quick, efficient service, this *dhaba* has between 200 and 300 customers eating at any time. A casual glance at the customers sitting at different tables show mostly families eating together – mother, father, and children; one parent and child; young men or women with aged relatives; couples; and less commonly, groups of young men. One of the service staff revealed that around 500 staff, which includes the cleaners, waiters and those manning the counters, work round the clock, and estimated that the daily turnover would be around 25 to 30 lakh rupees (approximately US$33,000 to US$39,000).

Other *dhabas* on the Murthal road, such as Shiva, Mannat, Dharam Garam, and Pahalwan (slightly smaller) are comparable in size, look, décor, and facilities. The Murthal *dhabas* get most of their footfall from highway commuters of Delhi and the three nearby states of Haryana, Punjab and Himachal Pradesh, but there are other categories of customers as well, such as school- and college-going students from the Delhi-NCR region, out to have a good outing and good food at budget prices (since *dhabas* are less costly than restaurants) and people from nearby towns and cities, who book tables for birthdays, anniversaries and family dinners.

While *dhabas* have always been a resting place for trucks carrying cargo as well as for interstate bus passengers, they have emerged in a different light in the new phase of massive highway construction underway all over India. *Dhabas* or highway inns previously existed to serve mostly truck drivers who ply their trucks on the highway through the night, and who require rest and refreshments before they can resume their journeys. The new *dhabas* that are fast emerging alongside highways and bypasses are, however, very different in look and character from the older *dhabas*. The *dhabas* that now dot the roadside have glossy exteriors, neat, capacious, air-conditioned seating arrangements, often divided into cubicles for greater privacy, and they also serve a more expanded menu that includes both local cuisine and non-local fare such as noodles pasta, or fried rice. The hoardings and signboards for these *dhabas*, often showing up more than ten kilometres before the actual *dhaba* appears, advertise them as '*dhaba* cum restaurant', evidently to enforce upon the customer that while they have roots in a local *dhaba* food culture, they offer no less variety than regular city-based restaurants. Termed '*dhaba*-restaurant hybrids' by Mayur Sharma and Rocky Singh, hosts of the popular NDTV channel show *Highway on My Plate*, these *dhabas* are usually visited by middle-class people commuting in cars between towns and states for work or holiday, politicians, businessmen, and tourists.

Drawing on conversations with customers, staff, managers and owners of such 'hybrid *dhabas*' along NH 1 (Murthal) and NH 37 (Nagaon), as well as my own observations and experiences, travel books and reviewers' comments on various travel sites, I show how the hybrid *dhabas* constitute new sites of middle-class consumption on the Indian highway. While roads are studied both as an infrastructural form as well as conduit for other forms of infrastructure, I draw attention to how road passage can bring people and things together in new configurations through the focus on *dhabas* (Harvey and Knox 2015). I depart from Marc Augé's (1995) conceptualization of highways as one of the spaces of supermodernity where social interaction is contractual rather than organic – he lists highways among empirical non-places where the user of such spaces has contractual relations with it. My approach is closer to Dalakoglou (2010), who analysed how spatial practices and narratives of people on the Greek-Albanian cross-border motorway imbue the roads with meaning, and in this way, subvert the concept of non-place by dealienating space. *Dhabas* similarly embed meaning in seemingly homogenous highway spaces by spatializing social relations. By looking at *dhabas* not just as a material construction but as one imbued with a particular social character, I show how highways generate or regenerate social meanings and relations.

Jack Kerouac writing about the American road journey in *On the Road* (1957) depicted the road trip as symbolizing an escape from the strictures of domesticity and societal conventions. Although Kerouac's road narrative was mostly about the male quest for freedom (Ganser 2006), he shows how travel is generative and reflective of social meanings. The new *dhabas* not only provide an opportunity for leisurely, convenient stops in specially designed spaces but in their habitation by a particular class, they produce a social meaning of travel that is different from what existed before. In the wake of India's infrastructural boost in the last decade, and particularly road expansion, the highways have become a site to observe the reproduction of middle-class habitus (Bourdieu 1977).[2] Through this chapter I show how hybrid *dhabas* reveal the highways as hierarchical spaces. Along with the mode of travel, I argue that the stops on the highway are equally important as a measure of differential mobility.

The rapid growth of *dhabas* on Indian highways expose a particular class character of Indian highways. A number of scholars have described the classed character of infrastructure and connectivity (e.g. Anand 2017; Gupta 2015). Nikhil Anand (2017), for example, argues that while highways (or other infrastructural forms, such as airports, flyovers) facilitate different forms of (auto)mobility, they also afford selective passage or movement, displacing and bypassing many people, so that road connectivity for the elite and middle classes comes at the cost of the disconnection of lower-income groups. Murton and Sigdel (this volume) report similar polarized effects of rural roads as well, as they show how caste and class asymmetries are not flattened but reinforced as a result of new roads-based mobility in rural Nepal. In India, while highways allow speed of travel and connectivity between places, in the absence of public transport, it does not give everyone equal access to mobility.

I show how highways not only serve mostly middle-class commuters by facilitating auto-mobility, but also generate spaces of exclusion. By contrasting the new hybrid *dhabas* with older *dhaba* types, which now cater primarily to truck drivers, I show how the former type is constituted only by excluding the latter. By signalling their preferred customer type, hybrid *dhabas* demarcate boundaries of belonging, and segregation. In this regard, they resemble some material spaces in urban areas, especially metropolitan and megacities, such as malls, shopping plazas, multiplexes, theme parks, and gated communities, which are sites of middle-class consumption (e.g. Bal et al. 2017; Srivastava 2015), and exclusive in that they are not equally accessible to all sections of the urban population. I argue that *dhabas* are similar spaces where one can trace exclusion in the emerging highway-scapes across peri-urban and rural India.

---

2   I use 'habitus' – Pierre Bourdieu's (1977) concept that explains how social order is internalized by people and manifested as dispositions – to explain how *dhabas* clarify the spatialization of class habitus in highway spaces, just as shopping malls and gateway complexes do in urban spaces.

Figure 4.1 Amrik Sukhdev Dhaba, Murthal, NH 1

Photos by author

Figure 4.2 Anurag Dhaba, Nagaon Bypass, NH 37

Photo by author

Hybrid *dhabas*

As India has progressed, especially since the economic reforms of the early 1990s, dhabas have changed too. What were once just dusty joints for sleepy truckers have become throbbing highway destinations, some with air-conditioned dining areas, clean washrooms and an array of food choices, including, of course, dal and roti. The transformation reflects the changing food habits, mores and middle-class preferences of 21st-century Indians. (Mazumdar 2016)

Traditionally, in the Persian world, including Mughal India, caravanserai or roadside resting places would provide the weary traveller some respite from the road. The word *serai* is of Turkish and Mongol origin and primarily means a shed. They were located particularly along the connecting roads, where a military regiment or a group stayed for a short period of time during a long surface journey. Caravanserai served the flow of commerce, information and people on trade routes. It acted as a transit place where travellers met and exchanged views.

In modern India and Pakistan, *dhaba* was the name given to the roadside restaurants which were also resting points for, mostly Punjabi, truck drivers; and they typically served simple fare like dal, roti and vegetables. Usually rustic structures, they had basic chairs or *charpoys* (cots) in front of them for truckers to lie down and take rest. The front of these shops would usually have large steel or aluminium pots and pans in which food would be continuously cooking. Journalist Charmaine O'Brien writes in her guide to regional food in India:

> The highways of north India are dotted with basic eateries called *dhabas* that provide meals to truck drivers and other travellers. Punjabis dominate the ranks of truck drivers in India; [...] hence there is a strong association between Punjab and *dhabas*. [...] The presence of a contingent of trucks outside a *dhaba* is usually a sign that the food is good – though it can also suggest the availability of liquor and gambling! (O'Brien 2013)

In peri-urban highway spaces of India, the traditional *dhabas* have now given way to the new *dhabas*. The traditional features are maintained only in those *dhabas* that are frequented by truck drivers. In many places in India, such *dhabas* are known as 'line *dhabas*' or 'line hotels' today, most likely in reference to the fact that truck drivers would park their trucks in rows outside the *dhaba* where they stopped. Since most cities in India ban entry for heavy commercial vehicles and trucks during the day time, in order to avoid traffic congestion – for example, in Delhi, trucks are not allowed to enter the city between 7 AM in the morning and 11 PM at night – trucks have to be parked a few kilometres away from the city's entry barricades. In the absence of any government or privately owned truck terminals or depots, the grounds outside the line *dhabas* function as parking spaces for trucks, when they are not moving. The line *dhabas* serve as eating places, washing and resting areas for truck drivers, who grab food and a few hours of sleep here after driving continuously for, sometimes, 20 days on the highway. Most of these *dhabas* are single-room tenements, with a row of *charpoys*, and food cooking on one side.

Figure 4.3   Trucks parked outside a line *dhaba*, NH 37

Photo by author

The new *dhabas* that are fast emerging alongside highways and bypasses
are quite different in look and character from the line *dhabas*. Anurag,
Sugandhi, and Midway *dhaba* on the Nagaon bypass, or Amrik Sukhdev,
Gulshan, Garam Dharam and Zhilmil *dhaba* in Murthal are *dhabas* are of
this type. It is true that many of these *dhabas* have humble beginnings, as
a shack or small roadside joint, but with sustained success over the years,
helped greatly by the increased traffic on improved roads, these old *dhabas*
reinvented themselves into their swanky new avatars. For example, Amrik
Sukhdev, which began as Sukhdev Vaishno *dhaba*, used to serve mostly truck
drivers on NH 1 but later changed its name and expanded and upgraded to
a luxurious *dhaba*-cum-restaurant.

Charmaine O'Brien writes with regard to the *dhabas* on Murthal road:

Dhabas have nestled alongside the highway in Haryana for at least half a
century, providing decent meals to the drivers of the thousands of trucks
plying the route every day. The otherwise nondescript highway town of
Murthal (near Sonepat) has become quite renowned for its *dhabas* and
people now drive there just to eat. You can't miss the string of *dhabas*
along NH1 here because of the mass of the parked vehicles of patrons. All
these places serve 'pure vegetarian' food and most are open round the
clock – and are reportedly busy even at 3 a.m. Sukhdev Vaishno *Dhaba*
claims to be the biggest *dhaba* in the world. Its success has seen it develop
a 'multi-cuisine' menu. (O'Brien 2013: 28)

Figure 4.4   Inside a line *dhaba*, NH 1

Photo by author

The emergence of the new *dhabas* are a by-product of the fast-expanding network of four-lane and six-lane highways across India. In the north-eastern part of India, for example, highway construction has seen a spurt in the last decade. Regional economic cooperation and integration (RCI) have become buzzwords in the North Eastern Region, because it is a borderland where several international boundaries intersect, and through which cross-border roadways can serve as conduits for international trade. The process of RCI in Asia has been driven by several factors, including reduced barriers to intra-regional trade and investment, renewed emphasis on formal regional integration initiatives (e.g. ASEAN, Asia-Pacific Economic Cooperation [APEC]), the spread of free trade agreements, and regional infrastructure investment in roads and energy (Madhur et al. 2009). The Asian Highway, the Kaladan Highway, the India-Myanmar-Thailand Trilateral Highway are some of the interregional cross-border networks that have become partly functional or are in the pipeline, which promise to connect the landlocked region of Northeast India with national as well as international roads. The emphasis in most of these road projects is to upgrade existing networks that had been funded in the past. For example, India signed the inter-governmental agreement on the Asian Highway network with United

Nations Economic and Social Commission for Asia and Pacific (UNESCAP) in April 2004; according to this agreement, signatory countries have to work for the coordinated development of those highway routes in their country which fall on the Asian Highway network.

The National Highways Authority of India (NHAI) has taken initiative to develop four-laned roads in Northeast India through its two major projects – the East-West Corridor and the Special Accelerated Roads Development Programme (SARDP), which cover road networks included in the Asian Highway megaproject. The Ministry of Road Transport and Highways (MoRT&H), the Border Roads Organisation (BRO), and the state Public Works Department (PWD) are some of the other agencies involved in road construction in Northeast India. In 2014, I had met and interviewed Alok Kumar, an NHAI official in the organization's office in Nagaon, when he shared documents and presentation slides with me from meetings, which were mostly reports of the progress made by NHAI in these two road projects in the states of Assam, Meghalaya, and Nagaland. The four-laned highways have replaced the older single lane roads that often ran through rural settlements.

As lands were acquired, and quarries were set up for building materials, some people in nearby rural areas saw *dhabas* as a new opportunity for business. Pranjit Sarmah, of B&B *dhaba* in Nagaon, told me how he bought the land from people of Sutara village (he belongs to an adjacent village) in 2010 when he saw the road being constructed (interview, 12 September 2014). The four-laning of NH 37 was completed in 2012 and in 2013, Pranjit opened his *dhaba*. Pampu Baniya, owner of Midway *dhaba*, did not own the land; he had leased it from Pranab Saikia, a resident of Nagaon (interview, 15 September 2014).

In Murthal, money for building and maintaining the luxury *dhabas* comes from remittances. In most cases, land was bought by businessmen from nearby Punjab from farmers of Haryana when the highway was in its inception stage. All over India, these new *dhaba* types have taken on global characteristics by adding international features of food and look to their traditional structures.

Dhabas are found not only in highways but inside cities, too. In millennial India, where globalization has brought the formal and informal sectors in closer affinity than before – for example, Mike Davis (2005) argues that slums, which house many of those working in the informal sector, appear to be an inevitable part of urban growth globally today – *dhabas* have mushroomed in many new city spaces. A case in point is Gurgaon, a major satellite town of New Delhi, where numerous *dhabas* have sprung up to cater to the employees of the several business process outsourcing (BPO) units of multinational companies located there (Tewari 2007). The open access, 24 hours availability, low-cost fare and variety of food served make these informal *dhabas* a huge success among the BPO workers. Situated next to towering glass buildings with sophisticated design and technologies, these small, informal *dhabas* often housed in shacks, stalls or mobile kiosks offer starkly contrasting visuals to Gurgaon's high-rise landscape. Many city-based restaurants also have a separate *dhaba* outlet, where they claim to serve traditional food.

However, the highway *dhabas* are different from the BPO *dhabas* and other city-based restaurants because they serve a larger sample of highway commuters across the class spectrum. While their menu card contains both *desi* (local/Indian) and *videsi* (international) items, the owners know that it is the local dishes that attract the average customer. As one of the managerial staff of Shiva *dhaba* on Murthal told me, city *dhabas* and restaurants cannot serve the fresh home-made butter that the highway *dhabas* are able to source daily from local people – a thali, or set meal, of tandoori (oven baked) parathas topped with white, home-made butter, with mint and garlic chutney on the side that the manager of the Shiva *dhaba* offered us hospitably, is one of the most popular fares of highway *dhabas*, which city *dhabas* find hard to replicate. The twinkling lights, colourful decor and bright advertising of these *dhabas*, notwithstanding, they have a very homely, warm and relaxed ambience. Apart from taste and quality of food, this is a major factor that attracts the highway commuter. Three young girls in their early 20s, all business administration students from Bhopal in Madhya Pradesh, who were on an all-girls' road trip to Himachal Pradesh, told me that highway *dhabas* are places where they can relax, and literally put up their feet without being bothered about what people think. Unlike the formal atmosphere of restaurants, where one has to be mindful of etiquette, *dhabas* afford a home-like feeling where they can savour food that reminds them of home, they said. As domestic tourism in India grows, these *dhabas* also provide essential infrastructural services for tourists, since they offer not just food but sanitary conditions for eating and clean washrooms.

The plazas, parking spots and other provisions in each *dhaba* complex mark the latter as not just resting areas during highway breaks but as attractive spots of recreation. These *dhabas* cater primarily to a middle-class clientele, and advertise accordingly. Garam Dharam, a sprawling *dhaba* in Murthal, just adjacent to Amrik Sukhdev, apparently owned by a relative of Bollywood actor Dharmendra, has a unique theme inspired by the actor's cinematic career. It has graffiti, dialogues, posters, and props (trucks, autos, lorries, jeeps) from Dharmendra's films as well as large posters, drawings and cut-outs of the actor himself on the inside walls and pillars. With a seating capacity of more than 1000 and around 700 employees, it is packed with customers day and night. A particular dialogue inscribed on one of the columns caught my attention. Taken from the 2011 Bollywood film *Yamla Pagla Deewana*, it said 'Discount middle-class logon ke liye hota hain' ('Discount is only for the middle classes'). On NH 1 and NH 37, I saw that quite a few *dhabas* have rooms on the upper levels, which serve as venues for more private business meetings apart from providing lodgings. In Nagaon, one *dhaba* owner proudly reeled off the names of two famous ministers (names withheld) of Assam who patronise his *dhaba*. In Murthal, too, the multistoried *dhabas* double as hotels either under the same name or assume a different name. Amrik Sukhdev advertises rooms for its hotel wing, called Hotel Home In. Many people from smaller towns in Punjab use the Murthal *dhabas* as a resting point if they have time to kill before a flight or train. Some *dhabas* provide additional services, such as a wedding hall for customers from the nearby towns.

These *dhabas* provide a get-away for residents of nearby cities and small towns who look for forms of leisure outside their congested city. School children from nearby towns and cities, out to feast on fresh, plentiful food at costs much cheaper than city-based restaurants, are also frequent customers. Many people come to celebrate birthdays, anniversaries, and other family parties in these *dhabas*. Couples from towns who come for a drive on the highway treat these *dhabas* as points for a romantic rendezvous. *Dhabas* provide an adequate midway meeting point for businessmen and politicians coming from the opposite direction or for those who may not wish to meet inside the city either for reasons of privacy or convenience.

The term *dhaba* has thus changed in connotation. If earlier they were like inns offering respite to the weary traveller, they have changed their form as well as function in a neoliberal context where they are now spaces of middle-class consumption. These new hybrid *dhabas* are more in sync with *dhabas* inside city spaces, except that they are set apart from the latter by their location on the highway, fairly reasonable prices, and traditional food.

In 2008, Dabur, an Ayurvedic and natural healthcare company, adopted 150 *dhabas* on the highways from Delhi to Jaipur, Agra, Chandigarh, Dehradun and Haridwar to market *hajmola*, a post-meal digestive candy (Shukla 2008). In a move aimed at popularizing the brand, Dabur took the initiative of designing the interiors of these *dhabas* with branded chairs, tables, umbrellas and wall paintings. Dabur's innovative move, an attempt to tap into the marketing potential of *dhabas*, was a further recognition of the middle-class customer base of the latter.

Infrastructure and mobility effects

Philosophers and sociologists (e.g. Wirth 1938) in the early twentieth century studied the different effects of urbanization and mobility forms. For example, in 1903 Georg Simmel (2002) wrote about the changes in personality that accompany migration from rural areas to the modern industrial city, arguing that the typical urban attitude is a blasé attitude, characterized by indifference. Excess of physical factors – too many people and external stimuli of lights and noises – and rapidly shifting stimulations of the nerves by city life, lead to incapacity to react to new stimulations and consequently, the urban dweller develops a blasé attitude. Writers have also looked at how consumerist modernity generates specific responses and types, such as the flâneur (Benjamin 1999), who strolls the streets of Paris, observes and witnesses the commodity-based modern market.

Other scholars have focused on how the introduction of new infrastructure and mobility forms give shape to or change existing habitus of the people who could afford such modes of travel. A specific class then uses these newly available spaces to reproduce its distinctiveness. In his foreword to Wolfgang Schivelbusch's *The Railway Journey*, Alan Trachtenberg (1986) notes that this book belongs to the same genre as other works that explore the new forms of consciousness that arise out of encounters with new structures and things. Schivelbusch showed how the railways gave birth to panoramic vision. The speed and mathematical directness with which the railroad proceeds through the terrain destroy the close relationship between the traveller and the travelled space (Schivelbusch 1986: 51). This loss of landscape also affected the senses, and particularly the sense of sight. But if there was a loss of immediate landscape it gave rise to a new vision – the visual ability to perceive the discrete, as it rolls past the window, indiscriminately, and allowed the scenery that the railroad presents in rapid motion to be viewed as a panorama.

> Panoramic perception, in contrast to traditional perception, no longer belonged to the same space as the perceived objects: the traveller saw the objects, landscapes, etc. through the apparatus which moved him through the world. That machine and the motion it created became integrated into his visual perception: thus, he could only see things in motion. (Schivelbusch 1986: 56)

Railway mobility created certain sensory, perceptual experiences and gave rise to new habits and expectations.

Rashmi Sadana (2010), writing about the Delhi metro, shows how it changed people's attitudes and forced them to behave differently. In the metro, people mostly sit quietly, do not eat, drink, spit and generally follow order. This civic sense is in contrast to the somewhat aggressive and disorderly behaviour that the same people exhibit in less regulated public spaces. The Delhi metro is responsible for imposing in passengers a uniform 'bourgeois civility' (Thiranagama et al. 2018: 163) irrespective of social class, so that anyone violating this behaviour code becomes the object of opprobrium.

Shopping malls in cities also inculcate a new set of dispositions or benchmark of civility. Thus, customers in a mall or supermarket like a Big Bazaar outlet will not haggle (Srivastava 2015: 227). This does not reduce malls in India to more impersonal spaces. Sanjay Srivastava notes through ethnographic inquiries that the increase in the number of malls in Delhi-NCR has actually increased opportunities for family socialization. Earlier due to the paucity of sites where families could go for an outing or picnics (with India Gate and Qutub Minar being a few of these limited sites), and the problem of safety, families did not find many avenues to socialize. Now with malls, this has changed and also led to a greater shift to outside dining. In this sense, malls have become sites for a middle-class sociality.

My argument regarding *dhabas* follows similar lines, where I trace the reproduction of class effects. Highway construction brings great transformations in the lives, livelihoods and lifestyles of many; those whose land and residence are directly affected as well as those who form the category of users. I categorize the effects of highway construction into two types, divergence and emergence, which, though seemingly apart, are interrelated. Divergence is the friction that arises during highway building. Friction occurs when policy-level ideas and practices conceived in higher official circles encounter obstacles or obstructions on the ground, such as in the case of land acquisition, which brings public and private developers and local populations, especially rural landholders, directly into confrontation. Looking at highways from a divergence perspective, one sees the highway as dividing villages and alienating people from one another. While highway construction is a much vaunted concept in the idea of cross-border connectivity and overall development, it carries its own exclusions. Although a matter of pride for many people, four-laning of highways has created different experiences. The highway, evidently, caters to the different classes in very opposite ways. The euphoria of road construction is largely limited to the burgeoning middle classes for whom highways signal increased automobility. In contrast, for the less privileged, highways could mean bifurcation of households, disruption of livelihoods, loss of rural markets, and, overall, greater rather than fewer restrictions on mobility, both social and geographical. Many residents along NH 37, to whom the road appeared to be a saviour, were disappointed as they were displaced and uprooted from their older homes and forced to relocate somewhere where the road no longer went.

Rosy Ahmed, a homemaker in one of the villages affected by highway expansion reported experiencing a loss of community and increased disconnect as the highway bifurcated villages and sent the nearby marketplace, formerly a hub of gossip and sociality, into decline. She mourned before me the loss of her kitchen garden, fish pond and trees, which had to be given up to the road (interview, 13 September 2014). In the absence of proper public transport and service roads, highways not only bring disconnection instead of connectivity but also take a toll on people's lives through road accidents.

In this chapter, my focus has been on what I term the emergence effect of highway building. Emergence characterizes the unintended and secondary consequences of highway construction. Rather than seeing the highways as singular, empty space, or non-place (Augé 1995), I am interested to see how social relations, social differences, and habitus become manifest here. In the highways of India, social relations develop in various roadside spaces, which include bus depots, truck depots, gas stations, or *dhabas*. Each of these emergences characterize sets of social relations and provide indicators about the social character of highways. In the *dhabas*, which are a ubiquitous presence on every small or major highway of India, class relations already visible in the consumption patterns of the city are reinscribed.

Dhabas have many positive consequences. Rural areas gain when *dhaba* owners buy products from local farmers, marking a point of intersection between urban and rural settlements. In his account of the Pradhan Mantri Gram Sadak Yojana (PMGSY), India's programme to provide rural connectivity, Edward Simpson (Rankin and Simpson, this volume) cites an informant – 'this rural road-building scheme enlivens the dynamic connections between village and the market, the market and the highway, the highway and the nation'. The three-way connection between village, market and highway applies well in the case of the *dhabas*, which, in both physical and economic terms, represent the meeting point between village, market, and highway. *Dhabas* also create employment opportunities for predominantly young migrant workers. My fieldwork revealed that the service staff in the *dhabas* are mostly recruited from the migrant workforce, youth from small towns in Bihar and Uttar Pradesh in search of urban employment.

For others more financially able, *dhabas* are sites of speculation which have fuelled local entrepreneurship in real estate (see also Khan, this volume, for a comparative case in Pakistan). While highways may supplant local livelihoods, such as farming, they may bring alternative livelihoods in the non-farm sector. Here, both divergence and emergence appear to be two sides of the same coin. When land is taken over from local populations for the construction and expansion of highways, it is invested by entrepreneurs in businesses such as *dhabas* by the roadside. In both the sites I studied (Murthal and Nagaon), many of the lavishly designed, hybrid *dhabas* were owned by people who belonged to the wealthier sections of society. They were absentee owners, who did not personally oversee their functioning, and the management of these *dhabas* rested with their salaried employees, who manned the reception desks.

In Assam, however, several smaller or mid-sized *dhabas* were owned and operated by individuals who found in them a source of income in the absence of other employment opportunities in the private sector or the much-coveted *sarkari* (government) jobs. For example, Pampu Baniya, owner of Midway *dhaba*, is a college graduate who got the land for his *dhaba* on a fifteen-year lease from a teacher in Nagaon College. He told me that the highway had given a boost to local entrepreneurship as many, previously unemployed, educated youth like himself seized the opportunity to start *dhaba* businesses, investments in hardware, welding, motor parts and road contract work (interview, 15 September 2014).

Dhabas are not always lucrative sources of income for the local population. In Murthal, for example, businessmen from the neighbouring Punjab state bought up large plots of land from the local people for building *dhabas*. In the case of the Maldives, documented by Heslop and Jeffery (this volume), entire islands were obtained through road projects. In the next few sections, I discuss how highway *dhabas* highlight and reinforce social relations based on class.

Dhaba culture and middle-class consumption

The new highway *dhabas* have changed how people making road trips now approach travel. Wolfgang Schivelbusch showed how with the invention of steam-powered rail, it was not just the railways per se, but the technological additions of telegraph wires and poles that became as central to the visual landscape of railways as the railways themselves and mediated the outer world beyond the compartment to the traveller (Schivelbusch 1986: 36). Just as the telegraph wires and poles became part of the railway-scapes, hybrid *dhabas* have also become almost synonymous with road trips. A question posed by the editors of this book: *How have people come to think about roads in the ways that they do?* (Heslop and Murton, this volume) finds one answer in the imagery of *dhabas*: when people in India think about travel on the highway they think about *dhabas. Dhabas* provide a common element in highway-scapes of India. For college-going youth or other groups out to have a good time, the highways provide an exciting destination, or travel goal, in the form of the *dhabas.*

A number of travel and food guidebooks and TV shows, which advise viewers and readers about the best *dhabas* along specific highways, go to prove how deeply embedded roadside *dhabas* have come to be in the imagination of highway commuters. The most well-known example is the show *Highway on My Plate*, hosted by Rocky Singh and Mayur Sharma on India's NDTV, who later brought out two books with the same topic and name (Singh and Sharma 2010, 2014), which document their *dhaba*-hopping journey across the country. These books give a state-wise division of the author's culinary explorations and contain maps showing the rough location of the *dhabas* and a brief note about each state, its food culture and signature dishes (Malhotra 2014). The book description on the back cover of Singh and Sharma's book, describes it as follows:

> Driving through India and want to know where to eat on the road? Try *Highway on My Plate*: the Indian guide to roadside eating, the country's first guide to *dhabas* and roadside restaurants. Adapted from the hit TV series on NDTV Good Times, 'Highway on My Plate', it lists the top eats on almost every major Indian highway and routes as presented by the popular anchors Rocky and Mayur. Packed with information, *Highway on My Plate* is an indispensable guide for all road trips. (Singh and Sharma 2010, back cover)

Like Singh and Sharma, Charmaine O'Brien's food guide includes many reviews and recommendations about *dhabas* and other eating joints. A search on the Amazon India site reveals multiple books on highway *dhaba* food that were published in recent years. A good number of newspapers, magazines and travel blogs regularly publish articles on *dhaba* eating; and the appreciation for such writing is evident in the customer reviews of books published on the online store's website. Mostly from people in the 20s to 40s age group, these reviews and feedback reflect how *dhabas* have enthused the imaginations of a large number of the travelling population.

They make it evident that people on road trips are not just interested in the end destination of the highway journey, but also in the breaks in the form of *dhabas*. Here we encounter a less noticeable, yet no less significant, aspect of infrastructure development and highway expansion.

These *dhabas* fulfil the need for clean and hygienic eating in between the journey. Quite often, the customers are not only travellers stopping for breakfast, lunch or dinner but also people who specifically come to eat in the highway *dhabas*, after reading or hearing good reviews of the latter. Interestingly, many of these *dhabas* have become brand names as seen in the fact that other aspiring *dhabas* seek success by imitating their names. For example, Zhilmil and Amrik *dhabas* have spawned many *dhaba* names that closely resemble theirs. Customers who might have heard of the big names are lured into the duplicate ones by the superficial resemblance of the names.

The new *dhabas* have generated different kinds of expectations from road travellers: clean restrooms, computerized receipts or bills, local flavours, etc., which were absent in the more basic traditional *dhabas*. They have created a new code of travel, but one which is biased towards the middle-class consumer. As one male customer in his late 20s, a Delhi-based business-man travelling with his partner, told me, 'We now expect better services from these *dhabas*, such as purified water, tissue papers etc.' (interview, 12 June 2019).

As more and more people are finding mobility through the improved road infrastructure across the country, they are also seeking new outlets for rest and recreation. The new *dhabas* on highways have fuelled a surge in not just outside dining but also dining away from the rush of the main city. *Dhabas* cater to this middle-class clientele seeking new avenues for consumption.

In India, 'middle class' is a flexible term that in the post-independence period was seen to be composed of 'Nehruvian civil service-oriented salariat', benefiting from the expansion of higher education, government, and the public sector during this period, its social and economic base rooted in the state (Deshpande 2003: 144-146; Fernandes 2011).[3] Post-liberalization India

---

3   Sociologist D.P. Mukerji (2002) contends that the middle class in India was a product of the colonial economy and the colonial pattern of education since British rule changed the very basis of the Indian social economy. The middle class mediated the relationship between the colonial rulers and colonial subjects by subordinating to colonial power but at the same time providing cultural leadership to the indigenous people. In post-independence India, the middle class were the Nehruvian middle class, whose role, Satish Deshpande (2003) suggests, was to 'articulate the hegemony of the ruling bloc', which it did through its control over the developmental state and the legitimizing ideology of development.

saw the rise of a new middle class, better defined as an upper segment of the middle class, consisting primarily of managerial-professional elites. In the contemporary period, the new middle class, as a social group, is depicted as negotiating India's new relationship with the global economy in both sociocultural symbolic practices of commodity consumption, and economic terms – the beneficiaries of the material benefits of jobs and business in India's new liberalized economy. They are the ones who are connected to a global circuit through education, jobs, and travel, and aspire to be participants of a global modernity. While the old middle class was dependent on public sector jobs, the new middle class locates itself primarily within the rapidly expanding private sector and the globalized economy (Fernandes 2011). From the 1990s onwards, India has seen rising incomes, diversification of occupations, an influx of foreign consumer goods, and growing consumption among the middle classes, who are flooded with new media images and advertisements sponsored by corporations wishing to promote their brands.

'Middle class', then, represents a class and a status group,[4] converging around lifestyle, purchasing power and prestige. Leela Fernandes (2011), while refusing a singular identity to the Indian middle classes, shows how the new middle classes provide a hegemonic model to which lower-middle-class youth of small towns and rural areas in India aspire. They try to acquire the cultural capital by honing their (English-)speaking skills, acquiring marketing or other professional diplomas from unaccredited institutes, purchasing certain commodities to project upward mobility. The new middle class represents a normative standard for the rest of this social group, who seek symbolic access to the upper tier through various consumption choices.[5]

In the regional context of Assam, the middle class is visible mostly through certain consumption habits and lifestyle practices. Along with the rest of the country, Assam, too, has seen a gradually burgeoning middle class

4   In his essay 'Classes, Status Groups and Parties', Max Weber (1978) differentiated between class situation, which is the way in which property is distributed among a population and determines their life chances in the market, while status is the way in which social honour is distributed in a community between different groups. While class and status are frequently opposed, they can also merge in some situations, when classes become status groups.

5   Scholars (e.g. Baviskar and Ray 2011) have argued that India's middle class is a represented category, that is, it is a diverse group composed of people who identify as middle class. This group has appropriated the identity of the *aam aadmi* (common man) in order to gain legitimacy for projects that eventually benefit the elite. Hence, popular politics in urban India revolve not around basic needs of food, clothing and shelter – which still remain significant in the lives of poor people – but around *bijli, paani* and *sadak* (electricity, water and roads) – all infrastructural forms that mirror aspirations of a particular class for inclusion in a global modernity.

since the 2000s. As in the all-India scene, this new regional middle class, whose identity rests on their economic purchasing power and consumption styles, is different from an earlier, salaried middle class, and are often called *natun dhoni* (new rich) – a term used by a *dhaba* manager to describe his customers – or those who acquired their wealth through contracting or business and are distinct from older, respected gentry. *Dhaba* owners solicit such moneyed clients. However, the very fact that the new *dhabas* invite and attract a particular kind of customer, also makes them spaces of exclusion.

Whose highway? *Dhabas* as spaces of exclusion

Seven Sisters Dhaba on NH 37, which is relatively small but with fancy lights, has a huge signboard that explicitly states that its hospitality is 'only for family and officers', and that 'wine (drinking) is not allowed'. It is a clear proclamation of who is allowed and legitimately belongs and who does not belong. The term 'officer', locally used to refer to bureaucrats, indicates a preference for a salaried and status-bearing middle-class customer. The signboard, in this case, is more than an advertisement, but is about being known in a particular way (Heslop 2015: 16). It is a communication sign that indicates a preferred customer type.

I read the use of 'officer' on the signboard of Seven Sisters Dhaba as the hangover of the post-independence period. Rather than referring only to the person of the officer of an older, salaried middle class, who is certainly not the only kind of customer frequenting these *dhabas*, the term 'officer' appears to be an indexical sign – the label for an amorphous and aspirational category that we call the 'middle class'.

Secondly, the pointed reference to 'family and officers' is clearly intended to convey a particular message. The fact that the *dhaba* extends an invitation to 'family' should not be read to mean that officers without families are excluded; rather, it speaks of a specific form of respectability, legitimacy and middle-class values that the *dhabas* in question seek to appropriate in order to project a particular image of themselves. The context for this is the widespread conception of highway *dhabas* and small hotels as dens of illicit, underground activities, such as the liquor trade and sex work, heightened by media reports about raids on roadside *dhabas*. In June 2018, acting on a tip-off, Haryana police raided Jannat, one of the smaller, less glamorous *dhabas* on Murthal road and arrested a team of sex racketeers, who were engaged in illegal trade from the *dhaba*'s hotel rooms. While such reports bring a bad name to highway *dhabas*, *dhabas* like Amrik

Sukhdev preserve their image as respectable and safe spaces for families or women travelling alone. This, I maintain, is possible because the new *dhabas* distance themselves, both physically and figuratively, from other *dhabas*, especially line *dhabas*, and by implication, the activities associated with the latter. Not only are the new *dhabas* different spaces from previous *dhabas*, but they are also quite specific in excluding those who are not perceived to belong in their target category.

The liaison role that line *dhabas* play in connecting truck drivers and commercial sex workers has been discussed in many reports. During their long journeys, truckers pick up women from the *dhabas*, have sex with them, and then drop them at another *dhaba*. Many reports attribute a huge incidence of AIDS transmission to unprotected sex rampant among truck drivers who move between different regions (Rao et al. 1999). Line *dhaba* owners are sensitive to such prejudices. I was regarded with unease whenever I tried to put questions to owners of line *dhabas*. One particular owner was hostile to me when I entered his *dhaba*. He gave brief, unwilling responses to my innocuous questions about food and the number of customers, and he insisted that I leave the *dhaba* and visit his other business of fixing car tyres, which he ran from a nearby shack. When I tried to reassure him that I meant no harm, he reacted defensively and said, without any prompt, 'Why should I be afraid of your questions? It's not as if I am running any *dhanda* [referring in this context to illegal businesses of sex and drugs].' On the one hand, thus, the stereotypical association of line *dhabas* with the sex trade make them a convenient foil for the new *dhabas*, as the management in the hybrid *dhabas* attempt to differentiate themselves from the former type. On the other hand, the imputed difference to line *dhabas* mark them as not belonging to the emerging middle-class spaces of the highways.

Dhaba owners openly admitted to me that they discouraged truck drivers from parking their vehicles outside, which naturally meant that truck drivers could not stop to eat in these places. One of them said, 'Truck drivers have their own *dhabas* nearer to their taste and community', adding that they do not allow in truck drivers, for they spoil the atmosphere of the place. According to Pranjit Sarma, proprietor of B&B *dhaba*-cum-restaurant on NH 37, truck drivers do not come to the fancier *dhabas*, preferring to go to another area – Kothiatoli, where line *dhabas* are clustered (interview, 12 September 2014). All over India, such line *dhabas* are found at safe distances – at least five kilometres – from the more mainstream *dhabas*. Pranjit Sarma's telling statement, 'families usually shirk from *dhabas* but won't hesitate to enter a *dhaba*-cum-restaurant', shows that the difference and exclusion of line *dhabas* are necessary for upholding the middle-class character and image of the hybrid highway *dhabas*.

The highways not only mark the line *dhabas*, but also the category of truck drivers who frequent these *dhabas*, as outsiders. Before the expansion and four-laning of the highways, and their gradual opening up to an increasing number of motorists, these roads were used mostly by the community of truck drivers, who provide essential transport services to the manufacturers and traders and, literally, are the main drivers of interstate ground transport. The reinvention of the Indian highway and the emergence of the new *dhabas* have meant that for truck drivers the highway has shrunk as a space for them. As the highways are sanitized as a space for middle-class consumption, truck drivers are restricted to particular corners, that is, the line *dhabas*. They eat, wash up, and rest in extremely unsanitary conditions, because public conveniences are not available and private ones are denied. The increased (auto)mobility of a large section of middle-class people have meant a more circumscribed movement for the truck drivers, as they are restricted from many spaces. The exclusion of the truck drivers further points to how highways are hierarchical spaces in terms of the conditions of mobility. Moreover, mobility, hierarchy and amenities on the roadside illustrate how the contemporary Indian economy is read through sites of consumption, while the work of production is largely hidden away: lorries travel at night and must not be seen at the restaurants themselves.

How highways reproduce urban hierarchies: Tracing middle-class habitus

Sociologist Amita Baviskar (2011) calls the Indian city a middle-class city and the site of bourgeois activism, that is, social activism oriented to serving the needs and demands of the middle class at the expense of lower-income city populations.[6] Anthropological studies of Indian cities (e.g. Baviskar 2011; Sadana 2010; Srivastava 2015) have shown how a particular middle-class habitus is produced by and is visible in certain consumption practices in the city.

6   Sanjay Srivastva gives a broader explanation of middle-class activism as connoting that middle classes are the agents of change; hence, the middle class may include the resident welfare associations (RWAs) that are an integral part of all housing societies in urban areas, which are urban associations of mostly middle-class base, which try to secure a certain material standard either through private means or by negotiating with the state (2015: 85). But middle-class activism could also be pro-poor lobbying, such as fighting for the rights of slum dwellers.

Post-liberalization, many urban spaces in India have been transformed by the shift from small shops concentrated in commercial areas and traditional markets to shopping malls, supermarkets, and designer stores. Changes of consumption is also evident in housing preferences. Many software professionals in cities like Bangalore want to stay in apartment complexes or gated communities with amenities like swimming pools, security guards, gyms or ATMs. The landscapes of cities such as Bangalore and Hyderabad have been transformed almost overnight by expensive apartment complexes and gated communities, posh shopping malls with multiplex theatres, upscale restaurants and specialty stores, the multiplication of luxury cars clogging the roads, and a range of leisure and support services catering to the global lifestyles of the new middle class – all testifying to the enhanced purchasing power and changing consumption patterns of this segment of the urban population.

Sanjay Srivastava (2015) identifies several spaces within cities, including malls, supermarkets, and gated communities, as well as refurbished and glamorized temple complexes, as spaces of consumption for the (self-identifying) middle classes. In many instances, these spaces are sites through which a middle-class status is claimed. This is particularly evident in the fact that shopping malls in cities are something of a tourist attraction for small-town visitors, who claim middle-class status through their identifica-tion as a mall-going public (Srivastava 2015: 225). But the point to note here is that these are not spaces to which all have access.[7] Not only are malls spaces of exclusion but also there is a particular way of navigating these spaces, which is available to the middle-class customer, and is facilitated by ways of dressing, speaking, behaving and so on. Those who do not inhabit a middle-class habitus are not welcome in these spaces.

Bal, Sinha-Kerkhoff and Tripathy (2017) describe how gated communities in many Indian megacities are favoured by return migrants who wish to recreate their experiences and lifestyles abroad in the country, and, in doing so, they create a divide between residents and the outside world. These authors note how residents are characterized by large incomes,

---

7   I recall a particular scene from the film *Mumbai Meri Jaan* (2008) which illustrates how malls are spaces of exclusion in India, where only the rich and the middle-class public are welcome. In this scene, internationally famous actor Irfan Khan plays a Malayali coffee vendor who takes his wife and child to a shopping mall but is humiliated and thrown out. His fault is that he is identified by the security guards in the mall as the person who regularly wanders around the mall, aimlessly picking and sniffing expensive perfumes, or touching the merchandise on offer, but is not able to actually afford buying them. Irfan takes his revenge by making hoax phone calls warning of a bomb in the mall that results in scare and evacuation.

exposure to the West, and high levels of civic sense, i.e. similar habitus (2017: 18).

Highways, which lie across or between city and village, reproduce or rather, extend this middle-class habitus of the cities to the space of the *dhabas*.[8] In the example of the Delhi metro I previously cited, the metro produces in passengers a bourgeois habitus by imposing a certain code of behaviour. When *dhaba* practices reflect and cater to urban middle-class consumer expectations, they too support and market this particular class habitus for competitive advantage. The stress on clean, purified water, sanitized restrooms, and hygienic, air-conditioned room by both *dhaba* management and clientele invite the observer to visualize the *dhabas* as middle-class spaces.

In this chapter, I have argued that like the middle-class sites in the cities, *dhabas* mark hierarchical spaces and unequal access in the highways. Highways in India serve the interests of a particular class by giving access to owners of cars and those who can afford travel in private vehicles. The segregation of *dhabas* into those meant for middle-class customers and those meant for truck drivers point to how inequalities are spatialized in the middle of the highway journey. Thus, highways mirror the inequalities and exclusions visible in India's urban spaces.

Here, I have highlighted only one kind of inequality, that is, class inequality. Other parameters of inequality – caste, gender, or religion – are equally present in highway spaces, although I have not explored those here. While highways are being built at a hasty pace, adequate public transport to accompany these developments is not provided. People who do not own cars and cannot afford private taxis are forced to rely on shared, overcrowded tempos, which make unscheduled stops on the highway and are generally regarded as an unsafe means of transport.

These highway trends are characteristic of neoliberal distribution. Akhil Gupta (2015), writing about electricity, shows how neoliberal government policy has prevented a more vigorous redistributive agenda. Even if there

---

8   Habitus is an ambiguous concept, formulated by Pierre Bourdieu himself and his later commentators, in many different ways. However, one attains a better grasp of it by seeing how Bourdieu differentiates habit from habitus: habit denotes mechanical behaviour, a stimulus-response reflex, whereas habitus implies a flexible disposition which, though pre-reflective, remains commensurate with purposive action and in no way precludes intelligence, understanding, strategy or knowledge on the part of the actor (Crossley 2013: 139). Habitus has a social, sociological quality, whereas habit is an individual matter. In my understanding, further, habitus is interactional; it is an interaction between individuals and the physical-social environment and, hence, it is also evolving, as individuals respond as socialized beings to the experience each environment exposes them to. In short, habitus shapes and is shaped by the external environment.

are more areas that have been electrified in theory, as governments in many developing countries claim, so that those who were formerly off the grid now have formal access to electricity, yet they cannot derive any actual benefit as they do not have the money to pay for its use. Poor people are forced to resort to various paralegal methods of getting power in their homes, such as paying intermediaries to cut and divert electricity lines for their use.[9]

Hence, with respect to India, Ravi Ahuja (2009) questions the logic of calling any public work or infrastructure 'public', for they do not cater to the requirement of the common public but only fulfil industrial or private needs. During colonial rule, many roads and railways were built to connect industry or plantation to ports and metropolitan destinations, and seldom increased rural connectivity. This situation continues in the postcolonial period, and has been aggravated by the neoliberal policies adopted by various governments, which has increased the disconnect between rich and poor. Like Ahuja, Nikhil Anand also questions the publicness of public infrastructure, stating: 'Public spaces are not designated for an ambiguous public but a defined one. Therefore, in modern cities, public spaces are not "open" spaces in which everyone can do what they wish' (2006: 3424).

I have tried to show in this chapter how *dhabas*, which appear to be secondary developments of highway expansion, are actually part of this general climate of neoliberal distribution. Like the gated communities, malls and other urban sites, highway *dhabas* spatialize social hierarchies and reproduce differential class habitus. As *dhabas*, and gradually, other, pay-for-use areas begin to dominate the landscape of the Indian highways, they irrevocably change the latter's character.

List of works cited

Ahuja, R. (2009). *Pathways of Empire: Circulation, 'Public Works' and Social Space in Colonial Orissa (c. 1780-1914)*. Hyderabad: Orient BlackSwan.

Anand, Nikhil (2006). 'Disconnecting Experience: Making World Class Roads in Mumbai'. *Economic and Political Weekly* 41 (31): 3422-3429.

Augé, M. (1995). *Non-Places: An Introduction to Super-Modernity*. London: Verso.

9   This is depicted in the documentary *Katiabaaz* (2013; in Hindi, the title's literal meaning is 'he who cuts electric cables'), which is a story about Kanpur, a small town in Uttar Pradesh, India, where residents regularly face lengthy power cuts up to fifteen hours long every day, forcing many to attempt to steal electricity and giving rise to informal middlemen who connect slum dwellers to the services of the city, such as Loha Singh, an electricity thief whose services are much sought after.

Bal, E.W., K. Sinha-Kerkhoff and R. Tripathy (2017). 'Unequal Mobility Regimes of Indian Gated Communities: Converging Regional, National and Transnational Migration Flows in Indian Metropolitan Cities'. *New Diversities* 19(3): 13-27.

Baviskar, A. (2011). 'Spectacular Events, City Spaces and Citizenship: The Commonwealth Games in Delhi'. In *Urban Navigations: Politics, Space and the City in South Asia*, ed. by J.S. Anjaria and C. McFarlane. Delhi: Routledge, 23-49.

Baviskar, A., and R. Ray (2011). 'Introduction'. In *Elite and Everyman: Cultural Politics of the Indian Middle Classes*, ed. by A. Baviskar and R. Ray. Delhi: Routledge, 1-27.

Benjamin, Walter (1999). *Illuminations*. London: Pimlico.

Blakely, E., and M. Snyder (1997). *Fortress America: Gated Communities in the United States*. Washington, DC: Brookings Institution Press.

Bourdieu, P. (1977). *Outline of a Theory of Practice*. Cambridge: Cambridge University Press.

Cresswell, T. (2010). 'Towards a Politics of Mobility'. *Environment and Planning D: Society and Space* 28: 17-31.

Crossley, N. (2013). Habit and Habitus. *Body and Society* 19(2-3): 136-161.

Dalakoglou, D. (2010). 'The Road: An Ethnography of the Albanian-Greek Cross-Border Motorway'. *American Ethnologist* 37(1): 132-149.

Davis, M. (2005). *Planet of Slums*. London: Verso.

Deshpande, S. (2003). 'The Centrality of the Middle Class'. In *Contemporary India: A Sociological View*. New Delhi: Viking, 125-150.

Fernandes, L. (2011). 'Hegemony and Inequality: Theoretical Reflections on India's Middle Class'. In *Elite and Everyman: Cultural Politics of the Indian Middle Classes*, ed. by A. Baviskar and R. Ray. Delhi: Routledge, 58-82.

Ganser, A. (2006). 'On the Asphalt Frontier: American Women's Road Narratives, Spatiality, and Transgression'. *Journal of International Women's Studies* 7(4): 153-167.

Gupta, A. (2015). 'An Anthropology of Electricity from the Global South'. *Cultural Anthropology* 30(4): 555-568.

Harvey, P., and H. Knox (2015). *Roads: An Anthropology of Infrastructure and Expertise*. Ithaca, NY: Cornell University Press.

Heslop, L. (2015). 'Signboards and the Naming of Small Businesses: Personhood and Dissimulation in a Sri Lankan Market Town'. *South Asia Multidisciplinary Academic Journal* 12: 1-16.

Kerouac, J. (1957). *On the Road*. New York: Viking.

Lefebvre, H. (1991). *The Production of Space*. London: Blackwell.

Low, S. (2001). 'Edge and the Centre: Gated Communities and the Discourse of Urban Fear'. *American Anthropologist* 103(1): 45-58.

Madhur, S., G. Wignaraja and P. Darjes (2009). 'Roads for Asian Integration: Measuring ADB's Contribution to the Asian Highway Network'. Asian Development

Bank Working Paper Series on Regional Economic Integration, No. 37, November. https://www.adb.org/sites/default/files/publication/28511/wp37-roads-asian-integration.pdf (accessed 1 July 2014).

Malhotra, A. (2014). 'How to Pick a Good Roadside Eatery in India'. *Wall Street Journal*, 13 August. http://blogs.wsj.com/indiarealtime/2014/08/13/how-to-pick-a-good-roadside-eatery-in-india/ (accessed 10 April 2021).

Mazumdar, S. (2016). 'Looking for Delicious, Authentic Cooking in India? Head to a Truck Stop'. *Smithsonian Magazine*, 21 January. https://www.smithsonianmag.com/travel/roadside-highway-dining-india-dhaba-cuisine-tradition-180957795/ (accessed 10 April 2021).

Mukerji, D.P. (2002). *Indian Culture: A Sociological Study*. New Delhi: Rupa and Company.

O'Brien, C. (2013). *The Penguin Food Guide to India*. New Delhi: Penguin.

Rao, K.S., R.D. Pilli, A.S. Rao and P.S. Chalam (1999). 'Sexual Lifestyle of Long Distance Lorry Drivers in India: Questionnaire Survey'. *BMJ* 318(7177): 162-163. https://doi.org/10.1136/bmj.318.7177.162.

Sadana, Rashmi (2010). 'On the Delhi Metro: An Ethnographic View'. *Economic and Political Weekly* 45 (46): 77-83

Schivelbusch, W. (1986). *The Railway Journey: The Industrialization of Time and Space in the Nineteenth Century*. Oakland: University of California Press.

Shukla, T. (2008). 'Dabur Adopts 150 Highway Dhabas'. *DNA*, 16 October. https://www.dnaindia.com/business/report-dabur-adopts-150-highway-dhabas-1198463 (accessed 10 April 2021).

Simmel, G. (2002). 'The Metropolis and Mental Life'. In *The Blackwell City Reader*, ed. by G. Bridge and S. Watson. Oxford: Wiley-Blackwell, 155-168.

Singh, R., and M. Sharma (2010). *Highway on My Plate: The Indian Guide to Roadside Eating*. Noida: Random House India.

Singh, R., and M. Sharma (2014). *Highway on My Plate-II: The Indian Guide to Roadside Eating*. Haryana: Ebury Press.

Srivastava, S. (2015). *Entangled Urbanism: Slum, Gated Community and Shopping Mall in Delhi and Gurgaon*. Oxford: Oxford University Press.

Tewari, S. (2007). *Informal in Formal: Mushrooming of Dhabas next to BPOs/MNCs in Gurgaon*. Dissertation, Sushant School of Art and Architecture, Gurgaon.

Thiranagama, S., T. Kelly and C. Forment (2018). 'Introduction: Whose Civility?' *Anthropological Theory* 18(2-3): 153-174.

Trachtenberg, A. (1986). 'Foreword'. In *The Railway Journey: The Industrialization of Time and Space in the Nineteenth Century*, by W. Schivelbusch. Oakland: University of California Press, xiii-xvi.

Veblen, T. (1899). *Theory of the Leisure Class*. London: Macmillan.

Weber, Max (1978). 'Classes, Status Groups, and Parties'. In *Max Weber: Selections in Translation*, ed. by W.G. Runciman, trans. by Eric Mathews. Cambridge: Cambridge University Press, 43-56

Wirth, L. (1938). 'Urbanism as a Way of Life'. *The American Journal of Sociology* 44(1): 1-24.

About the author

SWARGAJYOTI GOHAIN is Assistant Professor of Sociology and Anthropology at Ashoka University, Haryana. Dr. Gohain has done research in Northeast India and the Himalayan region on borders and the state, culture, migration and infrastructure. She is the author of *Imagined Geographies in the Indo-Tibetan Borderlands* (Amsterdam University Press, 2020).

5 The edge of Kaladan

A 'spectacular' road through 'nowhere' on the India-Myanmar borderlands

Jasnea Sarma

Abstract

Using the case of India's mega-infrastructure build-up, the Kaladan Multimodal Transport Project (KMMTP) in the 'remote' and ethnically contentious borderlands between India and Myanmar, this chapter takes an ethnographic approach to understand the meaning of spectacular connectivity and infrastructure on remote borderlands. Based on six months of fieldwork, the chapter explores the voices, visions, spatial and ethnic worlds of border residents who subsequently have to position themselves and their remoteness to absorb the Indian state's spectacular new connective infrastructure. The chapter narratively traverses along this newly constructed road, to the very edge of a hitherto informal and flexible border with Myanmar. In doing so, it highlights the need to investigate the banal, unspectacular and interethnic lived realities of the borderland. The chapter argues that spectacular infrastructures such as the KMMTP are harnessed in the pursuit of territorial control, making the remote legible and for extracting profits. The chapter introduces the analytic of the 'spectacle' to demonstrate how powerful states and ethnic communities rely on grand infrastructural spectacles and cross-border projects often at the expense, erasure and displacement of those at the edge of borderlands, who have the least stake in shaping such spectacular infrastructures.

Keywords: India, Myanmar, Kaladan, spectacle, remoteness, infrastructure

Introduction: A road through 'nowhere' from India to Myanmar

Borderlands and frontiers have always been the archetypal 'remote' place in popular imagination yet they rarely vanish from the powerful gaze of

Heslop, Luke, and Galen Murton (eds), *Highways and Hierarchies: Ethnographies of Mobility from the Himalaya to the Indian Ocean.* Amsterdam, Amsterdam University Press 2021
DOI: 10.5117/9789463723046_CH05

empire rulers and state leaders. In the past, imperial courts tried to rein them in and colonial merchants wished to market them. Today, state authorities hope to govern them, zoning the peripheries as transformative spaces responsive to development agendas and new sovereign orders.
– *Zhang* (2014: 376)

On a late winter night in 2015, we arrived in the quiet town of Lawngtlai after an arduous seventeen-hour road journey from Aizawl, the capital of Mizoram state, in Northeast India. Sparsely populated, it was a cold, whispery district sitting at 1132 feet above sea level bordering Chin State in Myanmar to the south and the Chittagong Hill Tracts in Bangladesh to the west. Despite being the district capital, Lawngtlai was not an easy place to arrive at by road, as the roads U-turned often, sharply biting into the loose red soil of the Lusei[1] hills, making landslides common. Our muddy Suzuki 'Gypsy', one of the most preferred modes of transport in these hills advertised to power through the harshest hilly terrains, skidded dangerously in the red sand. Embarrassingly, we became stuck on landslides frequently during fieldwork. On that day, as we pulled in, we saw U Tawa,[2] my contact with the Mizoram state government's DRDA (Department of Rural Development). Sitting on the porch with his elderly father, undeterred by the deep fog surrounding them, U Tawa, who was probably used to his guests arriving much later than expected, came out remarking, 'Welcome to nowhere, sister.'[3]

His greeting surprised me. I had explored the Myanmar side of the border just a month ago, which I felt was undoubtedly truly like 'nowhere', boat rides on the Kaladan River being the only mode of travel anywhere north of the town of Paletwa in Chin State. But local residents in these parts of Mizoram on the Indian side of the border seemed to feel at home with this self-ascribed remoteness. U Tawa was quick to press the point further, saying that this must be the most remote place I had ever seen. Before 2010, this part of the Indian side of the border in the south of Mizoram had yet to be touched by the state or neoliberal capital. The Kaladan River, which flowed through this territory and across the border, was then one of the most pristine rivers in India, and in 2017, the fifth-largest un-dredged and un-dammed river in the world.

1   The anglicized form of Lusei is Lushai. 'Lushai' will be used only referring to the colonial period.
2   All names of informants used in this chapter are pseudonyms unless otherwise stated.
3   The fieldwork was conducted using a combination of English, Hindi, Burmese and Mizo languages. Quotes used here have been translated by the author as closely as possible to match the vernacular tone.

But things were changing in the hilly, remote borderlands. Something 'spectacular', both material and discursive, was disturbing its indubitable 'remoteness', catapulting the hills into action, albeit quite slowly in the initial years. Here, in the 'middle of nowhere', India had invested US$484 million to build a 'multimodal' river and road transport infrastructure, as part of the Act East Policy to connect Northeast India to the Bay of Bengal through Mizoram state in India and the conflicted borderlands of Chin State/Rakhine State in Myanmar. These were terrains ill-suited to the safe construction of infrastructure. They named the project the Kaladan Multimodal Transport Project (KMMTP), after the Kaladan River. It was called 'multimodal' because of the project's complicated use of both land and riverine geographies to build the transport routes, including the side work of ancillary port building and river dredging on the Myanmar side. One engineer tasked with the job, perhaps sensing the spectacle, with both pride (for the project's grandeur) and frustration (for its difficult implementation), described it as an 'impossible engineering marvel in the jungle, in the middle of nowhere!'

Through this grand 'multimodal transport project', India aimed to develop and globalize the remote state of Mizoram (and all of India's landlocked North Eastern Region) and transform it into an important hub of regional cross-border connectivity, and as a future resource transit zone.

The state's geopolitical imagination travels down the chain from state to technocracy and finally to real-life materialization; in this case, to the 'middle of nowhere'. Successive state and central governments committed to completing this impossible task as part of India's ambitious Act East Policy,[4] widely promoting and celebrating it as a cross-border development that would optimize transportation linkages and create regional border markets, jobs and connections with a long forgotten and unexplored neighbour (Egreteau 2008). Behind such claims, it was clear that the Indian motives were geopolitical/economic and rather more strategic than altruistically developmental. Access to resources via the oil-rich Sittwe Port of western Myanmar notwithstanding.

How to build such an ambitious road and river project over such hilly terrains? The plan was to first dredge the river near Sittwe Port to accommodate boats with a six-metre draft, install a brand new port facility across from the town of Paletwa, 158 km up the river, construct a new 'multimodal' road connecting Chin State to Mizoram and create a border trading area between India and Myanmar with border gates, customs and checkpoints. In other words, to build what an Indian intelligence bureau officer (Aizawl,

---

4   For a discussion on this policy, see Jaishankar 2019.

2016) referred to as, 'an almost impossible road', seemingly going through 'nowhere', the construction for which no land, hill, forest or river was to be spared. As the planners got to work, the landscape began to change. Just the announcement of the project caused the borderland with Myanmar to become a spatial resource, readied to serve as an even more resourceful border trading zone. This formerly remote 'nowhere' would then potentially become India's largest border market and transit zone to Myanmar, a landscape where big Indian state-led dreams of infrastructure would materialize, where new border regimens would be created and the border would slowly turn into one of the many resource assemblages that Cons and Eilenberg (2019) have recently situated in many other Asian landscapes. What then lies behind a state's talismanic aspirations of a connectivity and infrastructure spectacle on a hitherto 'remote' borderland? And how do remote subjects perceive themselves as receivers, co-interpreters and as the audience of such spectacles transforming their spatial, communal and economic lives? That is the ethnographic focus of this chapter.

Now that the 'remote', 'nowhere', and 'the end of the road' would inevitably become somewhere, many of the spaces through which the project traverses will still continue to be seen as 'nowhere' when seen from the state's top-down perspective. Thus, here is where the chapter derives its title – 'A Road through Nowhere'. The mega 'multimodal' project is not plotted to go to Mizoram as its raison d'être, but rather, to go 'through' it – en route, crossing a hitherto un-securitized border surrounded by lush hills and forests between India, and the ports and markets of Myanmar. Both the 'remote' and the notion of 'nowhere' are problematized here in their specific and contingent micropolitical geographies, ecologies, ethnic identities and border landscape. In so doing, I pay particular attention to the meanings and implications of remoteness and nowhere-ness from the perspective, vision and voices of the actual spaces and people 'through' which the spectacular KMMTP crosses.

The next section begins with a conceptual framing clarifying the meaning of building a 'spectacular' infrastructural resource frontier (Cons and Eilenberg 2019) in the midst of lived 'remoteness' on the border regions along the Kaladan River road assemblage between India and Myanmar. Empirically, I start at the beginning of the road in Lawngtlai town (in Mizoram), and slowly travel south towards the last village on the India-Myanmar border, Zochachhuah, stopping along key sites where the KMMTP construction took place. As such, the chapter goes on to locate four microworlds, themes that are spatially arranged to deepen an analysis of the contentions, convergences and relationality between connectivity and remoteness. First, I locate the first few residential villages through the theme 'local positioning', examining the ways in which local residents have positioned themselves to negotiate, resist and profit from a road. Second, I travel further into the forest regions where the road is being built through the theme 'expediting ecology', in which I inquire into the ways in which environment, ecology and labour regulations were relaxed, or 'expedited', to engineer and quicken the construction of spectacular infrastructural projects, despite concerns raised. As I travel from Mizo-dominated parts to areas settled by other, smaller ethnic groups, I raise a third theme, 'shaky identities'; I deploy this term to examine how a political landscape of micro-ethno-territoriality traversed by a seemingly innocuous road to nowhere highlights the tensions between the various ethnic groups and their simultaneous feelings about the road and who gets to make a resource out of it. Lastly, I explore the theme 'border life at the edge' as I travel to the furthest reaches where the new road meets the border with Myanmar on the India side. Here, I reflect on the life worlds of undocumented, or locally termed 'paperless', people, who use the border as a 'safe zone' away from conflict in Myanmar.

The chapter demonstrates the scalar modes in which the macro (state spectacles, geopolitical connectivity and capitalist desires) clash and converge with minute micro-dynamics (life, mobility, identity, access and environment) when a mega-road meets a remote border. It thus offers a detailed empirical understanding of the contentions and convergences in the making of infrastructural resource frontiers/assemblages (Cons and Eilenberg 2019), with how they unfold in the actual lived space, identities and emotions of fast transforming Kaladan border region between India and Myanmar. The chapter ends with a concluding discussion where I argue that spectacular roads and infrastructural assemblages are very much bordering devices that create opportunities for states, capital and dominant groups to penetrate 'remote' border territory through mechanisms of legibility, erasure, and frontier expedition. One must look behind the spectacle, to the more banal, unspectacular microworlds of the borderland to document and gauge what such assemblages make or unmake for those on the ground.

Spectacular infrastructures, remote borders

When I first met U Tawa in 2015, road building was hardly a topic of discussion in Lawngtlai. But by 2017, dredging of the Kaladan River, which is critical to the livelihoods (fishing, water supply, transport) of over a million people both upstream and downstream in both India's Mizoram state and

Myanmar's Chin State and Rakhine State, had begun. The project rumbles on today (in 2020), almost finished after numerous central government budget cuts, and several years behind schedule. Slowly, its material arrival transformed the perception of the Lusei-Chin highlands from a forgotten, remote and unproductive place to one of opportunities, new governance and speculation. Or in other words, the region was experiencing the 'zoning the peripheries as transformative spaces responsive to development agendas and new sovereign orders' (Zhang 2014: 376). This in turn led to an influx of state-backed corporate investors, government officials, consultants, and low-skilled migrant labourers from the plains (primarily Assam, Delhi and Bihar) into the steep Lusei hills of Mizoram.

As expected of such geographies, problems soon arose. In 2018, several workers were reported to have died while working on the road due to illness (largely malaria) and injuries caused by accidents (landslides and mudslides) that could not be easily treated because of the infrastructural inaccessibility to healthcare (Bouissou 2015).[5] This is tragic and ironic in that these are the very challenges the completion of the road aspires to mitigate. Furthermore, in the same year, nearby conflict in Myanmar struck the project landscape. The Arakan Army (AA) destroyed construction materials in Myanmar's Paletwa township and declared that official ransom would be sought from big projects, including the Kaladan project, if they passed through the AA's self-declared territory within Myanmar. The conflict led to the displacement of several Chin and Rakhine villages to the Indian side of the border, who were reported as a 'security problem' (Bhattacharyya 2019). Local ethnic communities on the Indian side also assembled to demand land compensation for areas where the road was built, and where the IDPs and several undocumented people were now taking refuge (Sanga 2019).

Initial concerns were raised by local CSOs in Myanmar who argued that the road only fulfilled vested interests of the Indian state for which locals suffered (ARN 2009). The Kaladan multimodal road building went on for years at risk to everyone involved. Displaced farmers could be seen lining up in the local district commissioner's offices, carrying farm produce, chickens and sometimes goats as gifts, in order to get the demanded compensation for the land. Smaller communities, NGOs and borderland residents had started to question what the impact of the project would be for people living in Mizoram state, but, just like other boom-and-bust road projects in these parts, the activism never took off. Contra the suspicion and cynicism documented by Heslop and Jeffery in the Maldives (this volume; Heslop 2020), despite

5   Interviews with residents.

these controversies and setbacks, many in Mizoram still approached the project with a great degree of anticipation, seeing it as the harbinger of new opportunities. Enthusiasm for the road was reflected in op-eds and articles in the local Lusei newspapers, even church newsletters, and in interviews I conducted in Aizawl with government officials, and community leaders. Among topics discussed in these sources, the central role that Mizoram had to play in India's Act East Policy was the most heatedly discussed topic of conversation. Many interviewed in Mizoram displayed excitement at the prospects of creating a bridge out of Mizoram's landlocked status.

I started fieldwork in this region in 2015 (with three rounds of follow-up fieldwork between 2016 and 2018[6]) before such controversies began, when it was quiet and true to its sobriquet, remote. I was particularly interested in the villages in the final section of the road on the Indian side of the border crossing at a village called Zochachhuah.[7] This portion of the road was not yet completed, because this was where most undocumented people and refugees settled. In Aizawl and Lawngtlai, we spoke to a range of people, including journalists, ministers, intelligence officers, academics, civil service officials from various departments, paramilitary and police officers, ethnic leaders from ADCs (autonomous district councils), churches, members of prominent Mizo organizations like the YMA (Young Mizo Association) and members of student unions and women's unions. In the rural areas along the road, I interviewed village councils, farmers, local 'undocumented' residents and some refugees, among others.

Speaking to an array of actors, and observing the enthusiasm, alacrity and persistence with which the Indian state pursued such a topographically difficult project, as well as the way it was welcomed by a majority of the Mizo population, I started to get the impression that I was witnessing the production, sustenance as well as consumption of a grand spectacle over a largely, and hitherto 'remote', hidden and inaccessible territory. Such a spectacle, as conceptualized in this chapter, works at multiple levels. Aihwa Ong (2011) in her work on the Chinese state's 'megastructures', defines spectacles as instruments to enhance the state's 'self-assured sovereignty', in seeking to maintain appearances of its arrival and control at par with neoliberal capital

6   Not all these voices are represented in the chapter, but the overall narrative is informed by these interviews. In addition, while travelling with a team of four Mizo research assistants, I sought special permission from the government to access the Kaladan border, with an ILP (Inner Line Permit), which is mandatory for any travellers into the region, and then with further permits to access the road.

7   Zorinpui is the name given by the Mizo ethnic group to the non-Mizo border space where a Kaladan Road checkpoint is to be constructed.

(Ong 2011: 206). In competition with China's BRI infrastructures in Southeast Asia, the ability to pull off the Kaladan project provides fodder for India's own ambitions in infrastructure tied to its own BRI-like posturing. At the same time, it also lets the Indian state position itself in defence against critiques of keeping the North Eastern Region disconnected, or 'remote', and undeveloped for 'security' reasons (Gohain 2019). As a geopolitical spectacle, it is also meant to signal the Indian state's resolve to capitalize on their eastern border as an overland access route to a lucrative Southeast Asian market. In harnessing a remote region, its peculiar space, and contending border populations, the region offers ample geo-economic possibilities in state-sponsored capitalism's ever-present addiction to exploiting new, unexplored and 'unlikely' (Li 2009) terrains. These are solutions to what Harvey (2001) famously called the 'spatial fix'. Another spectacular aspect is the amount of what Scott (1998) calls 'high modernist' technocracy and bureaucracy the project mobilizes, as evidenced by the frustrated pride of the engineer interviewed. Most importantly, the spectacle also plays into the state's perpetual desire to make territory legible (Scott 1998), while also generating profits.

Guy Debord (2010), inspired by the Marxist concept of 'false consciousness', contends in his *Society of the Spectacle* (1967), that spectacles 'demands in principle [...] the same passive acceptance that it has already secured by means of its seeming incontrovertibility, and indeed by its monopoliza-tion of the realm of appearances' (Debord 2010: 15). 'Contemplation of the spectacle' (Debord 2010: 118) supersedes, and therefore deludes, the masses from the exploits of lived reality which, for Debord, is inherently capitalist and extractive. Following this classic publication, a body of critical work emerged examining the goal of spectacles (for both state and capital) in the study of a myriad of spaces that demonstrate the 'monopoly of appearance' in various spaces, including cities, metropoles, and borders (Venturi et al. 1972; Dyckhoff 2017). As Debord and others have argued, the affective textures of spectacles balance, enchant, delude and digress people and consumers away from the real questions of oppression and extraction.

In writing about the crisscrossing rush of newly instituted highland infrastructures in Asia, Rippa, Murton, and Rest posit that '[l]ong before their actual construction starts, such projects already work as a promise for future prosperity and connectivity and lend legitimacy to logics of the "state" in areas historically difficult to access and hard to govern' (2020: 84). In effect, these infrastructures create a new spectacle of connectivity leading to prosperity before anything is connected or anyone has prospered. In the Mizoram, the spectacular appearance of a grand road serves as an instrument of distraction, causing people to ignore the increased legibility

(Scott 1998), territoriality, and expansion of state control over a remote border and its bodies that these infrastructures bring.

Borders and borderlands have long been the locations of security spectacles, in the effective control of bodies (migrants, refugees, and crossers), space, and flows (Mezzadra and Neilson 2013; Jones 2017; De Genova 2013). Northeast India, which is surrounded by five other nations and highly militarized as a 'sensitive space' (Cons 2016), is unsurprisingly replete with (security) spectacles spun around discourses, perceptions, and production of identities (Jones 2017; Ghosh 2019; Brown 2017; Baruah 2007; Krichker and Sarma 2019). These infrastructures – including but not limited to border walls, biometric infrastructures, detention centres – all serve and become integral to the maintenance and fabric of border spectacles (De Genova 2013).

The Kaladan region located at the India-Myanmar borderland is not that kind of border. Or at least not yet, although the aspiration exists, as will be shown below. No security spectacle existed, there was no border, and no paramilitary were present there until the production of a security border spectacle became part of the road's aspirations.[8] Left untouched and unguarded, the region up until the road constructions, was a definitive 'Zomia' landscape, famously (and controversially) conceptualized as 'shatter zones', the last remaining terrains in the world that served as 'refuge' to state-escaping people (Scott 2009: 8). Scott's oft cited 'friction of terrain' deterred centralizing states from climbing up the ungoverned hills. Historically, Mizoram has always been a zone of subterfuge and escape (Jackson 2016). A rich history of routes that were used for hundreds of years by raiders, horsemen and tribesmen (Nag 2002), and then MNF (Mizo National Front) fighters (Pachuau and Van Schendel 2011) lay in this territory.

'These hills are not meant for roads and not development. They are too dangerous,' remarked a seasonal worker on one of Kaladan's construction sites, as if to echo Scott's (1998) thoughts through his own experience. The World Bank Group, for example, approved several other road-construction projects on the northern side of the Kadalan River, which started in 2014, but the bust soon outdid the boom. Stricken by difficult terrain, budget difficulties and inner corruption within ministries, these projects could never be completed as fully as they were intended. As such, without roads, these regions would not easily be bought under the state's complete vision of legibility. All that, as I will establish, was starting to change with the KMMTP.

8   Although Mizoram's border with Myanmar and Bangladesh are guarded by the paramilitary Assam Rifles and the BSF (Border Security Force), respectively, not all parts of these borders are fenced, including the Kaladan region.

In the context of Northeast India, an emerging set of critical literature has recently surmised that infrastructures in Northeast India remain half-baked and half-done, and they seem to be built in places where the people have less need (Ziipao 2020). For these reasons, infrastructure is often perceived with suspicion as being security- rather than people- or community-oriented for a cartographically anxious (Krishna 1994) and power-building state like India (Rahman 2019; Roluahpuia 2018). Despite suspicions of politically constructed remoteness, there is a drive to build in the region, such that, that 'Northeast India is littered with concrete' writes McDuie-Ra (2018) in his essay. This has left both a material debris on the region, as well as deeply impacted how people imagine their homelands in living memory. In her study of the India-China borderlands in Arunachal Pradesh, Gohain (2019) has recently termed such infrastructural makeover 'selective connectivity', where remoteness, she argues, is purposefully created and disposed of by the Indian state to secure particular kinds of national interest. Others have also argued how new roads, bridges and infrastructure, particularly in their pace and drive, have been either simply symbolic, appeasement oriented and selective so far as the states' and the majority's capitalist and territorial desires are met, in this case a Hindu majoritarian central party seeking to co-opt Hindu (and sometimes Christian and Buddhist) majoritarian regional votes in Northeast India. The following sections will locale the relationship between connectivity and remoteness in the micro-dynamics of lived experiences along the road.

Microworlds along a road that meets a 'remote' border

As of 2018, Lawngtlai is a fully connected and functioning district capital (connected by road, helicopter, and phones to Aizawl). In 2015, the population of Lawngtlai town was around 20,000 (the population of Mizoram state being around 1.1 million). Its ethnic composition is mixed, with a majority composed of the minority Mara, Lai, Pang, Mizo, Chakma, a few hundred Lusei Mizos, including several 'Vai'[9] settlers, officials and tradesmen. It hosts state government offices, a local college, district offices like courts, police stations, and, most importantly, three separate and fully constituted ethnic ADCs of the Lai, Mara, and Chakma communities with the unique

9   The exonym *Vai* is often translated as 'plains Indian'. However, its meaning can be deeply contextual and political. See Pachuau (2014: 4, 7, 11) for an analysis of the various ways in which the term is used, or abused.

constitutional guarantee of autonomy and rights to land ownership through India's Sixth Schedule (Wouters 2018; Doungel 2010). The town's sparse population allows quick mingling. It takes only one Sunday to encounter more or less everyone. Most importantly, nearly everyone uses social media platforms like WhatsApp and Facebook, each community with their own WhatsApp groups, often acting as the prime source of local news. As such, modern Lawngtlai is not as 'remote' as the majority Mizos would think.

The Kaladan frontier, on the other hand, characterized by lush, green, hilly terrain, a topography which is particularly challenging for infrastructure projects, like some of the other roads described in this volume (see, for example, Murton and Sigdel, this volume, as well as Huang, this volume) – was 'remote'. Here, the Kaladan River flows southwards from India into Chin State in Myanmar, through the townships of Kaletwa and Paletwa before entering Rakhine State and emptying out in Sittwe. On the Myanmar side, the only means to travel anywhere north from the town of Paletwa is by boat on the Kaladan River, or by motorbike or on foot over land. No real roads exist, the river serving as the only highway. The Kaladan road had changed this. Three years after my first trip on it, the road had transformed from a string of ochre earth dig sites full of goat herds and vehicles stuck in mud, to large portions of actual asphalt tracks that the district commissioner of Lawngtlai proudly posted about on journalists' WhatsApp groups. Almost concomitantly, many of my previous contacts from various research trips, including refugees and villagers in the last remaining villages, became uncontactable, dispersed to make way for the coming road. I sought out these people, hoping that they would provide insights into the forms of legibility and erasure that the new infrastructures brought.

During the construction years, the connectivity of the road paradoxically exacerbated the sense of further disconnection for local people and the landless labourers working on the project. This was because, from 2016 onwards, the terrain described above to the edge of the India-Myanmar border was cut off for 'security reasons'. This meant that in order to protect India's investments on the Kaladan Road, the area was demarcated as what became locally known as 'by permission only road'.[10] This made it mandatory for anyone wishing to travel in or out of the 90-kilometre tract of territory (on the Indian side), or the 130-kilometre tract (on the Myanmar side) to gain permission, including labour, locals, journalists or researchers like this author. The small ethnic and undocumented communities living inside those terrains found themselves suddenly turned into 'fixed' subjects. 'We

10   Interviews and observations on the KMMTP road, 2016.

have to take permission now from the road, sir. Sometimes we take to show we accept the rules, but why should I take permission to take my cycle out when I always did? This is not accepted by our people,' complained a Brue village chief.

Through such experiences, the Kaladan Road came to life in material reality in the region. As such, it became important to understand how spectacular geopolitical and economic 'frontiers' come alive from the perspectives of the people who have to live in the so-called development frontiers. By examining these everyday lives, narratives and microworlds of such voices living under the shadow of a spectacular megaproject, the chapter will now focus on the aforementioned themes of local positioning, ecology, identities and border life. I will illustrate how certain groups support and welcome such spectacular projects, while others do not, or feel ambiguous about them; and how the ongoing construction of roads and infrastructures in border spaces creates similar forms of securitization as much as securitized border enforcement regimes do.

Local positioning

I begin my research in the villages along the border where agriculture and subsistence farming are the way of life. Schools are makeshift mud houses with thatch roofs and solar panel toilets (that locals believe came 'free' with the road for the labourers). Electricity is supplied for around 8 out of every 24 hours, as are toilets (powered by small solar panels distributed by aid organizations). On the Indian side, except for the traditional *jhum* (shifting agriculture), central government development schemes dominate the economic landscape, dispatched by the ADCs and a few international Christian organizations. While bamboo grows prolifically, its potential, locals lamented, was not 'developed'/'harnessed'. Education for those who live here is a complete privilege, often not at all feasible in the depths of remoteness. Dropout rates are high because of the lack of further education or economic opportunities after primary and secondary education. There is only one higher education institution between Lawngtlai and the Myanmar border. The situation is even worse across the border in Myanmar, where there are barely any secondary schools, and only one post-secondary institution much further along, in the capital of Chin State, Hakka. When I interviewed residents of several of these villages, they described their desires for 'development', and expressed sentiments that reflected their life at the edge – geographically but also socioeconomically. They were preoccupied with problems of access to basic welfare systems – healthcare, education, sanitation, electricity, and water – and indeed, the guarantee of the next meal.[11]

Similar conversations and grievances were voiced when local officials came to visit. The desire for 'development' was invoked and reflected in the village residents' impressions of the Kaladan Road. Some were anticipated opportunities the road might bring and moved their houses down near the road with makeshift shops for the labour. While many others were oblivious to the road developments taking place, or at least chose to act this way. When I asked one of the village residents about the development of the Kaladan Road and border market only a few miles away, he seemed surprised. 'What road? Who is building?'

I explained that the government of India wants to connect the villages to the rest of India and across the border into Myanmar, and he replied,

> I hope they will bring a road. Last time I lost my wife because we had to carry her on a stretcher and wait for the bus to take her to hospital and she was really suffering. With a road at least we can travel. But where is this road going? Will they have a bus? (Lai farmer, 2017)

From the majority Mizo perspective on development, these rundown, remote regions and their people seem backward. But these stereotypes, and the prejudices they impose, gave rise to a craving for development among some of the Kaladan people, which was sometimes vaguely defined and lacked a clear direction. It is therefore no surprise that locals, who were far from the Myanmar border and cross-border market opportunities, welcomed the Kaladan project so long as their demands for land compensation were met. Still, many were also ambivalent (if not cautiously opportunistic), believing the project to be, at best, a good way to make some money from the road compensation. They knew that access to transport, health, and education would come at a cost, and that the project was not the best thing for the environment. Several men in these villages voiced such perspectives:

> Here the Kaladan is everything. We have fish. We have forests. Even the officers here say to me, so sad we have to cut the forest. (Brue fisherman, 2016)

11 From field observation in Paletwa up to the Indian border, and as well as on the Indian border.

Road, no road, who will come here? Also, they bring all the people from outside. Local people, we will still be making *zu* [rice wine] and drinking at 6 pm. (Lai wage labourer, 2017)

See we have to ask for compensation because if we don't ask, they will just take it like it's theirs. Already they took. We know very well our history is written by foreigners. (Lai village council leader, 2016)

By 2017, many of the Mizoram villagers would form a long queue outside the district commissioner's office with cash and gifts, to present their cases for land compensation. But not everyone had the means to get land passes from the Lai Autonomous District Council (LADC), the authorizing agent. The lines were smaller than they could have been as many did not even know that a project of such gravity was even being constructed in their backyards, due to intentional concealment by the authorities. 'We don't want too many people to know about the road, what will happen will happen, already there is too much compensation headache' (district commissioner, Lawngtlai, 2017).

Those who did know built small huts on the side of the road so as to partake in its economy, and also claim land where possible. But the locals face a conundrum. On the one hand, it is tempting to stall the project through union blockades until compensation is paid, but on the other hand, there is a desire to avail of the goods of state connectivity.

Expediting ecology

Although many lived off of nature and the environment on the Indian side of the Kaladan region, and even as the road construction passed through the vast hilly dense forest landscape, I found during interviews that ecology on the Kaladan has been the least of the planner's concerns when they have a spectacle to build. When civil society organizations got wind of the construction, they deemed the project as disregarding the actual borderland environment, the mangrove ecology in the Araken coast, and in neglect of a transparent environmental impact assessment (EIA). A report by the Kaladan Movement asserted that the local communities in Mizoram, Chin, and Rakhine States were not consulted about the impacts of the project. The central government of India confirmed this in 2013 when it argued that consultation was not necessary as the dredging of the river involves 'minimum intervention'. Reporters informed me that large portions of the project still did not clear the EIA.[12]

Ecological and labour exploitation, as other frontier assemblages have shown, often goes hand in hand so long as expediency for resources and geopolitical/economic grandeur can be extracted quickly (Cons and Eilenberg 2019). There are many who specialize in various forms of frontier expediency (Watts 2018; Duncan Baretta and Markoff 1978). In the case of Kaladan, and the pursuit of the grand spectacle of the project, the state and its officials and technocrats acted as the expediting force. 'How was it carried out?', one might ask; to which, a reporter in Mizoram responds: 'The environmental impact assessment has been a joke, and everybody knows it.' They explain further that when the first feasibility study was conducted, on orders from the government, by the Indian state-run Rail India Technical and Economic Services (RITES), journalists spotted several mistakes in this assessment; among others, this included an underestimation of the road length in Myanmar, and did not account for hydroelectric dam construction on tributaries to the Kaladan in Myanmar (Macleod 2017). No less than a year after the project was announced, the Araken Rivers Network (ARN) published a report that claimed the project would lead to the displacement of at least a million people living along the river (where the river portion of the project was being constructed), further militarization, and massive environmental destruction in the Kaladan environs. The report placed the blame squarely on the Indian and Myanmar governments, and by extension the latter's Tatmadaw (Burmese military), collaborating in resource exploitation at the expense of the land and people. While many of these claims have not been substantiated further, my interviews with officials indicate that the Indian government instructed the Mizo state government and forest department to relax environmental assessments in the areas where the roads cross in order to expedite the project (ARN 2009). However, even those relaxed standards were ignored. For example, in a 2015 report (which was not made public[13]) the chief conservator and nodal officer of Mizoram admonished the chief engineer, stating that the 'compliance report cannot be submitted to the ministry as the report is incomplete and none of the conditions have been complied with till date'.

The environmental impact has been considerable as the project nears completion. There are several reasons for this, including a tenfold increase

12   Interviews with officials and reporters in Aizawl and Guwahati.
13   However, I was able to acquire copies of the original report from undisclosed sources which are available on request.

in capacity of the Sittwe Port relative to the 2000-to-3000-ton ships it used to handle. In another interview, an NGO representative explained that dredging, which deepened the river by removing sediment, was disruptive to the environment and could potentially lead to the dispersal of toxic contaminants from the upturned sediment, bioaccumulation, and a lack of dissolved oxygen, all of which in turn is often fatal to fish populations.[14] Construction delays caused the port to be silted up again, in turn causing the whole river to be dredged a second time in 2018, which forced India and Myanmar to sign a new memorandum of understanding appointing an unnamed private operator to carry out that task. That same year, another phase of the project, the 90-kilometre extension of the Aizawl-Saiha National Highway to Zochachwa, was nearing completion, and the consequences of not conducting an EIA and ignoring stakeholders were felt. Landowners in Lawngtlai initiated a blockade of the project due to a lack of compensation for the use of their land. These included 303 landowners who had received approval for compensation of 50 crore rupees (500 million rupees), but had still not been paid out even nine years after the approval. They lamented that the road bulldozed through forests, community centres, and churches, but brought few of the touted benefits.[15]

Alongside a reconfiguration of ecological space, I encountered another unspectacular dimension of spectacular political connectivity. This was the use and abuse of labour, as experiences with road development elsewhere also show (Murton 2019), bodies tasked with the difficult and exploitative job of expediting and engineering nature and ecology in building infrastructure. A workforce of around 2700 employees was recruited by the multiple firms responsible for implementing the project (Bhattacharyya 2019). Relative to the massive project budget, the number of employees is actually rather low, and labourers have faced unsafe conditions. Labour is seasonal, as workers are usually discharged during the May monsoon and asked to rejoin in October. Wages have remained low and most of the workers are not from Mizoram but instead are recruited from other states, such as Bihar. One engineer told me, 'Lawngtlai hospital is about 65 kilometres away. People would get fever and die. The camp office didn't have a doctor. And initially they didn't know of malaria.' This was one of the main reasons, the engineer said, that workers did not want to live on site, especially in summer. Workers from another site said that their camp had only been provided with a proper water purifier a year after work started. Workers also told me that labourers

14   Interview with local environmental CSO leader, Hakka, Myanmar, 2018.
15   Interviews with farmers, Lawngtlai, Mizoram, India, 2017.

had died of accidents on site and due to untreated malaria. A journalist who was reporting on the road lamented: 'It's like one of those old movies where labour has been brought to Africa to build a road and tons of them die. In Kaladan, at least 60 workers have died so far, maybe even more' (reporter, Assam, 2017).

What I have examined in this section demonstrates and confirms that in the pursuit of success for the spectacle of infrastructural connectivity – which is convenient and necessary for the state to make territory legible – many forms of frontier expediency have been mobilized. Importantly and still more devastatingly, the ecological aspects and people at work explored above have found the least voice of all, and yet these conditions and experiences may well create the longest-lasting impacts on the region. Rather than improving lives for local workers, the project has led to an increase in casual and contractual labour, resulting in lowered wages and safety standards for workers in Mizoram. These unspectacular dimensions, however, are routinely lost beneath the spectacular story of India's Act East Policy.

Shaky identities

Although Mizoram state is named after the majority ethnic group, the Mizos, the southern area, south of Lawngtlai all the way to the last Indian villages in Zochachhuah, is a shaky social terrain populated by smaller but politically significant ethnic communities like Lais, Maras, and Chakmas. These communities enjoy constitutional protection from the Indian government guaranteed by the Sixth Schedule, a policy which is exercised through the ADCs. Since the road crosses through these complicated Lusei-Chin-Rakhine borders terrains along the Kaladan River – or a Zomian 'shatterzone', in Scott's formulation (1998) – the KMMTP was naturally bound to clash and congeal with a complicated micro-identity landscape. As I moved south from the start of the road at Lawngtlai, I therefore examined how these interethnic relations were tied to political and land rights, framed and mediated through their historical relationship with each other, and how they impacted the desires, demands and perceptions about the KMMTP at local levels.

My interviews revealed that when looking at the KMMTP, mutually contentious feelings among ethnic groups were momentarily kept aside for some (especially for the Mizo, Lai, and Chakma, all who have guaranteed territorial and political rights under the constitution), but that the perceived benefits were not necessarily expected to reach all others. In gazing upon the spectacle, this allowed, on the one hand, for a view and engagement with the state that was shaped by anticipation, optimism, contemplation and desire – a chance to profit and benefit from the promised road on what many referred to as their 'landlocked' and 'ignored' homelands.[16] But on the other hand, for those who did not have political rights (the Christian Brues and the undocumented settlers, and refugees who cross during conflict), fear and suspicion guided how they perceived the road. This anxiety was particularly acute because of the uncertainties surrounding how these communities would continue to exercise their flexibility on what has hitherto been their safe space, or places enveloped by remoteness. Despite deep-seated interethnic differences, the Mizo, Lai, and Chakma's aspirational sentiments, I found, took precedence over questions of environment, labour safety, and the actual needs of refuge for people who often 'run away' from Myanmar's many border skirmishes between various ethnic armed organizations (EAOs) and the Tatmadaw. This story of relationships between land access and political rights, is, however, far more complex.

A particular, but perhaps popular, Mizo view emerged as I travelled from village to village with U Tawa. He described himself as having come from 'nothing', of having 'no education, no books', to being a highly posted officer in the Mizoram state services. He earnestly believed that he sacrificed his own happiness to bring development to what was perceived as 'backwardness' in the remote frontiers of his state.

> I came top in the exam. I could have worked anywhere, gone up to Delhi, but no, I choose here, because this is the most difficult area, people are so backward. We have brought so much progress here. Before they were wearing only necklaces; now they are sending their children to school. When this road comes, you will see for yourself. (U Tawa, Kaladan Road, 2016)

In this region, men like U Tawa are often addressed as *unaupa* (big brother), a moniker he seemed to enjoy. Over several weeks, I spent long hours travelling on the roads between Lawngtlai and the border with him and his team. He insisted on driving, often breaking the eerie silence of remoteness with loud 'picnic parties'. On such days, the banks of the Kaladan reverberated

---

16   The discourse in Northeast India has always been one where the states feel ignored by Delhi. For more on this in the Mizoram context, see Pachuau 2014. For a comparative South Asian example, see Heslop 2020.

with 1990s Burmese love songs as local residents delivered pre-ordered (by district officials) meat delicacies and freshly brewed *zu* (rice wine), reporting the latest village council gossip for the district officials. U Tawa seemed to perceive that he was not liked, that people found him loud. 'So what if I am loud? I know these people,' he would explain further, 'Lais are a confused lot who wanted to deny their Mizo origins. Chakma are merely recent settlers, but basically illegal Bangladeshis now claiming their own council and Union Territory, not as hardworking as the Mizos. Brues are Burmese infiltrators' (U Tawa, Kaladan Road, 2016).

In one broad sweep, U Tawa summed up the micropolitics of the region from an arguably majoritarian 'Mizo' point of view.[17] His narrative revealed the interethnic tension with which the KMMTP now had to negotiate. One aspect of this sentiment is a desire for Mizo-led development and control over legibility, including and enabling the mobilization of both borders and infrastructures. This was especially pertinent since the Kaladan project was being constructed in the LADC. In this case, all land passes, leases, and compensation papers were to be negotiated directly with the LADC. A dominant Mizo way of seeing this policy is, accordingly, a way to extend good governance and integrate the 'mistakenly separated' Lais. A police officer in Lawngtlai explained how this road would fix the issue of illegibility with increased cooperation with the Assam Rifles[18] and thereby allow provisions for tighter security, while the paperless problem would also be 'in control'.

In fact, a majoritarian Mizo view ultimately reflects a desire for legibility and a securitized border via the KMMTP's connectivity promise. The existing border crossing with Myanmar on the eastern edge of the state at Zokathar-Champhai is one of the least used border posts in the country, with few listed items traded. It is still dreaded by the Mizos who also largely harbour negative stereotypes against Chin refugees (Son and Singh 2016). A Mizo excise and narcotics officer described the Zokathar-Champhai border and explained how the 'regulated' Kaladan border would be different:

That place is for criminals. The customs house is like a cowshed! In Zorampui (Kaladan), we will have full border [facilities] like your Singapore with custom, camera, fingerprint, Assam Rifles, automatic things, electronic

---

17   I use this example from U Tawa as it represents a dominant discourse that I heard among various other Mizo officers. This is not to say that all Mizos think in this way, but the local officers I met seem to have this opinion, by and large.
18   Paramilitary forces.

posts, and scan machines like they use in 'Adhar',[19] even an escalator!
(Former excise officer, Aizawl, 2017)

Fundamental to this view is a fear of the 'other' or outsider (Chins are seen as the 'other' around Lawngtlai while, further south, Chakmas and Brues receive this treatment). By extension, this sentiment also highlights a desire for better border securitization in order to keep out what Mizos largely feel are 'unwanted' or 'undesirable' people. As the Kaladan frontier has developed, the Mizo disdain towards the Chin has transferred to the Chakma, Brue, and other Burmese refugees, and even the Lai. Importantly, the majority Mizos themselves are not as directly or culturally reliant on the border for their cultural, ideological, and economic needs as are the Lai, Chakma, and Brue. When asked about these 'others', most Mizos were quick to react that such people are nothing short of 'illegal refugees' living on the Indian side, and an aberration that can be 'removed' once the road is built. A Young Mizo Association leader in Lawngtlai proudly proclaimed: 'They [Chin] already take advantage of border trade to stay in Mizoram. Why should we only take the burden?'

The Lai perception which I encountered on the road, however, was completely opposite to the Mizo perspective. Rather than associating road development with opportunities to securitize the border, the Lai hope was for more immediate connectivity and development of the local regions, a sort of reversal of the remoteness which they believe is an unfair colonial and post-colonial condition of state demarcation. The emotional and political desire for unification with the Chin hills, I found in my interviews, really framed the Lai perception with the other side of the border. As explained to me by a Lai historian, they hoped the road would finally integrate them with their Chin 'brothers and sisters' and resolve an 'historical wrong imposed by an international boundary'. Many Lais have thus seized on the promise of the road to bring prosperity to the LADC and give them the clout to resist Mizo dominance.

Tellingly, many of my Lai informants refused to give interviews or speak freely in front of my Mizo-Lusei research team. At these meetings, I often asked, 'Who are the Lais?'

We are not Mizo! The Chin and we are the same people. Our rights have been transgressed when they made the international boundary and you

---

19   A controversial biometric card which provides a unique identification number which can voluntarily be sought by residents and passport holders in India.

have Lai on this side, India, and on this side, Burma. Lai dominated this area before the colonial period. We had superior gene complexes. Now, inferior gene complex... (LADC officer and former student leader, Lawngtlai, 2016)

Church leaders also talked about the road as a way of achieving their own goals for Lai-Chin unification (under the watchful aegis of the cross-border Baptist networks). They hoped it would help relieve the Lais of ethnic 'Mizo dominance' and disinherit the Chakmas of their 'illegally acquired lands'. Such efforts were also thought to work as an antidote to remoteness, which they largely identify and blame to be the cause of their stalled progress. As such, the strong support for the road from the Lais stems from the widespread belief among many inhabitants of the north-east that they are neglected by the central government. In a focus group interview with LADC officers, I heard the following perceptions on the KMMTP:

> We also need to connect the border with infrastructural development: good roads, air transport. We welcome Kaladan because we welcome economic stability. We have bamboo, medicinal plants, and so many tourism opportunities. We could use tourism here, human resource development centre. Jobs.

But If the government of India is not addressing the concerns of us indigenous people, in the future, if knowledge, education, scholarship does not reach us, or contribute to the development of our situation, what's the use of this road?

> When I think of this remoteness of our area. When an international highway is constructed and vehicles plying on a regular basis, our remoteness will be mitigated. (Group of LADC officers, Lawngtlai, 2016)

The Lai's affinity with the Chins, however, has not caused them to feel a similar fear of the Chakmas and Brues, as was expressed by the Mizos: 'They [the Chakma] came here as voters, now they are immigrants, now they have autonomous district councils. Somewhere we also have to protect ourselves' (LADC officer, Lawngtlai, 2016).

Outnumbered by the Mizos and the Lais, the largely Buddhist Chakma in this region feel increasingly threatened, which is one reason that prospects of a connected road bring hope for acceptance:

> Even our politicians don't have a big vision, they don't know the value of our land. We are persecuted. We need to have infrastructural development,

we need communication, connecting different ethnic communities living in excluded areas. If there is a good road, people-to-people contact is very easy, maybe we will understand each other. It could be very conducive to nation building and we will be accepted. (CADC officer, Lawngtlai, 2017)

Despite acknowledged differences between the three major ethnic groups in the region – the Lai, the Chakma, and the Mizos – the communities have all respectively instilled talismanic hopes in the road to provide development and transform the border to their benefit. Across these groups, there is agreement, but in different forms, that the road is an integral part of Mizoram, and should become, through sanitization and securitization, Northeast India's biggest 'gateway to the east'. As such, a connectivity project from above becomes a mechanism to help control flows, spaces, mobilities and access on the borderland. But paradoxically, in so doing, a road can also engender the erasure of an 'other's' safe space, allowing for greater security or legibility in one's own place.

Border life at the edge of the road

As I travelled further along the road that was being built in 2015, leaving behind the Mizo, Lai, Mara, and Chakma regions and arriving at the last parts of the road near the border, I met a truck driver, Rawat, from Uttar Pradesh, who had been contracted by the company that won the road-construction bid. He was stuck in a landslide, alone and without food, for more than a day before my research team arrived with a few DRDA vehicles (which also got stuck). He was mortified that we wanted to go further down the road, 'What have you come to research here? There is nothing, no people, nothing, no food, go back, madam. This is not a place for ladies' (Rawat, Kaladan Road project site, 2017).

Yet, on the very same day, I counted at least fifteen small settled villages along the road all the way up to the border with Myanmar comprising mainly Brue Christians or Chakma Buddhists towards the India side, and several undocumented people (who believe themselves to be a mix of Rakhine, Chin and Rohingya) on the Myanmar side. Here, in the frontier of the frontier, at the border's edge, locals say that people in Mizoram's capital of Aizawl ignore the people of the border much the same way as locals in Aizawl say that Delhi ignores the state of Mizoram. Many of these families identified and utilized the still incomplete road as a resource to sell small items from Myanmar to the construction workers. It was fascinating to find that that, contrary to media portrayals of the Rakhine-Rohingya tragedy in Myanmar, this was the only place where the Rakhine Buddhists shared space quite amicably with the Rohingyas – two groups of refugees, each staying away from the violence in Myanmar's Rakhine State. Here, the groups shared space with each other, and with others who have made this frontier's frontier their home. U Tawa defined them as 'paperless people who came to Mizoram illegally from Myanmar', but I refer to them instead as 'border residents'.

As I encountered and came to know more of these border residents, Rawat's words, 'there is nothing' lingered on my mind. The erasure of living histories of those in the borderlands tend to be subsumed by states seeking to secure borders. It was therefore telling that even as a precarious wage earner from the plains, largely outside the realm of micro-ethno-politics in Mizoram, Rawat also knew (but consciously or unconsciously failed to mention) that so many people have now turned the border into a resourceful safe space.

Before modern borders were drawn, the region comprised jungle and villages running across a contiguous green landscape. And when the border was demarcated, neither the Indian nor the Burmese governments thought it necessary to fence this particular region. In the post-independence era following the Partition of India in 1947, the border had been marked only by a small, dilapidated three-foot-tall concrete post. In other parts of Mizoram, topographical changes between hills and plains do impact the physical nature of borders; but such is not the case here, where an overgrown patch of greenery has formed a grander route for crossings. As noted above, this borderland has traditionally been defined by movements, evasions, and motility. Institutionally, the physical border here still matters little, with humans, animals, and goods crossing it informally. On both sides, remoteness, subsistence farming, and the ability to visit families, churches, and festivities across boundaries inform everyday practices. Of course, these practices are occasionally disrupted by official visits from Indian government officials, or by small skirmishes on the Myanmar side. And yet here the border has managed to sustain a rich life: providing space for refugees and borderland dwellers to move around freely. Its remoteness, however, has also rendered the space illegible, and its liminality and fluidity has long offered those fleeing persecution with a safe space to settle down.

Being extremely poor and excluded from basic services like healthcare and education, communities of the borderland have developed their own cross-border culture and modes of interdependent survival. Much of this has been sustained through pre-established kinship links and newly established Rakhine Buddhist links. Villages on the Indian side of the border were all Buddhist and linguistically Burmese. Schools were set up by Buddhist monks who fled Myanmar during military rule in the early 2000s and sustained entirely through religious affiliations from Myanmar. They were open to all refugee children, including the Rohingya. The village residents on the border were fiercely protective of these relations and would answer my questions differently in front of state or security agents than in the presence of an independent observer.

Such invisibility then, so far preserved because of remoteness, was in fact perceived as a boon for many of the undocumented border residents. From their perspective, remoteness kept the borderland conveniently safe for their livelihoods and mobile lives. It made space flexible and transactable between India and Myanmar, which is the extent to which they wanted to use it. While the overall refugee policy in Mizoram, like in many other borderscapes (Rajaram and Grundy-Warr 2007), has been to 'fix' people (particularly Burmese Chins), these residents showed no desire to go beyond their homes and farms. Therefore, they were inclined to be self-restrictively territorial about the border space. When I asked how they felt about road building, I heard various iterations of 'this road is not for us', or 'ours'. Halok, an ethnic Brue man living in Zochachhuah village, broke it down further:

> When 'road sir' comes, we know we have to move from there because they say we get eviction and a paper problem. I don't have a *patta* [title deed]. So, I am just coming and going all the time. My family has eight old people. We have moved five times since this new road building came. I am finishing a good batch of *zu* [rice wine] now. I sell to the workers. Once the road comes, who will want to buy? They will just get rid of us. (Halok, Zochachhuah, 2016)

U Zaw, one of the Rakhine residents, said that when the Assam Rifles or Rural Department officers arrive, they often spin clever tales of horror about what is happening on the other side of the border:

> When the police come, we say the Burma Army makes a huge bomb there that day, then they run away. The sirs [DRDA officers] don't go to the other side because they are afraid many guns and bombings are there, [...] but we never see it, we just fool them. (U Zaw, Zochachhuah, 2016)

Many of these people had moved not because of conflict, but simply to create liveable, everyday lives, in fluid conditions of mobility. After living with U Zaw's family for a few days, away from the gaze of the Mizo officers, another story emerged. Before 2018, when the road wasn't fully constructed, families like his could freely move across the border without any documents. They did so whenever they wanted to farm on the India side of the border, or find some shelter, or gain temporary education for their children. But as the road made the terrain more legible, documentation has become essential to prove one's nationality. The villagers feared that the regularization of a new border trade zone and the construction of a new road cutting right through their villages would curtail the fluidity of movement they had relied on for decades. The widespread dreams of spectacular and big regional connectivity in Mizoram instead represented fears for a persecuted, and micro-regional minority community who had survived on informal connectivity inherent in borderlands, but always in unspectacular ways.

The KMMTP thus was more an aberration than a need for U Zaw and his community. Numerous other informants also reiterated that they want to live off the land through subsistence farming and hunting, and preferred to be mobile rather than sedentary. While border residents in the villages identified that what they need is the freedom to live off the land, and be connected in a limited fashion to their immediate support based in India and Myanmar, they expressed no desire or even hope that being part of a grand connectivity project would bring much of anything to them. Faced with the challenges of top-down state infrastructures, these borderlanders therefore did not share the majority's dreams of connectivity for the region.

Naturally, the ways in which invisibility is perceived by the border resident is different from those tasked with the completion, implementation, and governance of the KMMTP assemblage (both the road and border security.) That is, rather than treating the existence of the flexible (Rakhine and Rohingya) as part of the borderland's lived or organic history, Mizo leaders and members of legislative assemblies who were interviewed for their familiarity with the project, saw the existence of the Rakhine and the Rohingya as 'a temporary problem in need of a permanent governance solution'.[20] I heard such sentiments often. An interviewed politician suggested that 'those without papers' be best 'removed' and 'repatriated' once the road concretized the border and installed a large border trading post connecting the road. A senior Assam Rifles officer was convinced that someone studying borders must only be worried about the border's 'security', and tried to 'reassure me': 'It will have all modern facilities to protect the border, so we will bring the Mizoram police, don't worry. We will have a customs gate and no illegal activities will be tolerated' (Prashant, Aizawl, 2017).

---

20   Interview with a police officer.

Thus, where and when remoteness affords the agency to remain invisible, the road and border infrastructure assemblage works to erase border settlement and mobility. And this is, of course, all a part of the spectacular project of the KMMTP.

Conclusion

This chapter introduced how one of India's spectacular border connectivity infrastructures, the Kaladan Multimodal Transport Project (KMMTP), promised to bring connectivity and development to a landlocked, remote region on its Myanmar borders, while also serving as India's Act East Policy's success story. However, through an ethnographic exploration along the new road towards the border, it becomes apparent that these promises of connectivity bring with them other forms of border enforcement which regulates, limits, and fixes border crossers and migrants. What this chapter shows is that the road acts as another border to make territory in a remote place legible. This legibility is then harnessed to extract and access resources and markets from previously unexplored resource frontiers, in this case, from Myanmar. In seeking to create spectacular projects and to further spectacular geopolitical/economic agendas, the Indian state, I suggest, selectively chooses hitherto remote and flexible border regions for modernization, development, and connectivity projects.

As this conclusion is being written (in 2019), the KMMTP on the Indian border is nearly finished. Undoubtedly, there will be an opening ceremony where leaders from India and Myanmar gather and declare that a new day has dawned in Mizoram. Just as assuredly, the hundreds of people whose land claims have yet to be paid, and the environmental impact assessments that remain undone, will remain unmentioned while hands are shaken, ribbons cut, and the Kaladan project is added to the spectacle surrounding India's Act East Policy. Meanwhile, for the refugees, undocumented people, and flexible locals, the road will continue to pose larger existential threats of erasure and displacement for those whom it has made legible. Infrastructure will act in tandem with border regularization, as a new 'secure' border trade zone is readied alongside the road. The remoteness of the border, which has so far sheltered the border villages, schools, and makeshift tents, and the border spaces that kept space safe for floating populations seeking refuge will be washed away in the making of spectacular projects.

Not surprisingly, when I tried to get in touch with Halok and many of the refugees and villagers interviewed in this article, I could no longer contact them. Refugees had recently been shuffled around, to other locations along the border. As I write, one of the engineers interviewed here was abducted by the AA (Arakan Army), who sought to hit the media and Indian government where it hurts, to make a spectacle out of a non-spectacular remote space, so as to match the state's own spectacle of constructing the Kaladan Road. He died in their custody, erased as another worker dead on the Kaladan, adding yet one more reason why the border ought to be more secure. These ambiguities and clashing realities from such unlikely places remain as debris to new and spectacular highways and hierarchies developing across Asia. In the making of spectacular state projects, the unspectacular will be forgotten.

List of works cited

ARN (2009). 'Kaladan Multi-Modal Transit Transport Project: A Preliminary Report from the Arakan Rivers Network, Chiang Mai'. Arakan Rivers Network. http://www.arakanrivers.org/wp-content/uploads/2019/02/ARN-Preliminary-Report-of-Kaladan-Multi-Modal-Transit-Transport-Project-red.pdf (accessed 15 August 2020).

Arora, V., and R.R. Ziipao (2020). 'The Roads (Not) Taken: The Materiality, Poetics and Politics of Infrastructure in Manipur, India'. *Journal of South Asian Development* 15(1): 34-61.

Baruah, S. (2007). *Postfrontier Blues: Toward a New Policy Framework for Northeast India*. Washington, DC: East-West Center.

Bhattacharyya, R. (2019). 'India Deploys the Army to Check Rebel, Refugee Influx from Myanmar'. *The Diplomat*, 15 March. https://thediplomat.com/2019/03/india-deploys-the-army-to-check-rebel-refugee-influx-from-myanmar/ (accessed 15 August 2020).

Bouissou, J. (2015). 'India's Long Highway to Myanmar Starts to Take Shape'. *The Guardian*, 27 September. https://www.theguardian.com/world/2015/sep/27/india-myanmar-road-mizoram-tribal-areas-modi (accessed 15 August 2020).

Brown, W. (2017). *Walled States, Waning Sovereignty*. New York: Zone Books.

Cons, J. (2016). *Sensitive Space: Fragmented Territory at the India-Bangladesh Border*. Seattle: University of Washington Press.

Cons, J., and M. Eilenberg, eds. (2019). *Frontier Assemblages: The Emergent Politics of Resource Frontiers in Asia*. Hoboken, NJ: John Wiley & Sons.

Debord, G. (2010). *The Society of the Spectacle*. Detroit: Black & Red.

De Genova, N. (2013). 'Spectacles of Migrant "Illegality": The Scene of Exclusion, the Obscene of Inclusion'. *Ethnic and Racial Studies* 36(7): 1180-1198.

Doungel, J. (2010). *Evolution of District Council Autonomy in Mizoram: A Case Study of the Lai Autonomous District Council*. Guwahat: Spectrum Publications.

Duncan Baretta, S.R., and J. Markoff (1978). 'Civilization and Barbarism: Cattle Frontiers in Latin America'. *Comparative Studies in Society and History* 20(4): 587-620. https://doi.org/10.1017/S0010417500012561.

Dyckhoff, T. (2017). *The Age of Spectacle: Adventures in Architecture and the 21st-Century City*. London: Random House.

Egreteau, R. (2008). 'India and China Vying for Influence in Burma: A New Assessment'. *India Review* 7(1): 38-72.

Ghosh, S. (2019). '"Everything Must Match": Detection, Deception, and Migrant Illegality in the India-Bangladesh Borderlands'. *American Anthropologist* 121(4): 870-883.

Gohain, S. (2019). 'Selective Access: Or, How States Make Remoteness'. *Social Anthropology* 27(2): 204-220.

Harvey, D. (2001). 'Globalization and the "Spatial Fix"'. *Geographische Revue* 2: 23-30.

Heslop, L. (2020). 'Runways to the Sky #roadsides'. *Allegra Lab*. https://allegralaboratory.net/runways-to-the-sky-roadsides/ (accessed 10 April 2021).

Jackson, K. (2016). 'Globalizing an Indian Borderland Environment: Aijal, Mizoram, 1890-1919'. *Studies in History* 32(1): 39-71.

Jaishankar, D. (2019). 'Acting East: India in the Indo-Pacific'. Brookings, 24 October. https://www.brookings.edu/research/acting-east-india-in-the-indo-pacific/ (accessed 10 April 2021).

Jones, R. (2017). *Violent Borders: Refugees and the Right to Move*. London: Verso.

Krichker, D., and J. Sarma (2019). 'Can Borders Speak to Each Other? The India-Bangladesh and Spain-Morocco Borders in Dialogue'. *Journal of Borderlands Studies*. DOI: 10.1080/08865655.2019.1676813.

Krishna, S. (1994). 'Cartographic Anxiety: Mapping the Body Politic in India'. *Alternatives: Global, Local, Political* 19(4): 507-521.

Li, T.M. (2014). *Land's End: Capitalist Relations on an Indigenous Frontier*. Durham, NC: Duke University Press.

Loomis, E. (2015). *Out of Sight: The Long and Disturbing Story of Corporations Outsourcing Catastrophe*. New York: The New Press.

Macleod, A. (2017). 'Kaladan woes reflect frustrated Indian vision for Myanmar and Southeast Asia'. Global Risks Insights, 14 September. https://globalriskinsights.com/2017/09/kaladan-reflects-frustrated-indian-vision/ (accessed 26 April 2021).

McDuie-Ra, D. (2018) 'Concrete and Culture in Northeast India.' Raiot, 14 February. https://raiot.in/concrete-and-culture-in-northeast-india/ (accessed 26 April 2021).

Mezzadra, S., and B. Neilson (2013). *Border as Method: Or, the Multiplication of Labor*. Durham, NC: Duke University Press.

Nag, S. (2002). *Contesting Marginality: Ethnicity, Insurgence and Subnationalism in North-East India*. New Delhi: Manohar.

Oh, S.-A., ed. (2016). *Myanmar's Mountain and Maritime Borderscapes: Local Practices, Boundary-Making, and Figured Worlds*. Singapore: ISEAS-Yusof Ishak Institute.

Ong, A. (2011). 'Hyperbuilding: Spectacle, Speculation, and the Hyperspace of Sovereignty'. In *Worlding Cities*, ed. by A. Roy and A. Ong. Oxford: Wiley-Blackwell, 205-226.

Pachuau, J. (2014). *Being Mizo: Identity and Belonging in Northeast India*. Oxford: Oxford University Press.

Pachuau, J.L.K., and W. van Schendel (2016). 'Borderland Histories, Northeastern India: An Introduction'. *Studies in History* 32(1): 1-4.

Pau, P.K. (2018). 'Transborder People, Connected History: Border and Relationships in the Indo-Burma Borderlands'. *Journal of Borderlands Studies*. DOI: 10.1080/08865655.2018.1438914.

Rahman, M.Z. (2019). '"Pickled" Infrastructure and Connectivity: Locating Community Engagement in Northeast India's Infrastructural Transformation'. Heinrich Boll Stiftung. https://in.boell.org/sites/default/files/uploads/2019/06/pickled_infrastructure_and_connectivity_locating_community_engagement_in_northeast_indias_infrastructural_transformation.pdf (accessed 15 August 2020).

Rajaram, P.K., and C. Grundy-Warr, eds. (2007). *Borderscapes: Hidden Geographies and Politics at Territory's Edge*. Minneapolis: University of Minnesota Press.

Rippa, A., G. Murton and M. Rest (2020). 'Building Highland Asia in the 21st Century'. *Verge: Studies in Global Asias* 6(2): 83-111.

Roluahpuia (2018). 'Hydro-Nation, Discourse and Discontent in Northeast India: The Case of Tipaimukh Dam, Manipur'. *Society and Culture in South Asia* 4(2): 255-277.

Roluahpuia (2020). 'Whose Border Is It Anyway? Control, Contestation, and Confluence in Indo-Myanmar Borderlands'. *Contemporary South Asia* 28(1): 74-85.

Sajjad H.M. (2008). *Building Legitimacy: Exploring State-Society Relations in Northeast India*. New Delhi: Oxford University Press.

Sanga, Z. (2019). 'Landowners Threaten Stir over Kaladan Project'. *Assam Tribune*, 11 July. http://www.assamtribune.com/scripts/detailsnew.asp?id=jul1119/otho56 (accessed 15 August 2020).

Scott, J.C. (1998). *Seeing Like a State: How Certain Schemes to Improve the Human Condition Have Failed*. New Haven, CT: Yale University Press.

Scott, J.C. (2009). *The Art of Not Being Governed: An Anarchist History of Upland Southeast Asia*. New Haven, CT: Yale University Press.

Son, B. and Singh, N.W. (2016) 'The Chin State-Mizoram Border: Institutionalised Xenophobia for State Control' in S. Oh, ed. *Myanmar's Mountain and Maritime*

Borderscapes: Local Practices, Boundary-Making and Figured Worlds. Singapore: ISEAS-Yusof Ishak Institute, 2016.

Tsing, A.L. (2003). 'Natural Resources and Capitalist Frontiers'. *Economic and Political Weekly* 38(48): 5100-5106.

Van Schendel, W. (2016). 'A War within a War: Mizo Rebels and the Bangladesh Liberation Struggle'. *Modern Asian Studies* 50(1): 75-117.

Venturi, R., D.S. Brown, and S. Izenour (1972). *Learning from Las Vegas.* Cambridge, MA: MIT Press.

Watts, M.J. (2018). 'Frontiers: Authority, Precarity, and Insurgency at the Edge of the State'. *World Development* 101: 477-488.

Woods, K. (2020). 'Smaller-Scale Land Grabs and Accumulation from Below: Violence, Coercion and Consent in Spatially Uneven Agrarian Change in Shan State, Myanmar'. *World Development* 127: 104780.

Wouters, J.P. (2018). *In the Shadows of Naga Insurgency: Tribes, State, and Violence in Northeast India.* New Delhi: Oxford University Press.

Zhang, J. (2014). 'Remote Proximity.' In 'Remote and Edgy: New Takes on Old Anthropological Themes', ed. by E. Harms, S. Hussain and S. Shneiderman. *HAU: Journal of Ethnographic Theory* 4(1): 361-381.

Ziipao, R.R. (2020). 'Roads, Tribes, and Identity in Northeast India'. *Asian Ethnicity* 21(1): 1-21.

About the author

JASNEA SARMA is a postdoctoral research fellow at the Institute of South Asian Studies (ISAS), National University of Singapore (NUS). She works on borderlands, ecologies, and resource frontiers in India, Myanmar (Burma), and China.

6 The making of a 'new Dubai'

Infrastructural rhetoric and development in Pakistan

Mustafa A. Khan

Abstract

In Tharparkar, south-east Pakistan, over 300 kilometres of roads are being constructed to facilitate access to a coalfield intended to provide power to an electricity-starved country. The new roads are often sold as harbingers of great change and signs of modernity. Industry and the sought-after prize of foreign direct investment are presented as being just around the corner. I was often told that Thar (Tharparkar) would become 'a Dubai', which represented an ultimate symbol of modernity. Scholars have argued that neoliberalism's achievements are double: narrowing the window of political debate, while promising prospects without limit. In Tharparkar, the immediate roads effect has been increased land speculation, with little tangible improvements with regards to local employment. I argue that the 'transition rhetoric' being used by the state and the local political elite has no relation to the actual economic and political processes, except to veil interests of the elite groups. The material from Tharparker demonstrates that roads as symbols of 'modernity' can be used to deconstruct some of the contradictions at the heart of many modernization myths.

Keywords: Pakistan, modernity, speculation, promise, economic corridors

Introduction

The many gatherings held in the offices of Mahesh Kumar,[1] president of the Taluka[2] Council of Islamkot in the district of Tharparkar in Pakistan,

---

1   Pseudonym used.
2   The term *taluka* is used for a subdistrict in Sindh.

Heslop, Luke, and Galen Murton (eds), *Highways and Hierarchies: Ethnographies of Mobility from the Himalaya to the Indian Ocean*. Amsterdam, Amsterdam University Press 2021
DOI: 10.5117/9789463723046_CH06

were often attended by local businessmen, largely Hindu, and one's absence meant that the individual was no longer part of the informal network of Hindu traders who dominated local politics. During one such meeting held in December 2016 at the municipal offices, to which I had invited myself, Mahesh was effusive: 'We are very happy with the developments. It's going to be a Dubai. You will see. There is talk of a special economic zone. And, of course, now we are in the China-Pakistan Economic Corridor.'

There was genuine excitement among those present, including the opposition leader on the town council, Nikhil Vanya.[3] The men were known to be rivals, changing parties but never a member of the same party at the same time, yet here they were in this crowded room in complete agreement. Dubai has come to acquire a 'symbolic power' as the ultimate marker for modernity in Muslim Asia (Acuto 2010). The district of Tharparkar in south-eastern Pakistan is the site of a large coal mining project which has entailed the construction of a 360-kilometre-long road. The region is undergoing tremendous social and economic dislocation, yet I observed widespread optimism about its future, even among those already suffering from the consequences of the mining project. Indeed, this infrastructure-induced optimism was not restricted to Tharparkar but was affecting Pakistan as a whole. The expected billions of dollars of investment from the China-Pakistan Economic Corridor (CPEC) are regarded as a 'game changer' (Chaziza 2016) for the 'beleaguered country', said to be overwhelmed by insurgency and political instability (Ali 1983; Lieven 2011). The rhetoric that Pakistan will now become a 'new Dubai' is increasingly being used as justification by the state for the tremendous loans that are being sought as part of the CPEC (see Garlick 2018 on the financial aspect of CPEC). Plays are being written, songs sung, and adverts produced, all in the service of this bright future.[4] Timothy Mitchell has argued that neoliberalism is the triumph of the political imagination. Its achievements are double: while narrowing the window of political debate, it promises from this window a prospect without limits, allowing for the neglect of the concerns of local communities, 'while encouraging the most exuberant dreams of private accumulation' (1999: 28). In this chapter, I will explore these dreams of 'private accumulation', which mask a contradictory reality on the ground, with much of the new wealth being concentrated in the hands of 'outsiders' and concealing a long history of discriminatory state policy towards the region.

3   Pseudonym used; Nikhil sadly passed away during the course of my fieldwork (September 2016-July 2017).
4   For example, a Pakistani advert for a biryani mix had around 2 million views within two days and showed a Chinese family moving to Lahore. See SBS Urdu 2019.

Throughout the period after independence in 1947, Tharparkar, with its location as a region almost surrounded by India, saw little state investment in infrastructure (Siddiqi 2018). Political developments in a borderland are determined simultaneously by the situation in two neighbouring states, and by the social, economic, and political interactions between them (Baud and Van Schendel 1997). Relations between India and Pakistan have been largely hostile due to a number of historical and political events, starting with a violent partition of British India in 1947, the unresolved dispute over Kashmir, and the numerous military conflicts fought between the two nations (Mitra 2001). The few roads that exist in the India-Pakistan borderlands have been built by military agencies, such as the Frontier Work Organization (FWO) in Pakistan (Ispahani 1989; Haines 2012) and the Border Roads Organisation (BRO) in India (Aggarwal 2004; Demenge 2011), reflecting a view that roads are 'strategic assets'. Pakistan has also suffered territorial fragmentation, with the secession of East Pakistan in 1971, which led to the creation of the independent state of Bangladesh (Athique 2008). Reflecting these concerns, the first asphalt road in Tharparkar district was only built in 1987, which connected the district headquarters of Mithi with the city of Mirpurkhas. However, things changed with the discovery of coal in 1991. With an area of 19,638 square kilometres, however, the district still only has 743 kilometres of roads, and the quality of these is still among the lowest for any Sindh district (see iMMAP 2014). Roads remain a rare commodity in Tharparkar, with sandy tracks still the main way to get to many of the larger villages.

The (hi)stories of the road and the coal project are intertwined in Tharparkar, with the exploitation of the Thar coal field very much spun in the national and local press as a harbinger of prosperity. However, in regions of resource extraction, 'road construction may be oriented less towards territorial integration and the promise of political incorporation than with facilitating the "off-shoring" of mineral wealth by connecting mines to seaports' (Reeves 2017: 712). Roads can, as Dalakoglou shows, 'promote hope or hopelessness, expectation or fear, love or hate, stability or instability, mobility, loss, suspicion or subordination' (2017: 13). It is also important to consider why the Pakistani state has been so anxious to build roads in its southern borderlands. Given Pakistan's continuing description in articles and books as a 'failing' or 'failed state' (see Ali 1983; Lieven 2011), the state has been particularly sensitive about its margins. Road-making is clearly a contentious process (Harvey and Knox 2012), however, as I will argue, state-sponsored rhetoric can influence those being affected by these infrastructural interventions to view a particular project with 'hope' or 'hopelessness'.

In the Global South, government rhetoric often concedes that to achieve this 'good life', 'out of the way place[s]' (Tsing 1993) must sacrifice themselves for the 'greater good' (Padel 2011) of the nation, by acquiescing to large infrastructure projects. Development of the extractive kind in South Asia commonly involves displacing ethnic minorities and 'tribal' populations (see Rycroft and Dasgupta 2011). However, often many of these communities have been unwilling to be sacrificed, as demonstrated by the large- and small-scale protest movements, which in some cases have led to governments making compromises (Baviskar 2004; Caron and Da Costa 2007; Padel 2011). In South Asia – starting from the colonial period – the state has encroached upon the land for the construction of railways, mines, and plantations. Infrastructure development has led to land loss in Pakistan, with the state acquiring land for large-scale infrastructure, mining, and industrial projects, often funded by the World Bank (Shaikh 2005), with mass dispossession of local populations. Large-scale infrastructural developments in other parts of the world have also been sites of violent conflict, with different and contradictory interests often colliding (Ascher and Mirovitskaya 2016). Meanwhile, state and multinational donors promoting infrastructure argue that such developments represent the 'good life', with dreams of equality and universal access (Anand et al. 2018). Resistance to the coal project has largely been missing in the district, despite the fact that the situation on the ground is full of contradictions, with the benefits of both the road and the coal project patchy at best. Rather, between 2016 and 2017, when I was carrying out my fieldwork, there was a sense of optimism that the changes brought about by the infrastructural interventions would bring prosperity to the district in the 'future'. Pelkmans (2006) proposes the term 'transition rhetoric' to capture the way in which the rhetoric used by the state and local political elite has no relation to the actual economic and political processes, but functions to veil the interests of elite groups. By taking a historical and anthropological perspective, I locate infrastructures within larger political and economic processes that Tharparkar is undergoing.

Tharparkar: Road-making in a borderland

Administratively, Tharparkar is subdivided into six *talukas* (subdistricts), one of which, Islamkot, is the site of the coal fields. The district headquarters are in the city of Mithi (Hasan and Raza 2011: 79). Tharparkar gets its name from two regions: Thar, the vast desert that extends into Rajasthan, and the mountainous region of Parkar, which forms an 'island' within the Rann of Kutch (Ibrahim 2009: 82). In terms of its history and caste make-up, it shares links with Kutch and western Rajasthan (Ibrahim 2009), both regions in India. Tharparkar is also unique in Pakistan in that it has a high Hindu population: 41% according to the 1998 census (Population Census Organization Statistics Division 1998), which in the coal mining region reaches a majority of 60% (see Hagler Bailly 2012). The low position of the Hindu community in Pakistani social hierarchy has been influenced by external factors, such as the state's poor relationship with India (Mahmood 2014; Schaflechner 2018). The predicament of Pakistan's Hindu minority is best explained by Schaflechner (2018: 12):

> [T]he structural exclusion of Hindus within the governmental education system, their demonization in parts of popular culture, and the very foundation of the two-nation theory itself, the Pakistani Hindu identity exists in a kind of purgatory, caught betwixt and between.

Many of the Tharparkar Hindus belong to Dalit communities, who are doubly disadvantaged: as members of a religious minority, they confront a hostile majoritarian state and civil society; being Dalits, they are also marginalized within their own religious communities (Jodhka and Shah 2010). Also, Dhatki, the most widely spoken language in the district, has no official status (Hammarström et al. 2017), further adding to its marginality.

In 1947, when Pakistan gained independence from Britain, the boundaries between the province of Sindh and the princely state of Kutch, which had joined India, were unclear. These conflicting territorial claims between the new neighbouring states led to periods of negotiation, confrontation, and arbitration (Bajwa 2013). Tharparkar district, thus became the site of two of Pakistan's three wars with India, and during the Indo-Pakistani War of 1971, most of the district was occupied by the Indian Army, and only returned to Pakistani control in 1972, after the Shimla Agreement that formally ended hostilities. The region is what Martínez (1994) terms an 'alienated borderland', where the borders are functionally closed and cross-border interaction is almost or completely absent. Tharparkar is very much a borderland locale, where the border often intrudes in a violent manner on the everyday lives of its inhabitants.

Infrastructural development in Pakistan has been closely related with a process of territorialization at the geographic margins of the state (Haines 2012; Jamali 2014). To this end, Bouzas (2012) shows how road development in Baltistan, which seeks to improve connection with the rest of the country, has been interpreted as the 'first step to cut off of Baltistan's traditional ties with the Himalayan-Tibetan milieu' (Bouzas 2012: 881). Bouzas also argues that the borderland status of Baltistan imposes an imprint of silence and fear on the local population, in what is a heavily militarized region bordering the contested region of Indian-controlled Kashmir. Similarly, Jamali's (2014) study of the construction of a container port in the city of Gwader, located on the Iran-Pakistan border, shows how people were marginalized from decision-making as the project was presented in the language of national integration and security; as part of a common good, greater than local concerns, in a region prone to insurgency. The government of Pakistan has not shied away from 'stating' the importance of the CPEC to 'national integration'. An article in the *Pakistan Observer* gives a taste of the rhetoric being used:

> The China-Pakistan Economic Corridor, linking Gwadar Port to the Chinese province of Xinjiang, will be a game changer not only for Balochistan and Pakistan but also for the world trade. In Balochistan, development activity has picked up with the return of peace after years of insurgency and violence. A few countries are trying to sabotage the mega project, but Provincial Minister for Home and Tribal Affairs, Sarfraz Ahmed Bugti has more than once said the provincial government would do its part in providing fool-proof security to workers during the construction period. With the development efforts of the federal and provincial governments and efforts of the Army Balochistan youth having been inducted in the army, who will frustrate the designs of enemies of Pakistan. People of Balochistan and even Jirga are likely to support efforts for peace and development in Balochistan. (Jamil 2017)

Prior to independence, Tharparkar was presented in colonial discourse as a 'wild' region home to 'restless communities' that required pacification (Ibrahim 2009: 83). The existence of this discourse in colonial policy making has led to the creation of marginal populations, which are formed out of indigenous or natural subjects, who are at once excluded from the same identities by a sort of disciplinary knowledge that marks them out as racially and civilizationally other (Das and Poole 2004). Recent works in South Asia (Baviskar 2004; Haines 2012; Rycroft and Dasgupta 2011) have demonstrated that regions that have had histories of uneven inclusion by the colonial state, amplified by being marginalized by history, poverty, and vulnerability, have also been sites of large infrastructural projects involving large-scale population displacement. Tharparkar is rated consistently as one of the most deprived districts provincially and nationally, and historically has had very little investment in infrastructure (Khalti 2015). Marginal regions like Tharparkar have now increasingly been reimagined as resource-rich, unexploited 'wastelands' targeted for large-scale development schemes for economic integration and control (Cons and Eilenberg 2019). The optimistic infrastructural rhetoric in Tharparkar is masking a 'socio-material terrain' (Anand et al. 2018: 2) with a history of state making, that has treated the region with both suspicion and neglect.

Thar coal: Electrifying Pakistan

Progress on infrastructural development in Tharparkar remained slow in the 1990s and would have remained that way had an earthquake not occurred in 2001 in the region. According to the 1998 census report, the total 'metaled roads' in the district amounted to a 195 kilometres, with the 50-kilometre section between Mithi and Naukot being the only asphalted road. The 2001 earthquake led to massive state-led infrastructural intervention in Kutch, on the other side of the border in India, which included an extensive road-building programme. Prior to the 2001 earthquake, Kutch also had very little infrastructure investments in the border regions of the district, with a single road that ran northwards ending at the border with Sindh (Simpson 2006). The recent upsurge in the construction of infrastructure in the borderlands has amounted to something of a race between the two countries to control and develop their 'margins'.

Decades of infrastructural neglect in Tharparkar have now been replaced by an aggressive investment in roads, power plants, and coal mines. In 2008, the Thar Coal Energy Board was set up to oversee the coalfield, and the field was divided into twelve blocks, each to be given to a concession. In 2009, the Government of Sindh (GOS) granted the concession of Block II of the coalfield to the Sindh Engro Coal Mining Company (SECMC), a joint venture between the Sindh government and Engro Corporation of Pakistan. As part of the agreement between SECMC and the GOS, SECMC would mine 22.5 million tonnes of coal annually from Block II, with about 2 billion tonnes of reserves, and its subsidiary, the Thar Power Company, would subsequently develop 4000-megawatt mine-mouth power plants in two phases (Ali 2014). The total estimated cost of the project is US$1.3 billion, which is the biggest single investment undertaken by the GOS since independence in 1947 (Talpur 2017). The agreement requires that the GOS construct or improve 369 kilometres of roads, as well connecting the mine mouth to the rail network, transmission lines and arranging fresh water supply and mining-effluent disposal for Block II. The so-called Coal Road starts near the town of Badin, in southern Sindh, which connects to an existing road to the port of Karachi and ends abruptly at the mouth of a mine near the village of Thariyo Halipota. Although the sole purpose of this road is supposedly to serve the coal field, but in discussions with officers of the Thar Coal Energy Board, I was often told of the road's 'strategic importance'.

Investment in infrastructure is now seen in terms of 'public-private partnerships' (Gulyani 2001), with the GOS initially seeking out multinational investors. In the early days of the coal exploration, the GOS sought out multinational investors. However, it was unsuccessful and eventually entered into partnership with Engro Limited, a Pakistani company that is generally associated with fertilizers and petro-chemical production. The hegemonic discourse of the 'public private' has percolated down to the Sindh Coal Authority, whose website assures investors of the high returns in investing in coal (Sindh Energy 2019). A good example of this attempt to attract multinational investment was a document produced by the Pakistani embassy in Washington, DC, entitled 'Pakistan's Thar Coal Power Generation Potential Seeks Potential Foreign Investment' (Embassy of Pakistan 2008), which promised excellent infrastructure and a very attractive tax regime, two factors that seem to reoccur in many such projects in the Global South. Another document, this time produced by the Thar Coal Board, was equally enthusiastic, promising high returns and business-friendly policies. The language used in all of these documents is incredibly fervent, promising a neoliberal paradise. The idea that the private sector does things better was well established among the Sindh Coal Authority officials I spoke to. Their website makes reference to the fact that exploitation of the coal field will require the construction of an airport, road networks, a railway link, water supply, and electricity transmission lines, thereby acknowledging the large-scale state investment. Despite investing over US$2 billion in the project to date, the SECMC has needed further subsidies. These ups and downs of the coal project were certainly known to the local elites. Ashok Pundit,[5] a Mithi resident who ran a local NGO, and was also landowner, kept telling me that these difficulties did show that the project was perhaps unviable, but was still supportive of the coal project. As a landowner, Ashok was explicit that the speculation on land was something that benefited Tharis who were landowners.

By 2014, the GOS had invested over US$2 billion in the project already, but SECMC was still seeking further subsidies (Ali 2014). One of the reasons

---

5   Pseudonym.

for delay in the exploitation of the mine and the spiralling costs was the complete absence of roads in the district. However, road building in Pakistan is essentially a state-led enterprise, despite a rhetoric now increasingly being couched in the neoliberal language of encouraging investments from multinationals, with a whole host of acronyms such as BOT (Build Operate and Transfer) and PPP (Public Private Partnerships). The cost of the Coal Road was eventually borne by the GOS. Originally, the coal project was not part of the CPEC, but after the insistence of the GOS, it was included, after an initial Chinese reluctance to get involved, who only agreed after the government of Pakistan promised US$700 million worth of sovereign guarantee to underwrite the loan taken by the SECMC (Ahmed 2019). Mitchell (1999) argues that contrary to its rhetoric, the neoliberal state has neither removed the state itself from the market nor discouraged the profligate subsidies. These subsidies are no longer being used to protect the most vulnerable from the worst excesses of neoliberalism but are rather benefitting an ever-decreasing circle of individuals, most with close links to the state.

Building infrastructure in Pakistan is essentially a state-led enterprise, dependent upon loans from international lenders such the International Monetary Fund or the World Bank (Haines 2013; Jamali 2014). The CPEC is an opportunity for Pakistan to seek out alternative sources of funds, and a rebranding of the long-term cooperation between China and Pakistan, which has been in progress since the 1950s and included the construction of the Karakorum Highway between 1959 and 1979 (Garlick 2018). Chinese infrastructure investment in Pakistan has also been selective, and their reluctance to invest in the Thar coal project shows how the interests in both countries can and do diverge. Without the sovereign guarantee, it is unlikely that China would have given the required loans. The CPEC involves the upgrading of the Karakorum Highway, that will provide an alternative route to the sea for China. An anthropologist who had spent the last five years working in Gilgit Baltistan told me that weather conditions were so severe that it was unlikely the Karakorum Highway would be able to handle the large amount of truck traffic expected by the proponents of the CPEC. The Karakorum Highway lies in a seismologically unstable region which is often subject to landslides (Garlick 2018) and is now undergoing reconstruction because of a recent earthquake. It seems unlikely that the Karakorum Highway will ever be used as a major logistics route, yet the gap between the rhetoric and the reality allows for different actors to insist that the CPEC will be a 'game changer'. There exists in Pakistan a clear tension between the centralizing tendencies of the state, and the necessity for the state to negotiate with international lenders who demand that it seek private partners.

The CPEC and the land along the road

The Thar coal project clearly predated the CPEC by almost a decade, but during the course of my fieldwork in 2016-2017, I discovered that the 'symbolic power' of the CPEC was such that the construction of the Coal Road was often conflated with the CPEC. I had met a Karachi-based estate agent at his office, accompanying a relative who was in the process of selling his property. Discussions had drifted towards why I was in Pakistan, as I explained the nature of my research, his voice rose with excitement. The words 'China-Pakistan Economic Corridor' and 'special economic zone' kept coming up during the conversation, with incentives to buy land along the Coal Road. The estate agent was obviously keen for me to buy real estate in Tharparkar, despite the fact that there is no special economic zone or industrial park planned here, nor was the road project included in the CPEC. I asked him who the possible sellers would be, and he insisted that there were many Thari landowners who were keen to sell, and he had received interest from potential buyers as far away as Lahore in Punjab. Chandrabhan, a local activist and NGO employee, told me how in Islamkot, a large number of squatters had occupied the *gaucher*, common land used for pasturage by villagers, located next to the Tharparkar Coal Road. Rumour also had it that most were connected with a local political leader who wanted to grab the *gaucher* lands, which were technically in state ownership. The land along the Coal Road was said to have quadrupled in value. In the coal field area, I often saw tractors belonging to the Sindh Revenue Department ploughing up fields containing crops on *gaucher* lands in villages near Mithi, but I never witnessed anything like this on the Coal Road in Islamkot. There is evidence that the immediate effect of the CPEC discourse was the destruction of important pasture, which also heightened the tension between the local villagers and the squatters. Like other regions in South Asia undergoing infrastructural interventions, Tharparkar was seeing a shift in the idea of land 'from its productive use to its commodification' (Gardner and Gerharz 2016: 2), with land now becoming the central arbiter of power, and for those with access to the land, wild dreams of accumulation can be strategically encouraged.

Land in Tharparkar had not been surveyed or 'settled', to use the colonial government terminology, because it was considered unlikely to provide tax revenue. The construction of the Tharparkar Coal Road has completely changed this situation, thereby exciting the interests of the likes of my property developer friend. Jamali (2014) refers to something similar, albeit at a more advanced stage, in his field site in Gwader as a result of the construction of the East Gwader Expressway. Like Tharparkar, Gwader had not been surveyed and with the road arrived a plethora of real estate agents, brokers, and revenue officials. This is a type of state privatization, although perhaps not in the way the World Bank would conceive it, with the emphasis on selling off public assets.

Figure 6.1 Pictures of Container Hotel

Photos by author

The Container Hotel

Along the newly constructed Tharparkar Coal Road, most of the investment is not from Tharparkar residents. Even where residents are involved in investment, they do not always employ people local to the area to work in the business. For example, a petrol station built on the Tharparkar Coal Road between Islamkot and Mithi, near the village of Saund and the Container Hotel, is staffed by Sindhis from outside the district. An example of a large-scale investment along the Coal Road was the Shaikh Ziaul Haq & Sons Facilitation Centre, or commonly referred to as the Container Hotel, an air-conditioned restaurant built by a Karachi-based company S. Ziaul Haq & Sons (SZS). The restaurant has been constructed from disused cargo containers, hence the name. This restaurant is a visible symbol of the new Tharparkar, located some five kilometres from the town of Islamkot, the largest in the coalfield. The sort of capital required, both social and economic, to make an investment of this kind is beyond the reach of most in the district. Rumour had it that SZS had paid ten times the market value to buy the land from a Memon[6] landowner on which to build the Container Hotel. The presence of the road has already encouraged a great deal of land speculation, although the long-term effects on land prices are difficult to predict. Mohammadbhai, who was also Memon and had land along the

---

6   A local Muslim caste, traditionally associated with trade.

Coal Road had advised much of the land near the Container Hotel had been bought by 'outsiders'.

Traditionally, commerce in Tharparkar was in the hands of Hindu castes such as the Lohana and Baniya (Nadiem 2001), and some certainly have the capital to invest. I was often told, mainly by Muslims, that any kind of obvious display of wealth was regarded as risky by many wealthy Hindus. Large-scale investment from Hindu merchants in the district is also unlikely, as many have little confidence in state protection. Mohammadbhai, whose village was located opposite the Container Hotel, would tell me stories of kidnappings of wealthy Hindu traders in northern Sindh, and the press often ran stories as well (see News 18 2012). As nothing like this had happened in Thar, it is difficult to establish whether this was indeed the case. In South Asia, during ethnic and religious violence, businesses and property of minorities is often vulnerable to arson and looting (see Wilkinson 2006), therefore the Hindu businessmen in Tharparkar had good reason not to be very public about any investments. Although there had been some local investments from the likes of Mahesh and Nikhil, the two local political leaders mentioned at the start of this chapter. Both ran agencies representing large foreign companies – in the case of Mahesh, this included commodities as such as refrigerators and sugar – and as politicians, both had the necessary links to obtain the permits required by the state to operate the business. Indeed, some of the newly built petrol stations along the road are joint ventures; with the Hindus providing the funds and Muslims dealing with state officials of all types. However, I was repeatedly told by Mohammad Bhai and Ashok Pandit that the new petrol stations that had been built all had their ownership in the name of a Muslim, while the Hindus were said to be silent partners.

The Container Hotel resembles a lunar base, detached from the landscape, surrounded with a razor wire. Once inside, you would be hard pressed to find anything Thari or anything necessarily aimed at a local clientele. The menu was written in English and Urdu, and featured food such as club sandwiches. When I asked the manager, who was a Punjabi, and clearly not impressed by what he had seen so far in Thar, whether they employed any locals, his answer was a straightforward 'no', as they are, he pronounced, 'lazy' and 'dirty'. Interethnic relations are fraught in Pakistan, with Sindhis often depicted as lazy and unreliable (Ring 2006). These tensions are reinforced with existing economic disparities in Pakistan. Tharparkar is ranked lowest among the districts of Sindh for literacy, with rates in rural Tharparkar standing at 28% (Hagler Bailly 2012).

The village of Saund is located just behind the Container Hotel. I got to know Abdul, who lived in Saund and worked as a cook at the NGO I was staying with in Islamkot. Like many villages near the Tharparkar Coal Road, Saund lacked electricity and was not connected by a feeder road. It was a uni-caste village, inhabited entirely by Muslims, who had been pastoralists. Saund was a *dhani* (hamlet), built around a well and a watering hole, and did not appear on revenue records. Its absence on the official records meant that the public services, few as they were, that the GOS provided in other villagers, were not available in Saund. Abdul had been appointed a cook when the NGO had carried out a project in his village some two decades ago. His son and son-in-law also both worked at the NGO as cooks or caretakers. The land on which the Container Hotel was built had previously been used as pasture by many of Saund's residents and had been owned by a Memon from Mohammadbhai's village. Abdul was bitter about this, telling me that the Memon's father would never have sold the land, as land was something to be passed on, but now money was the only thing that mattered.

I asked Abdul whether he had applied for a job at the Container Hotel; after all, a job there would halve his commute. His response was that he had tried but had been unsuccessful. I asked whether he had told them that he had over 20 years of experience working as cook, and his response was that he was never allowed beyond the front gate. Indeed, the Container Hotel had a rather large security guard, and anyone going in had to sign a register in English or Urdu. Tellingly, the register was written in English, itself an exclusionary act, as most of the population could not read English. SZS markets itself as 'providing services par excellence and is serving major Oil & Gas Explorations in the most difficult remote areas in Pakistan' (SZS 2019). Its website is full of acronyms and demands that potential applicants possess a large number of formal qualifications. The recruitment policy involves submission of a CV typed in English to the human resources department. Even if Abdul could have somehow managed this, he lacked the requisite training to apply for a position as chef or indeed trainee chef. Bearing in mind that most of the population of Saund are pastoralist, with a district figure of 28% literacy itself is likely to be an exaggeration, the ability of villagers to get a job in the Container Hotel would be severely limited. Indeed, many of the waiters I encountered were from the Gilgit Baltistan, the northern-most region of Pakistan, where there has been a long history of both domestic and international tourism through which they have gained experience in the hospitality industry (Haines 2012). This saw a sharp decline after the September 11 Twin Towers bombing, when Gilgit Baltistan, bordering Afghanistan, became embroiled in conflict. Leading many residents to seek jobs in other parts of the country. The waiters were extremely dismissive of the locals, often using very derogatory language. The difficulty Abdul and I experienced tackling the SZS recruitment website had not led him to be dissuaded by the idea of Thar becoming a 'new Dubai'. Yet what I found was to the contrary; he seemed to be taken in by the discourse of better days that lay ahead.

The CPEC had now acquired a 'symbolic power', imposing a set of socially accepted meanings which in turn affected the actions of many Thari such as Abdul. The Coal Road was now referred to locally as the 'CPEC bypass', and any criticism of the coal project was seen somehow being critical of CPEC. Ashok Pandit in one of our many conversations made the point how important CPEC was bringing 'development' to the district. Urdu news channels, such as the ARY, a widely watched Urdu news cable channel also emphasized how the Thar coal project, and the CPEC (Engro Corp. 2019), and would bring benefits. The discourses of Thar becoming a 'new Dubai', the ultimate symbol of modernity, was also a recurrent theme on KTN, the largest Sindhi language TV channel. This channel was watched extensively in the district, including by Abdul, although the Sindhi news channels such as KTN sometimes did give more nuisance to the project then their Urdu counterparts such as the ARY (KTN News 2020; KTN News 2016). These metanarratives of infrastructural-led modernity and a 'better future' were widely consumed locally, and played an important role in reducing resistance to the project. They have also of been strategically encouraged by the state as shown by a statement by the governor of Sindh in 2017 published in a national newspaper, stating that the project will provide education, which in itself is slightly strange as this is one thing that even the project does not claim to do (Jamil 2017). The way the media can shape the public discourse has been well researched (see Besley and Burgess 2002; Dyck and Zingales 2002; Hamilton 2003), and in particular how it influences the public not only through the slant of a particular report (DellaVigna and Kaplan 2007) but also by choosing what to cover (George and Waldfogel 2006).

Conclusion

Following Gidwani (2002), this chapter has shown that 'development can – and should be – principally understood as a place holder concept that denotes regulatory ideals of a better life within specific time-space concepts' (2002: 5). The development of infrastructure in South Asia has always also required investors to take financial risks, something that is not just confined to the modern Pakistani state (Whitcombe 1996). The 'promise' of infrastructure is its future orientation and its generative impulses (Harvey and Knox 2012).

From these generative impulses emerge new symbols of status and change; for Heslop and Jeffery (this volume), concrete in the Maldives comes to stand as potent symbol of modernity and development. While in Nepal, Murton and Sigdel tie in road mobility with a new public-private future, in India, Gohain illustrates how the *dhaba* provides a new site for reckoning symbols of status and captures notions of development and modernity on the highway.

In the imaginative work of conjuring 'better' more 'modern' lives that is 'development', new infrastructures are created which reinforce pre-existing social hierarchies. In Tharparkar, we can observe both, as land emerges as an important commodity, yet the historic marginality of the region's Hindu minority is being reinforced. The daily wage work provided by SECMC in the open cast mine is precarious and the business that are now opening up along the Coal Road are not employing local Tharis. The coal project has allowed for an increase in land prices, which will clearly disadvantage most, with many sharecroppers facing eviction, as speculators buy the land along the Coal Road, which is subsequently fenced by the new owners. For Mahesh, it was about waiting and seeing if he could extract something from this state largesse, while Abdul hoped that the dreams of better employment opportunities he had seen televised on KTN would soon be fulfilled. However, as I argue, these tangible benefits are few and limited. The local political elites in Tharparkar, many of whom are landowners, clearly benefit from the increased speculation of land, which becomes an economic commodity, but even they lack the necessary social and economic capital to build something like the Container Hotel. The real beneficiaries are only the likes of SZS, with its experience of working within the oil and gas industry, which has allowed it to make the political connections required to obtain permits to operate in what is a highly securitized border region.

Infrastructure has clearly moved from the background to the foreground in the social sciences, and any 'explication' (Latour 2005; Sloterdijk 2009) of it requires an understanding of the contradictions, which are often masked by public rhetoric. There exists an uncomfortable space between the discourse and the reality in any infrastructure project; it is these spaces that need to be interrogated. As Pakistan undergoes a massive investment programme under the aegis of the CPEC, with words such as 'game changer' being used, the question one may ask is, what are these exuberant dreams of connectivity and economic prosperity really revealing? The 'transition rhetoric' of the creation of a new 'Dubai' has allowed both the state and local political elite to 'veil' the actual economic and political processes at play in Tharparkar, where the immediate effect of the mining project is the dispossession of local communities. There is now considerable literature on how past projects, with their assurances of modernity, have degenerated, leaving only decay and breakdown where there once was grandeur and optimism, however fantastical (Mitchell 2002; Pelkmans 2006; Larkin 2013). By foregrounding the contradictions between the grand narrative of infrastructure and its implications for the residents of Thar, this chapter has shown that the 'better future' imagined at the Islamkot municipal offices is ambivalent terrain indeed.

List of works cited

Acuto, M. (2010). 'High-rise Dubai Urban Entrepreneurialism and the Technology of Symbolic Power'. *Cities* 27(4): 272-284.

Aggarwal, R. (2004). *Beyond Lines of Control: Performance and Politics on the Disputed Borders of Ladakh, India*. Durham, NC: Duke University Press.

Ahmed, A. (2019). 'Pakistan Opens Its First Coal Power Plant in the Most Backward Area of Thar'. *Gulf News*, 10 April. https://gulfnews.com/world/asia/pakistan/pakistan-opens-its-first-coal-power-plant-in-the-most-backward-area-of-thar-1.63245988 (accessed 25 November 2020).

Ali, F. (2014). 'Thar Coal: Reality and Myth'. *Business Recorder*, 1 October. http://www.brecorder.com/articles-a-letters/187/1229452/ (accessed 10 May 2018).

Ali, T. (1983). *Can Pakistan Survive? The Death of a State*. Harmondsworth: Penguin.

Anand, N., H. Appel and A. Gupta (2018). *The Promise of Infrastructure*. Durham, NC: Duke University Press.

Anwar, N. (2015). *Infrastructure Redux: Crisis, Progress in Industrial Pakistan and Beyond*. Basingstoke: Palgrave Macmillan.

Ascher, W., and N. Mirovitskaya (2016). *Development Strategies and Inter-group Violence*. Basingstoke: Palgrave Macmillan.

Athique, A.M. (2008). 'A Line in the Sand: The India-Pakistan Border in the Films of J.P. Dutta'. *South Asia: Journal of South Asian Studies* 31(3): 472-499.

Bajwa, F. (2013). *From Kutch to Tashkent: The Indo-Pakistan War of 1965*. London: Hurst.

Baud, M., and W. van Schendel (1997). 'Toward a Comparative History of Borderlands'. *Journal of World History* 8(2): 211-242.

Baviskar, A. (2004). *In the Belly of the River: Tribal Conflicts over Development in the Narmada Valley*. Oxford: Oxford University Press.

Besley, T.J., and R. Burgess (2002). 'The Political Economy of Government Responsiveness: Theory and Evidence from India'. *Quarterly Journal of Economics* 117(4): 1415-1451.

Bourdieu, P. (1984). *Distinction: A Social Critique of the Judgment of Taste*. London: Routledge.

Bouzas, A.M. (2012). 'Mixed Legacies in Contested Borderlands: Skardu and the Kashmir Dispute'. *Geopolitics* 17: 867-886.

Caron, C., and D. da Costa (2007). 'There Is a Devil on Wayamba Beach: Social Dramas of Citizenship in North West Sri Lanka'. *Journal of Asian and African Studies* 42(5): 415-445.

Chaziza, M. (2016). 'China-Pakistan Relationship: A Game-Changer for the Middle East?' *Contemporary Review of the Middle East* 3(2): 147-161.

Cons, J., and M. Eilenberg, eds. (2019). *Frontier Assemblages: The Emergent Politics of Resource Frontiers in Asia*. Hoboken, NJ: John Wiley & Sons.

Dalakoglou, D. (2017). *The Road: An Ethnography of (Im)mobility, Space, and Cross-border Infrastructures in the Balkans*. Manchester: Manchester University Press.

Das, V., and D. Poole (2004). *Anthropology in the Margins of the State*. Santa Fe, NM: School of American Research Press.

DellaVigna, S., and E. Kaplan (2007). 'The Fox News Effect: Media Bias and Voting'. *Quarterly Journal of Economics*, 122(3): 1187-1234.

Demenge, J. (2011). *The Political Ecology of Road Construction*. PhD thesis, University of Sussex.

Dyck, A., and L. Zingales (2002). 'The Corporate Governance Role of the Media'. In *The Right to Tell: The Role of the Media in Development*, ed. by R. Islam. Washington, DC: The World Bank, 107-140.

Embassy of Pakistan (2008). 'Pakistan's Thar Coal Power Generation'. Private Power & Infrastructure Board. http://embassyofpakistanusa.org/wp-content/uploads/2017/05/Thar-Coal-Power-Generation.pdf. (accessed 15 September 2017).

Engro Corp. (2019). 'Impact of Coal Project in Thar Block 2'. *YouTube*, 13 April. https://www.youtube.com/watch?v=_sSKicNIeKo (accessed 20 June 2020).

Gardner, K., and E. Gerharz (2016). 'Introduction: Land, "Development" and "Security" in Bangladesh and India: An Introduction'. *South Asia Multidisciplinary Academic Journal* 13. https://doi.org/10.4000/samaj.4141.

Garlick, J. (2018). 'Deconstructing the China-Pakistan Economic Corridor: Pipe Dreams versus Geopolitical Realities'. *Journal of Contemporary China* 27(112): 519-533.

George, L.M., and J. Waldfogel (2006). 'The *New York Times* and the Market for Local Newspapers'. *American Economic Review* 96(1): 435-447.

Gidwani, V. (2002). 'The Unbearable Modernity of "Development". Canal Irrigation and Development Planning in Western India'. *Progress and Planning* 58: 1-80.

Gulyani, S. (2001). *Innovating with Infrastructure: The Automobile Industry in India*. Basingstoke: Palgrave Macmillan.

Hagler Bailly (2012). 'Environmental and Social Impact Assessment Final Report Block II (Volume 1 of 2)', January 2013. http://haglerbailly.com.pk/documents/reports/R2M03THP%20-%20Appendices%20-%20ESIA%200f%20Thar%20Coal%20Block%20II%20Mining%20Project%20(Vol%20II).pdf (accessed 10 July 2018).

Haines, C. (2012). *Nation, Territory, and Globalization in Pakistan.* London: Routledge.

Haines, D. (2013). *Building the Empire, Building the Nation: Development, Legitimacy and Hydro-politics in Sindh, 1919-1969.* Karachi: Oxford University Press.

Hamilton, J.T. (2003). *All the News That's Fit to Sell: How the Market Transforms Information into News.* Princeton, NJ: Princeton University Press.

Hammarström, H., R. Forkel and M. Haspelmath, eds. (2017). 'Dhatki'. In *Glottolog 3.0.* Jena: Max Planck Institute for the Science of Human History.

Harvey, P., and H. Knox (2012). 'The Enchantments of Infrastructure'. *Mobilities* 7(4): 521-536.

Hasan, A., and M. Raza (2011). *Migration and Small Towns in Pakistan.* Karachi: Oxford University Press.

Ibrahim, F. (2009). *Settlers, Saints and Sovereigns: An Ethnography of State Formation in Western India.* New Delhi: Routledge India.

iMMAP (2014). 'USAID Pakistan Emergency Situational Analysis: A Profile of District Tharparkar'. Islamabad: iMMAP Pakistan Services Desk. https://reliefweb.int/sites/reliefweb.int/files/resources/PESA-DP-Tharparkar-Sindh.pdf (accessed 25 November 2020).

Ispahani, M. (1989). *Roads and Rivals: The Political Uses of Access in the Borderlands of Asia.* Ithaca, NY: Cornell University Press.

Jamali, H. (2014). *A Harbor in the Tempest: Megaprojects, Identity, and the Politics of Place in Gwader, Pakistan.* PhD dissertation, University of Texas at Austin.

Jamil, M. (2017). 'CPEC: A Game Changer'. *Pakistan Observer.* http://www.cpecinfo.com/archive/news/cpec-a-game-changer-/Mzg3NA== (accessed 10 April 2021).

Jodhka, S., and G. Shah (2010). 'Comparative Contexts of Discrimination: Caste and Untouchability in South Asia'. *Economic and Political Weekly* 45(48): 99-106.

Khalti, S.A. (2015). 'Life in the Desert'. *Himal Southasian*, 29 July. http://himalmag.com/life-desert-tharparkar/ (accessed 30 September 2015).

Krishna, S. (1996). 'Cartographic Anxiety: Mapping the Body Politic in India'. In *Challenging Boundaries: Global Flows, Territorial Identities*, ed. by M. Shapiro and H. Alker. Minneapolis: University of Minnesota Press, 193-214.

KTN News (2016). 'Thar Coal'. *YouTube*, 10 November. https://www.youtube.com/watch?v=qG1qy6UwX00 (accessed 20 June 2020).

KTN News (2020). 'The Issues with Hussain Thebo'. *YouTube*, 25 February. https://www.youtube.com/watch?v=dKxP0AMRxIA (accessed 20 June 2020).

Larkin, B. (2013). 'The Politics and Poetics of Infrastructure'. *Annual Review of Anthropology* 42(1): 327-343.

Latour, B. (2005). *Reassembling the Social: An Introduction to Actor-Network Theory.* Oxford: Oxford University Press.

Lieven, A. (2011). *Pakistan: A Hard Country.* London: Allen Lane.

Mahmood, S. (2014). *Minoritization of Pakistani Hindus (1947-1971).* PhD dissertation, Arizona State University.

Martínez, O. (1994). *Border People: Life and Society in the U.S.-Mexico Borderlands.* Tucson: University of Arizona Press.

Mitchell, T. (1999). 'Dreamland: The Neo-liberalism of Your Desires'. *Middle East Report* 29(1): 28-33.

Mitchell, T. (2002). *Rule of Experts: Egypt, Techno-Politics, Modernity.* Berkeley: University of California Press.

Mitra, S.K. (2001). 'War and Peace in South Asia: A Revisionist View of India-Pakistan Relations'. *Contemporary South Asia* 10(3): 361-379.

Nadiem, I. (2001). *Thar: The Great Pakistani Desert.* Lahore: Sang-e-Meel Publications.

News 18 (2012). 'Three Hindu Traders Kidnapped in Pakistan: Three Prominent Hindu Businessmen Were Kidnapped Along with Their Driver by Unidentified Armed Men'. 14 July. https://www.news18.com/news/india/three-hindu-traders-kidnapped-in-pakistan-487751.html (accessed 15 May 2019).

Padel, F. (2011). *Sacrificing People: Invasions of a Tribal Landscape.* New Delhi: Orient BlackSwan.

Pelkmans, M. (2006). *Defending the Border: Identity, Religion, and Modernity in the Republic of Georgia.* Ithaca, NY: Cornell University Press.

Population Census Organization Statistics Division (1998). Tharparkar District Census Report. Islamabad: Government of Pakistan.

Reeves, M. (2017). 'Infrastructural Hope: Anticipating "Independent Roads" and Territorial Integrity in Southern Kyrgyzstan'. *Ethnos* 82(4): 711-737.

Ring, L. (2006). *Zenana: Everyday Peace in a Karachi Apartment Building.* Bloomington: Indiana University Press.

Rycroft, D., and S. Dasgupta (2011). *The Politics of Belonging in India: Becoming Adivasi.* London: Routledge.

SBS Urdu (2019). 'This Pakistani Ad Is Breaking the Internet with Around 2 Million Views in Two Days', 16 April. https://www.sbs.com.au/yourlanguage/urdu/en/article/2017/04/25/pakistani-ad-breaking-internet-around-2-million-views-2-days (accessed 25 November 2020).

Schaflechner, J. (2018). *Hinglaj Devi: Identity, Change, and Solidification at a Hindu Temple in Pakistan.* Oxford: Oxford University Press.

Shaikh, A. (2005). 'Pakistan: Development and Disaster'. In *Internal Displacement in South Asia: The Relevance of the UN's Guiding Principles*, ed. by P. Banerjee, S. Basu, R. Chaudhury and S.K. Das. Thousand Oaks, CA: Sage Publications, 62-112.

Siddiqi, A. (2018). *In the Wake of Disaster: Islamists, the State and a Social Contract in Pakistan*. Cambridge: Cambridge University Press.

Simpson, E. (2006). 'The State of Gujarat and the Men without Souls'. *Critique of Anthropology* 26(3): 331-348.

Sindh Energy (2019). 'Investment Opportunity in Thar Coal'. https://sindhenergy. gov.pk/investment-opportunity/investment-opportunity-in-thar-coal/ (accessed 15 May 2019).

Sloterdijk, P. (2009). *Terror from the Air*, trans. by A. Patton and S. Corcoran. Los Angeles, CA: Semiotext(e).

SZS (2019). S. Zia-Ul-Haq & Sons website. https://www.zias.com.pk/ (accessed 15 May 2019).

Talpur, M. (2017). 'Save Thar from Coal Projects'. *Daily Times*, 26 November. https:// dailytimes.com.pk/147162/save-thar-coal-projects/ (accessed 10 July 2020).

Tsing, A. (1993). *Realm of the Diamond Queen: Marginality in an Out-of-the Way Place*. Princeton, NJ: Princeton University Press.

Whitcombe, E. (1996). 'The Environmental Costs of Irrigation in British India: Waterlogging, Salinity and Malaria'. In *Nature, Culture, Imperialism: Essays in the Environmental History of South Asia*, ed. by D. Arnold and R. Guha. New Delhi: Oxford University Press, 237-259.

Wilkinson, S. (2006). *Votes and Violence: Electoral Competition and Ethnic Riots in India*. Cambridge: Cambridge University Press.

About the author

MUSTAFA KHAN is a social anthropologist researching the state, infrastructure, and contested borderlands of South Asia. Prior to coming to anthropology, he worked as a lawyer within the infrastructure development sector for over a decade. He obtained his doctorate in Social Anthropology in 2020 from SOAS, University of London.

7   Encountering Chinese development in the Maldives

Gifts, hospitality, and rumours

Luke Heslop and Laura Jeffery

Abstract
This chapter examines the longest and most developed road in the Maldives archipelago, a fifteen-kilometre-long link road connecting four islands of the Laamu (or Haddummati) Atoll. In the planning phase, there were tensions between those who argued that the road should connect houses to the school and the mosque and those who argued that the road should connect the harbour to the market. Such appeals, bifurcated along gender lines, reflect local mobility concerns and were tied to existing political rifts between the four islands that were intensified by the appearance of a new infrastructural asset. The built road facilitates a multitude of local encounters as people travel further and more regularly, but it is also through the road that islanders encounter the global forces of capital and construction that shape their islands. The Laamu link road was a 'gift' from the Chinese government, constructed by the Jiangsu Transportation Engineering Group (JTEG), and amidst local mobility concerns and inter-island politics swirl rumours and hearsay of land grabs and international power struggles between China, India, the US, and Saudi Arabia. This chapter, as well as being an ethnographic exposition of Chinese infrastructure development in a South Asian archipelago, explores the road as a social experience as it crosscuts competing visions of modernity, global connectivity, and anxiety about material change on remote coral atolls in the Indian Ocean.

Keywords: Maldives, encounter, geopolitics, rumour, gifts, link road

Heslop, Luke, and Galen Murton (eds), *Highways and Hierarchies: Ethnographies of Mobility from the Himalaya to the Indian Ocean*. Amsterdam, Amsterdam University Press 2021
DOI: 10.5117/9789463723046_CH07

Foreign encounters and changing infrastructure

Approximately 67 million years ago, the tectonic plate of what is now the
Indian subcontinent drifted northward over a particularly hot part of the
Earth's mantle, stretching from Reunion to the Deccan Traps of India,
and sprouted a row of volcanoes, which later cooled and subsided. For
millennia, coral has grown atop this sunken oceanic plateau, the Chagos-
Lakshadvip (formerly Laccadive) volcanic ridge, which stretches from the
Chagos Archipelago to the Lakshadvip Sea off the coast of Kerala.[1] As the
volcanoes subsided, they left upwardly growing fringing coral that had
formed around the peaks where they touched the surface of the water
(Darwin 1842). Fringing coral and calcified sediment became sandbanks
in the ocean, which eventually bore vegetation and became habitable.[2]
The outlines of these sunken volcanoes form the distinctive crescent
shapes of the 26 coralline atolls that comprise the Maldives archipelago
today.[3] Currently the Maldives national territory covers an area of 90,000
km², but only 300 km² qualifies as land (Bremner 2016: 289). The National
Bureau of Statistics (2015) reported that the 2014 census had enumerated
a total resident population of 402,071, of whom 157,693 (around 38%) lived
in the capital island, Malé, which has the fastest-growing population out
of any island in the Maldives, and is one of the most densely populated
cities in the world at 65,201 people per km² (Maldives National Bureau of
Statistics 2015: 13, 20, 21). The rest of the population is dispersed across 20
administrative atolls (encompassing 118 inhabited administrative islands)
and non-administrative islands (109 tourist resorts and 128 industrial islands
and islands used for other purposes) (ibid.: 15). Historically the Maldives has
been somewhat enclaved from the surrounding world by its perilous reefs;
islands are dispersed across the atolls, which in places are separated by large
deep-water channels. One such channel is the 'Equatorial Channel', which
separates the country's southernmost atolls (Addu and Fuvahmula) from
the rest of the archipelago to the north. The largest deep-water channel is
called the one-and-a-half-degree channel because it cuts laterally through
the atoll one-and-a-half-degrees north of the equator. This channel is 50 miles
wide and lies south of Laamu atoll. We will later return to this channel, but

---

1   Today, the ridge lies at a depth of 1000 m below sea level, bounded by waters which drop to
an oceanic floor of 2500 m on the east side and 4000 m on the west (see Forbes 1980; Rufin-Soler
et al. 2014).
2   The current layer of Maldives reefs began forming at the top of this coral platform about
7500 years ago (Kench et al. 2009).
3   Fuvahmula is the archipelago's only single island atoll without a lagoon.

for now, this is the fragmented geophysical environment that has come to shape the political terrain on which infrastructural encounters take place.

This chapter focuses on a more recent infrastructural encounter on the Maldivian atoll of Laamu, where the Chinese government developed a fifteen-kilometre-long link road connecting four islands on a north/south axis. The Laamu link road, completed in 2016, is the longest road in the Maldives, and is an instantiation, for people in the Maldives generally as well as in Laamu specifically, of a new modernity: a concrete symbol of development and a sign of things to come. The common Divehi word for 'development' (*thara'gee*) is a relatively new word, with *thara* said by some to derive from the English word 'tarmac'. *Thara'gee* is thus explicitly linked with concrete or asphaltic manifestations of change on the islands. The root word for 'progress' (*kuri*) by contrast, is borrowed from the word for the bud of a plant, forming a distinct linguistic split between conceptualizing ecological growth as progress and development as tar.

As a 'gift' from the Chinese government, the Laamu link road also represents for Maldivians a seemingly axiomatic connection to global power networks and to struggles between China, India, the US, and Saudi Arabia. The danger of 'the gift', as anthropologists following Marcel Mauss have illustrated, is that it is never pure, but rather embroiled in wider circuits of power, reciprocity, and 'total systems of exchange' (Mauss 1954; cf. Gregory 1982; Parry 1986). Gifts are loaded with risk, carrying a moral peril of indebtedness and injurious patronage: reciprocation of some sort is always expected and rarely unproblematic. Anthropological literature on 'gifts' in the context of development, whether philanthropic benevolence (Osella et al. 2015), or couched in terms of disinterested Christian charitable giving of 'pure gifts' (Stirrat and Henkel 1997: 77), or corporate social responsibility programmes that seek to do well by doing good (Dolan and Rajak 2016), similarly suggest that 'gifts' come with strings. Much of this literature draws on the Trojan Horse of Homeric myth by way of an explanatory metaphor. The Chinese state explicitly conceptualizes Chinese development projects as 'gifts' (Yeh 2013: 14), and analysts have pointed to the implications for recipients across South Asia not only in terms of 'indebtedness' (e.g. for Tibet Autonomous Region, see Yeh and Wharton 2016: 296), 'surveillance' (e.g. over Tibetans in Nepal, see Murton et al. 2016: 414), and 'influence' (e.g. for Kazakhstan, see Koch 2013; for Mongolia, see Jackson and Dear 2016: 357, 367). While infrastructure development funded by wealthy global powers such as China has the potential to transform the Maldives, it simultaneously gives rise to concerns about land grabs and lagoon colonization.

Suspicion of gift-laden strangers, foreign encounters, the arrival of distant seafarers and would-be colonizers, generosity, and the perils of changing island infrastructure (both physical and social), are pervasive themes of everyday life in the Maldives and popular tropes within Maldivian folk lore. Moreover, new arrivals to the islands, changing island infrastructure, and a threat to the sociopolitical order go hand in hand. This is perhaps most neatly encapsulated in 'The Sandbank of the Seabirds', a folk tale from the southernmost Addu Atoll. To paraphrase the version recorded by Xavier Romero-Frias (1999: 60-61): Seabirds fed, rested, and bred on an isolated sandbank surrounded by fish. One day the sandbank was visited by a Maldivian cuckoo called a *dīkoi*. The seabirds allowed the land bird to stay overnight, but the oldest seabird warned the others that this visit would be devastating for them. The following morning, when the cuckoo left, it had left its droppings in the sand. The seeds in the droppings began to germinate and eventually the island was covered in lush green bushes. The old seabird warned that the growth of bushes would mean that the seabirds would have to move away, but the other seabirds still dismissed him, enjoying the shade offered by the new vegetation. Soon, however, the lush vegetation attracted a passing fisherman, who then sought and was granted permission by the atoll chief to plant and harvest coconuts on the island. Seeing that the trees grew well, the fisherman built a hut and brought his children, who chased the seabirds and ate their eggs. The fisherman periodically caught seabirds, which he took home with their legs tied and wingtips cut, and eventually only a few seabirds remained. The wise seabird gathered the survivors and together they left the sandbank that had been their home for so long.

Read as an allegorical tale of warning, this folk story from Addu Atoll alludes to a long-standing wariness of outsiders and the fear of contamination. Here, the arrival of a seemingly harmless outsider contaminates the sand and encourages an infrastructural change that catastrophically destabilises the existing political and social order.[4] The story speaks to a pervasive xenophobia in contemporary Maldivian social life born from an inherited fear of *beyru miniha* (outsiders/outside people) that has been largely encouraged by the state (Colton 1999: 94). At the level of the household, *beyru* can refer to people from beyond the boundary wall of the compound (*beyru faaru*), notably those who enter the household through service or

---

4   The enclosure and isolation of the tourist industry to discrete islands for the first decades evinces wariness of integration on inhabited islands.

marriage.[5] At the level of the nation, this is bound up in a powerful histori-cally produced sense of duty to protect Islam – the one and only permitted religion – from contamination by the invading *kaffir* (a pejorative term for non-Muslim). While marriage can decontaminate outsiders entering the household, conversion to Islam decontaminates entrance to the nation and is a sine qua non for being Maldivian.[6] The idiom of contamination is particularly apt in the context of climate and environmental change: as the reefs become contaminated, the low-lying coralline islands become less resilient to sea-level rise (Baer and Singer 2014; Orlove et al. 2014: 259-260). One of the major contaminators in this regard is sediment produced from dredging and dumping sand on the reef flats, which is currently common practice in island infrastructural development in the Maldives.

As the islands sink beneath the surface of the ocean, much like the volcanoes that preceded them and gave the atolls their shape, the islands are resurfaced not with foliage, as in the folk tale, but with asphalt and concrete born from the seeds of Chinese foreign direct investment that have germinated within a changing economy. As some seabirds enjoyed respite from the sun under the foliage, unaware of what this lush greenery would mean for their future on the sandbank, people across the atoll today ride up and down on imported mopeds playing out a mobile and fast-moving vision of 'modernity' (*zamaanee*), on the asphalt roads, perhaps unaware, or unconcerned, with what this may mean for the future of the islands.

Like the anthropological literature on the gift, anthropological approaches to hospitality draw attention to the asymmetric relationships, expectations of eventual reciprocation, and potential dangers for hosts and guests alike (Herzfeld 1987; Marsden 2012: 119, 124; Delaplace 2012: 140-141; Kelly 2012: 150). In this literature, the (giving) hosts have power over their (receiving) guests. By contrast, both 'The Sandbank of the Seabirds' and our case study of the Laamu link road exemplify the opposite power relation to the hospitality literature: the danger is in offering hospitality to a guest whose powers may not be fully known from the start. Moreover, studies of hospitality tend to start with the host giving and the guest receiving (e.g. Delaplace 2012: 141).

---

5   This has been documented by Elizabeth Colton among elite families of Malé. Outside of Malé phrases such as '*keyo kewvaru engeynee bithu fangi negeema*' ('we'll know how many bananas were eaten when the [thatched] walls are taken down'), suggests that creating partitions shielding homespaces is more problematic than protecting the home from outsiders. This phrase has been taken up more recently as a reference to institutions and the importance of transparency to limit corruption.

6   The 1997 constitution designates Islam as the official state religion. The government interprets this provision to impose a requirement that citizens be Muslims (see also Maloney 1980: 175).

By contrast, the case of the Laamu link road presents the opposite process: the Chinese government (guest) first 'gives' development to the Maldives (host), with a view – perhaps, if the rumours are true – to 'taking' something else later.

Historically, built infrastructure on the Maldives has been shaped around harnessing or protecting against the wind and the ocean as it impacts on the islands. Houses were constructed at angles to channel the cooling wind as it comes off the sea. Routes commonly run east-west from the central point of habitation to the shore so that boats can dock and get their goods onto the island in rough seas during both the south-west and north-east monsoon seasons.[7] By contrast the fifteen-kilometre-long Laamu link road runs north to south. Infrastructure has been designed and built in response to the forces acting upon the islands themselves. If the link road stands as an infrastructural response to (and a product of) a different set of forces that impact the atoll, what are those forces? The rough seas of late capitalism, or the 'capitaloscene' (Tsing et al. 2017; Haraway 2015)? The changing winds of global power? How is the link road perceived to ready the islands, and for what kind of imagined future? What are the problems for which the link road is imagined as a desirable solution? This chapter explores the Laamu link road as a social experience, as it intersects competing visions of modernity, global connectivity, and anxiety about material change on a small island in the Indian Ocean. The chapter discusses the development of the Laamu link road, Chinese construction and Maldivian maintenance, the process by which projects beget projects, and associated rumours about geopolitical power struggles in the Indian Ocean.

Conceptualization of the Laamu link road

Laamu is the largest atoll in the Maldives and is an administrative division consisting of twelve inhabited islands with a total population of around 15,000 people.[8] Most of Laamu's islands are small and isolated farming islands used to grow cash crop vegetables or dedicated to industrial work such as fish packing, and are mainly occupied by Bangladeshi, Sri Lankan, and Nepalese labourers. The Laamu link road goes through four elongated islands running north to south on the eastern rim of the atoll: Gan, Maandhoo, Kadhdhoo, and Fonadhoo. Of these, the two islands that

7   South-west monsoon: June to September; north-east monsoon: October to April.
8   Not including expatriate workers.

are significantly populated are those at either end: the northernmost and larger island of Gan and the southernmost and smaller island of Fonadhoo. At the time the research was conducted (2016-2017), Gan was dominated by supporters of the opposition Maldivian Democratic Party (MDP), while Fonadhoo was dominated by supporters of the government Progressive Party of Maldives (PPM). Perhaps unsurprisingly, government largesse seemed to fall on Fonadhoo, as evinced by complaints that those from Gan have to travel to Fonadhoo for the cash machine and the petrol station. On the other hand, however, people from Fonadhoo have to travel to Gan for the atoll hospital and the college. As is common elsewhere on the archipelago's inhabited islands, the split between the two political parties' supporters is well broadcasted by the colour they paint their homes and compound walls: bright pink for the government party; yellow for the main opposition, MDP.

The two central islands, Maandhoo and Kadhdhoo, host a large fisheries company and a military airport, respectively. The fisheries company in Maandhoo is a gated industrial complex with a private harbour and accommodation for the 500 Bangladeshi, Sri Lankan, and Nepalese labourers that reportedly work there. The scale of the harbour is only evident when flying over the island; it is only from the air that one can see the harbour large enough to dock more than fifteen large trawlers, hidden behind a stretch of reclaimed land. Across the road from the factory, a coconut tree plantation spreads out towards the sea. Tucked away in some of the thicker scrub is an old Buddhist stupa, a relic of the pre-Islamic past of the Maldives.[9]

The excavation for the Iskandhar Military Airport in Kadhdhoo began in the early 1980s and was completed in 1986. It was one of the early projects of former President Maumoon Abdul Gayoom and went against the grain of his otherwise centralist national development policies, which focused heavily on Malé and the Malé region throughout his 30-year presidency (1978-2008). Kadhdhoo Airport also receives several flights a week from the domestic carrier Maldives Aero.[10] Tourists disembark, cross the highway to a small harbour, and are promptly taken to a nearby luxury resort. The

9   According to H.C.P. Bell, who documented Buddhist relics in Laamu in 1922, Buddhism spread from northern India to Sri Lanka around the third century BC and from Sri Lanka to the Maldives in the first century BC (Bell 1940), although Buddhism in Maldives was not thought to have taken root until the first or second century AD (see Forbes 1980: 44). In addition to the stupa mentioned, Bell also documented a *sanghārāma* (Buddhist monastery) on Gan.

10   The airport development was supervised by a member of Gayoom's parliament called Ilyas Ibrahim, who is a bit of a local hero, despite not originating from the island, or even the atoll itself: he is from Malé, is former President Maumoon Abdul Gayoom's brother-in-law (wife's brother), and was in President Gayoom's cabinet.

development of the central islands is geared towards export processing and tourism, representing a privatized model of economic development. The transport networks that emerged from this industry and cater for it are waterways and air travel. Public mobility concerns per se were not a priority in the infrastructural development of the atoll.

Historically, islanders had to take a small boat (*bokra*) from island to island across the reef flat.[11] By the 1990s, causeways linked Fonadhoo to Kadhdhoo, Maandhoo to Gan, and finally Maandhoo to Kadhdhoo. In the 1990s, the first petition for road development was put to the government in Malé through an island chief (*katheebu*), who could speak to the atoll chief (*atholhu verin*), who could speak to the president. Anything pertaining to infrastructure development and public planning was decided by President Gayoom and a close circle of national planners. Nothing happened, and it wasn't until 2005 that any major road work seemed possible. Somebody from the Ministry of Atolls Development visited Laamu to announce that the deputy minister for the then Construction Ministry had said that there was an offer of foreign aid to build a road. However, the amount on offer was rumoured to be only half as much as would be required to successfully develop the road. According to the atoll president, in light of this rumoured funding shortfall there were discussions of building either a two-lane road that went half the distance, or a single lane that could run the full distance of the atoll. At this time, nobody on the island really knew what could be done or who would do it. In the years that followed, nothing seemed to happen about this offer of foreign aid. Nevertheless, according to many Laamu inhabitants, discussions had started about how to build a road with only half the required money and where a connecting road should go. As a public good, who should the road serve? This question sparked conversations about contiguous land-based mobility, connectivity, how the islands should progress and develop, and what sort of political channels exist to participate in decisions concerning where such a road may run.

Chinese construction and Maldivian management

In 2008 the political landscape shifted significantly. Following the MDP's electoral success, petitions proceeded from a bureaucratic infrastructure of councils and community groups to MPs and cabinet ministers. The political

---

11   These boat trips are within living memory of people on the islands currently over 30 years old.

and economic conditions for the link road in Laamu seem to have been the perfect storm of a government that had become more open to foreign direct investment and grant-aid development projects combined with a programme of decentralization that saw larger infrastructure development on islands beyond greater Malé. Two influential MPs in the MDP government had also developed guest houses in Gan and wanted easy transportation for people and materials. This was perhaps the first time that the people of Laamu successfully petitioned through a political channel other than directly through the island chief.

In 2009, during MDP President Nasheed's term in office, the idea of the road was reinvigorated with community discussions and a survey. This was the early days of community-engaged participatory development and stakeholder consultation in the Maldives, when the development industry promoted 'partnerships' and 'dialogue' as opposed to top-down strategies (Linnell 2003): a step change in development practice very much on-message with the values of electoral democracy being pumped into the political bloodstream of every island during the MDP era. Before electoral politics and a multiparty governance system, islands would generally get what they were given by national presidents and their close circle of national planners, and before this by the sultan. At the island level, resources such as houses would be allocated to island inhabitants by the island chief, who had control over land disputes and could exile people from the island entirely under the authority of the sultanate (Maloney 1980). The atoll and island councils formed under President Nasheed supplanted the island chiefs to become the new administrative channel through which development would flow from the capital to the islands. However, many in Laamu felt that the islands councils were involved in the consultation and road discussion process at a very superficial level; as soon as the project began everything was reportedly deferred to the ministry level. It was made clear by an official on the island that formal discussions with island inhabitants regarding where the road should go was thought to be merely a performance of participatory practice on the part of the project proponent. According to officials who participated in these meetings and those who claimed to have attended them, there did not need to be a carefully selected and willing 'public' for 'public consultation'. To hold the consultation was enough. It was still the early days of the Maldives's foray with multiparty democratic processes, cooperation did not really need to be established, it was enough simply hold the consultation. It was still expected that the national government – referred to in such instances as the 'Malé government' – and the company would have the final say.

In 2012, towards the abrupt end of Nasheed's term in office, a Chinese company, China Communication Construction Company (CCCC) Ltd., the same company constructing the China-Maldives Friendship Bridge connecting Malé to Hulhulé, completed the road design and released some 'final drawings'. There was evidently a marked disparity between the specification for the link road that developed through the survey and the finished design for the road that finally emerged, with the effect that islanders became sceptical about public consultation processes. In 2014, following an agreement that China would build the road, the Maldivian government signed a contract with a Chinese subsidiary developer, Jiangsu Transportation Engineering Group (JTEG). Construction work was completed in two years as promised. Towards the end of the construction process islanders petitioned for additional new roads that would connect residential areas to local facilities: schools (reportedly favoured by women), mosques (reportedly favoured by men), and health facilities. However, members of the Gan Island Council, including the island president, who had access to municipal vehicles and needed to travel between islands, resisted such requests on the grounds that a link road was supposed to be an uninterrupted highway on which one could travel without worrying about slower vehicles attempting to merge onto the highway. Though the window for consultation had long since closed, island inhabitants also petitioned for pedestrian paths and cycle routes that were protected and shaded, but these requests seemingly came too late in the process to be realized within the scope of the construction project.

One aspect of the road that people seemed keen to change was on the southern cusp of Gan, where a sharp bend follows a long straight on which riders have built up speed. During fieldwork, discussion focused on a fatal accident that had already claimed the life of one young man. Whilst people were upset about the accident, criticism centred on the Maldives Road Development Corporation (MRDC), implying that there was confusion about who was responsible for such repairs before the official opening of the road had begun and while there was still a presence of Chinese workers on the island, diminished though it was.

In 2016, management of the Laamu link road was transferred from the Chinese contractors JTEG to the MRDC, a relatively young state corporation (see Heslop and Jeffery 2020). This marks an important transition in the life of a road from construction to maintenance. Maintenance of the road is the responsibility of the MRDC via its government budget allowance. Neither Gan nor Fonadhoo generate any kind of revenue that would allow them to service the roads or contract any specific work. Island residents fear that this has the potential to reopen the door for politically driven imbalances within budgetary allocations: that is, the concern that the government would prioritize road maintenance for islands that support the government. There is a history to this concern: in Addu Atoll, the southernmost atoll in the Maldives archipelago, the British military connected another island – also called Gan – to three neighbouring islands by building a ten-mile-long causeway, which was at that time the longest road in the Maldives (Maloney 1980: 203), the local council claim to have no way to pay the commercial rates of the MRDC to maintain the roads, and municipal councillors and islanders alike attribute the lack of budgetary support for road maintenance to the fact that Addu is a majority MDP atoll.

What comes to the fore in this section, is not only how the road is engaged with in the physical production process, but how new local political channels are explored, albeit with little success, as a means to participate in the road-construction process. Moreover, it shows that maintenance of the road is highly political and a key site to engage in politics. It also shows that public consultations and what comes out of them in respect to the actual road are two different things. Despite the changing political climate for participatory decision making and talk of a democratized and a locally enfranchised polity, once the road management became a gift and taken under the auspices of the ministry at the national level, newly established political channels became somewhat ineffectual locally. Dealing with the Chinese firm directly was near impossible, channels to make contact were ineffective, and the company itself operated behind gated compounds.

How (Chinese) projects beget (Chinese) projects

The Laamu link road was offered as a gift from the Chinese government to the Maldives government. Through contractual agreements and memorandums of understanding between China and the Maldives, a Chinese firm, JTEG, was contracted to undertake the construction. Other similar agreements include: a housing project funded through concessional loan financing by the government of China, and implemented by the China Machinery Engineering Corporation (CMEC); the expansion and upgrading of Ibrahim Nasir International Airport, contracted to the Overseas Business Department of the Beijing Urban Construction Group Company Limited; and the Malé-Hulhulé Bridge Project, contracted to CCCC. Gifting in this way gives Chinese infrastructure development firms an opportunity to expand beyond domestic markets and opens avenues for other projects and investment in overseas businesses.

The gift of the Laamu link road and the subsequent contracts awarded is a recognizable element of China's expansion into foreign markets, known officially as China's 'Going Out' (*zou chuqu*) strategy. By 2014, the Chinese Export-Import Bank and the China Development Bank had become a larger lender than the World Bank (Zhou and Leung 2015), with over US$100 billion of outward overseas foreign direct investment (OFDI) on the books (Yeh 2016: 275). As part of this outward-looking strategy, Chinese state-owned enterprises, like CCCC and CMEC mentioned above, were encouraged to open up new markets for its firms and facilitate access to credit (Yeh and Wharton 2016: 287). China doesn't simply create markets for its own infrastructure contracts and expertise in South Asia: it also creates new export markets for raw materials, notably steel and concrete.

Opposition MDP party members, interviewed in Colombo in 2016, pointed out that the company contracted to build the Malé-Hulhulé Bridge had been blacklisted by the World Bank Group: in 2009, CCCC was debarred for engaging in fraudulent practices during a national road project in the Philippines (World Bank 2011). The MDP questioned the transparency processes underpinning such large infrastructure gifts, and argued that the government politicians were pursuing their own financial interests. The MDP also explained that the flooding of the Maldivian economy by China's Export-Import Bank would tie up the country's GDP in servicing the debt, such has been thought to be the modus operandi in many other countries. Furthermore, they warned that China would take land as collateral and ensure the Maldivian government supplies contracts to Chinese firms.

MDP opposition politicians were vocal about the dangers of the Chinese debt trap, but the response this appeal evoked locally was not entirely coherent. Islanders often presented themselves as being reluctant to incur the resultant punishing levels of national debt, yet simultaneously unsure about what this might mean or how that might play out in real terms. Maldivians don't pay tax and have only since the construction of Hulhumalé (1997-2002) had the right to own and sell property; treasury accounts have historically been restricted to a select few at the centre of power. Those on the islands therefore focused on a few key concerns during construction work undertaken by foreign companies. Firstly, the work should be done to an acceptable standard (that is, the standard that would be appropriate for the capital, Malé, or better). Secondly, foreign companies should be bound by the dual imperatives not to take away anything that belongs to the island and to leave whatever is necessary to maintain the road. Thirdly, foreign companies should not attempt to turn Maldivian citizens away from the national religion of Islam. For many across the political spectrum, the environmental impact was perceived to be a more axiomatic and pressing issue than the inability to meet future debt obligations.

For the most part, what was expected from the Chinese workers on the islands was pretty much what was received. The road workers lived in a self-sustaining gated compound on Fonadhoo, built out of the shipping containers the equipment arrived in. They had a basketball court, a salt-water treatment facility, facilities to keep livestock, and a vegetable garden. The only time they left the compound was to work. There was very little opportunity for them to mix with island residents. Only very senior management could be seen taking a stroll up the link road at sunset. In the eyes of one young Maldivian employee of the MRDC, the discipline of the Chinese workers and the control that management had over them was one of the most admired attributes of the company.

In terms of everyday interactions on the Island, the presence of the Chinese workers, and what could broadly be referred to as China's impact on the island, appears almost minimal to non-existent. Life for the Chinese labourers on the island was contained within the compound and work outside the compound was confined to the link-road. Chinese workers were not seen hanging around at the coffee stalls on the beach or the restaurants along the roadside. While Chinese absorption into Maldivian social and economic life was not readily observable through day-to-day activities on the island, Chinese companies were expanding beyond road infrastructure in Laamu by developing links with other local sectors, such as the fisheries industry. Maandhoo is home to Horizon Fisheries, which has limited interest in road development since produce and labour enter and leave the factory by sea via an enormous private harbour. Horizon Fisheries is a Maldivian company owned by a conglomerate called Villa Group, which belongs to an entrepreneur and politician called Qasim Ibrahim.[12] Qasim founded a political party called Jumhoori in 2013 and ran in the presidential campaign. At the end of his unsuccessful campaign he found himself out of favour with the victorious President Yameen's PPM. According to the Maldives Prison Authority, Qasim is now a fugitive of the state (Maldives Independent 2017). Villa Group owns Horizon Fisheries, but half of the capital investments, and therefore half of the profits, go to a Chinese investment company that partnered with Villa Group shortly after the road project began. The company is a Chinese private investment outfit called Zhoushanshi Putuo Dongnani

---

12   Qasim started off as a clerk in a hospital and now has a net worth in the hundreds of millions.

Import and Export Limited (ZPD). ZPD is, on the surface, a small investment firm with a single page of info online (all in Mandarin). It has no registered capital in China, and a single point of contact in Beijing with a Yahoo.com email address.[13] The involvement of ZPD is significant, insofar as it evinces the range of interests in the Maldives, the flow between different sectors (private and state, as well as infrastructure and commercial export), and the scales at which this is taking place; for the Chinese government, for state owned enterprises such as CCCC, associated subsidiaries such as JTEG, and for private investment companies such as ZPD. 'Going Out', as has been argued by Emily Yeh, is 'a process through which the Chinese state itself is being made entrepreneurial, reterritorialized, and rescaled' (Yeh 2016: 280). This process is readily observable in the Maldives, where these actors not only have interests in road-development contracts, but have capitalized on bilateral infrastructure projects to gain a foothold in the local fisheries industry, land ownership, and the development of ports in the area.

The Indian press has reported feverishly on China's increasing influence in the Maldives specifically, and the Indian Ocean region generally. While the headlines point to a challenge to India's historical dominance in South Asia, they simultaneously emphasize it. Headlines such as, 'Asian Giants China and India Flex Muscles over Tiny Maldives' (Sanjeev and Aneez 2018) and international conferences polarizingly entitled, 'China in South Asia: Friend of Foe?' set the tone of India's concerns. The contract termination of GMR India for the for construction of the Maldives international airport in 2012, and the handing over of sixteen geostrategically located islands to the Chinese, are among the most commonly cited grievances leading to ostensibly strained relations between India and the Maldives (Guruswami 2018). One such geo-strategically important node in this scene is an island called Gaadhoo, to which we will now turn our attention.

Back in Laamu, it was rumoured that the Maldivian government – read, President Yameen – had gifted Gaadhoo to the Chinese government in return for the development of the Laamu link road. While there seems to be no official documentation or record of this exchange, certainly not that is available for residents on Laamu, it is presented locally, nationally, and even internationally as a social fact. Local rumour also has it that the Chinese will build an airport and a transhipment port. Such rumours were made all the more believable for residents on Laamu by the arrival of other structures on the island built by the Chinese government. In particular,

---

13   In China, company law stipulates that all enterprises must register a fixed level of operational capital (see Yao et al. 2014).

the housing in Fonadhoo for all who had previously lived in Gaadhoo. Underlying the Chinese housing provision is the assumption that for these structures something is sought in return. Here, we return to the 50-mile-wide one-and-a-half-degree deep water channel to the south of Laamu mentioned at the start of this chapter, to say something of its purported geopolitical/ economic importance. Gaadhoo is strategically important because it lies on this deepwater channel, through which the east-west sea traffic passes through the archipelago.[14] A transhipment port on this channel would apparently be advantageous for whoever established control. In the run up to the presidential election in 2018 the rumour of the transhipment hub in Gaadhoo has become a publicly discussed issue for the opposition MDP campaigning from exile and Indian think tanks alike. The port at Gaadhoo is thought to be a maritime node of connectivity in the Chinese government's Belt and Road Initiative (BRI).

Concerns about China's increasing investment and influence in the Maldives, as well as the acquisition of national territory, mirrored in some ways the rumours of land grabs in Sri Lanka in the development of the Hambantota Port during the post-2010 Mahinda Rajapaksa regime. These rumours have become a public conversation regarding China's political influence in South Asia, national security, indebtedness, and dispossession, with renewed vigour following a recent exposé in the *New York Times* (Abi Habib 2018). Informed by high-level government officials and anonymous Chinese economic policy makers, the article has been discussed on prime-time national news and used vociferously by Sri Lanka's leftist party (Janatha Vimukthi Peramuna, JVP) to highlight corruption under the Rajapaksa regime and threats to sovereignty. The article carves out a narrative of events recognizable to Maldivians; the Chinese government lends large sums of money to build a piece of infrastructure, that money is then used to contract Chinese state-owned enterprises to carry out the work. When fresh funding is required, which it almost inevitably will be, the initial fixed rates are renegotiated and are subsequently much higher. Unable to service the growing debt on the books, Sri Lanka is forced to handover a dominant equity-share of the port back to the lender (China), land around the Hambantota Port has also been given as a means of debt servicing (Abi Habib 2018). Sri Lanka now remains heavily indebted to China and no longer has a controlling stake in the infrastructure it borrowed to develop initially.

---

14   As well as being a conversation in Laamu couched in terms of rumour and hearsay, it is at the same time discussed in the Indian research centres and international press. It is also something being talked about by opposition politicians. So this is not *just* local rumour.

In the Maldives, Chinese investment evinced a stark political split between PPM and MDP supporters: the former were generally supportive of decisions made by President Yameen vis-à-vis infrastructure-financing schemes, while the latter were generally opposed to giving away islands for infrastructure. What complicated the picture a little more, at least during frequent arguments in the run up to the island council elections, was that it was the MDP that began the practice of giving islands to investors to subsidize the development of state infrastructure, such as the Vermillion inter-island/inter-atoll ferry system.

Rumours of geopolitical power struggles

Conversations about development and infrastructural change in the Maldives were awash with stories of espionage and international schemes of geopolitical empire building. Chinese equipment is kept in a casting yard in Fonadhoo, next to which is an American sea cucumber farm called Blue Ridge. According to a very public secret, confirmed by a senior Maldivian politician, Blue Ridge is thought to be a front for an American CIA outpost. The location was declared hopeless for a sea cucumber farm – the water was too warm and the site was where all of the garbage in Fonadhoo eventually washes up – and the farm has apparently yet to produce a single sea cucumber for sale. The rumour amongst Maldivians in Fonadhoo was that the CIA was there to spy on the Chinese contractors. The CIA was thought not to have an interest in the link road *per se*, but was thought to be positioned on the northern cusp of the island in order to monitor activities at the Iskandhar Air Base in Kadhdhoo.

While the Chinese were building a link road, taking over an island and planning to construct a transhipment port on the one-and-a-half-degree deep water channel, and the Americans were pretending to cultivate sea cucumbers while (not so) secretly watching planes land, the Indian government was also thought to have people on the island keeping an eye on the developments unfolding. The Indian government gifted the Maldivian government an impressive helicopter, based at the Iskandhar Air Base. However, with no Maldivian pilot trained to fly the helicopter, the Indian government also provided Indian pilots. The rumour here is that the Indians, while claiming to use the helicopter to take aerial photos for 'island development', are also using it to spy on the Chinese developments on Gaadhoo.

An article in *The Market Mogul* (since removed) suggested that the Maldives is 'set to become centre stage in world politics': the Maldives is being courted by Saudi Arabia, as Riyadh hopes to 'cosy up' to Beijing in a strategic move against Tehran. Meanwhile on the islands, people go to school, go to the mosque, drink coffee, sleep when it gets too hot, and ride up and down the road on mopeds when the heat of the day has dropped, taking a *fini buru*, a 'cool ride'. The rhythm of daily life in Laamu is incongruent with the world of hyper-politics, espionage, and global infrastructure domination considered to be going on around it. Though anthropologists tend to lose their grip on a situation when it scales up to the level of international conspiracy theory, what was particularly interesting about these rumours, however, was how they were retold as such a matter-of-fact way. It did not seem remarkable to island inhabitants that they were, by their own reckoning, surrounded by spies and embroiled in an international geopolitical power struggle.

Conclusion

The Laamu link road can at one level be understood as securing a node in the maritime expansion of the Chinese Belt and Road Initiative (BRI). By gifting the link road construction, many people across the atoll believed China has gained the island of Gaadhoo and access to the one-and-a-half-degree deep water channel. Whether this is true or not we do not know, but following the construction of the link road there has been evidence of Chinese expansion into additional sectors of local industry: house building, transhipment, and fisheries. This is a good example of the type of economic possibility that can be facilitated through an infrastructure project. Who this will benefit also remains to be seen.

Maldivian folk stories such as 'The Sandbank of the Seabirds' evinces a wariness of the potential power of outsiders to wreak unexpected changes on the existing social and political order. Our case study of the Laamu link road enables us to bring together the anthropological literatures on the gift and on hospitality to explore the opportunities and potential risks in accepting a gift from and offering hospitality to outsiders whose powers and intentions may not be fully known from the start. The Chinese gift of a link road heralded not only much-desired infrastructural development but also the destabilization of existing social and political orders at the local and national level. The construction of the link road exacerbated existing political tensions between and within the four island beneficiaries. Moreover, rumours of espionage and lagoon colonization demonstrates that this tiny remote Maldivian atoll is utterly embroiled in international geopolitical struggles, but crucially it also reveals how the political and economic interests of the Maldivian hosts are absolutely sidelined by more powerful gift-giving guests from abroad.

With the construction of one piece of connective infrastructure on the island we have also presented a series of disconnected and closed-off communities, notably, the fisheries harbour in Maandhoo, the compound of the Chinese workers, the Blue Ridge CIA base in Fonadhoo, the transhipment port of Gaadhoo – none of which rely on the link road for connectivity. While the construction of the link road introduced a language of consultation and participation, the new enclaved sites and the encompassment of the project within the state architecture at a ministry level redirected the management of the road at a local level away from island inhabitants. The enclaved sites are part of an ecosystem of differently closed-off circuits of capital, political, and social relations.

In this chapter, we have explored the road as a social experience as it crosscuts competing visions of modernity, global connectivity, and anxiety about material change on remote coral atolls in the Indian Ocean. The arrival of the link road has brought with it the need to conceptualize and (re)imagine the meaning of development in the Maldives; not just in terms of *thara'gee*, *kuri*, connectivity, and mobility along the atoll, but also about the risks of debt, corruption, and public interest in national territory. To this end, the chapter has also documented how the anticipation, arrival, and consideration of the link road opened up a new space in which to consider what is to be expected of a public good in the Maldives – and how 'public' this is. The road represents a resurfacing of the political landscape as much as the physical. As an experience of an infrastructural encounter with the global forces of capital and construction, the road has brought with it a consideration of the efficacy of political channels domestically, and the potential fate of Maldives in the global contemporary present. Undoubtedly the road connects, but what it connects people to goes well beyond the shores of the atoll.

List of works cited

Abi Habib, M. (2018). 'How China Got Sri Lanka to Cough Up a Port'. *New York Times*, 25 June. https://www.nytimes.com/2018/06/25/world/asia/china-sri-lanka-port.html?smprod=nytcore-ipad&smid=nytcore-ipad-share (accessed 16 December 2019).

Baer, H., and M. Singer (2014). *The Anthropology of Climate Change*. London: Routledge.

Bell, H.C.P. (1940). *The Máldive Islands: Monograph on the History, Archaeology and Epigraphy*. Colombo: Ceylon Government Press.

Bremner, L. 2016. 'Thinking architecture with an Indian Ocean aquapelago'. *GeoHumanities* 2: 284- 310.

Colton, E.O. (1995). *The elite of the Maldives: Sociopolitical organisation and change.* Doctoral Dissertation. London School of Economics and Political Science (United Kingdom).

Darwin, C. (1842). *The Structure and Distribution of Coral Reefs: Being the First Part of the Geology of the Voyage of the* Beagle, *under the Command of Capt. Fitzroy, R.N., during the years 1832 to 1836.* London: Smith, Elder and Co.

Delaplace, G. (2012). 'Parasitic Chinese, Vengeful Russians: Ghosts, Strangers, and Reciprocity in Mongolia'. *Journal of the Royal Anthropological Institute* 18(S1): s131-S144.

Dolan, C., and D. Rajak, eds. (2016). *The Anthropology of Corporate Social Responsibility.* Oxford: Berghahn.

Forbes, A.D.W. (1980). 'Archives and Resources for Maldivian History'. *South Asia: Journal of South Asian Studies* 3(1): 70-82.

Gregory, C.A. (1982). *Gifts and Commodities.* London: Academic Press.

Guruswami, M. (2018). 'India's Dilemma in the Maldives: Is It Time to Deal with Chinese Influence?' *South China Morning Post,* 24 February. http://www.scmp.com/news/china/diplomacy-defence/article/2134327/indias-dilemma-maldives-it-time-deal-chinese-influence (accessed 2 December 2020).

Haraway, D. (2015). 'Anthropocene, Capitalocene, Plantationocene, Chthulucene: Making Kin'. *Environmental Humanities* 6: 159-165.

Herzfeld, M. (1987). 'As in Your Own House: Hospitality, Ethnography, and the Stereotype of Mediterranean Society'. In *Honor and Shame and the Unity of the Mediterranean,* ed. by D. Gilmore. Washington, DC: American Anthropological Association, 75-89.

Heslop, L.A., and L. Jeffery (2020). 'Roadwork: Expertise at Work Building Roads in the Maldives'. *Journal of the Royal Anthropological Institute* 26(2): 284-301. DOI: 10.1111/1467-9655.13236.

Jackson, S.L., and D. Dear (2016). 'Resource Extraction and National Anxieties: China's Economic Presence in Mongolia'. *Eurasian Geography and Economics* 57(3): 343-373.

Kelly, A.H. (2012). 'The Experimental Hut: Hosting Vectors'. *Journal of the Royal Anthropological Institute* 18(S1): S145-S160.

Kench, P.S., R.F. McLean and S.L. Nichol (2005). 'New Model of Reef-Island Evolution: Maldives, Indian Ocean'. *Geology* 33(2): 145-148.

Kench, P.S., S.G. Smithers, R.F McLean and S.L. Nichol (2009). 'Holocene Reef Growth in the Maldives: Evidence of a Mid-Holocene Sea-level Highstand in the Central Indian Ocean'. *Geological Society of America* 37(5): 455-458.

Koch, N. (2013). 'Kazakhstan's Changing Geopolitics: The Resource Economy and Popular Attitudes about China's Growing Regional Influence'. *Eurasian Geography and Economics* 54(1): 110-133.

Linnell, D., ed. (2003). *Evaluation of Capacity Building: Lessons from the Field*. New York: Alliance for Non-profit Management.

Maldives Independent (2017). 'Gasim Can Be Declared Fugitive Says Prison Authority', 3 October. http://maldivesindependent.com/politics/gasim-can-be-declared-fugitive-says-prison-authority-132880 (accessed 2 December 2020).

Maloney, C. (1980). *People of the Maldive Islands*. New Delhi: Orient BlackSwan.

Marsden, M. (2012). 'Fatal Embrace: Trading in Hospitality on the Frontiers of South and Central Asia'. *Journal of the Royal Anthropological Institute* 18(S1): S117-S130.

Mauss, M. (1954). *The Gift: Forms and Functions of Exchange in Archaic Societies*. London: Cohen and West.

Murton, G., A. Lord and R. Beazley (2016). '"A Handshake across the Himalayas": Chinese Investment, Hydropower Development, and State Formation in Nepal'. *Eurasian Geography and Economics* 57(3): 403-432.

National Bureau of Statistics (2015). *Maldives: Population and Housing Census 2014: Statistical Release: 1, Population & Household*. Malé: Ministry of Finance and Treasury. statisticsmaldives.gov.mv/nbs/wp-content/uploads/2015/10/Census-Summary-Tables1.pdf (accessed 2 December 2020).

Orlove, B., H. Lazarus, G.K. Hovelsrud and A. Giannini (2014). 'Recognitions and Responsibilities: On the Origins and Consequences of the Uneven Attention to Climate Change around the World'. *Current Anthropology* 55(3): 249-275.

Osella, F., R.L. Stirrat and T. Widger (2015). 'Charity, Philanthropy and Development in Colombo, Sri Lanka'. In *New Philanthropy and Social Justice: Debating the Conceptual and Policy Discourse*, ed. by B. Morvaridi. Bristol: Policy Press, 137-156.

Parry, J. (1986). 'The Gift, the Indian Gift and the "Indian Gift"'. *Man* (NS) 21(3): 453-473.

Romero-Frias, X. (1999). *The Maldive Islanders: A Study of the Popular Culture of an Ancient Ocean Kingdom*. Barcelona: Nova Ethnographia Indica.

Rufin-Soler, C., N.A. Mörner, J. Laborel and J. Collina-Girard (2014). 'Submarine Morphology in the Maldives and Holocene Sea-Level Rise'. *Journal of Coastal Research* 30(1): 30-40.

Sanjeev, M., and S. Aneez (2018). 'Asian Giants China and India Flex Muscles over Tiny Maldives'. *Reuters*, 7 March. https://www.reuters.com/article/us-maldives-politics/asian-giants-china-and-india-flex-muscles-over-tiny-maldives-idUSKCN1GJ12X (accessed 10 April 2021).

Stirrat, R.L., and H. Henkel (1997). 'The Development Gift: The Problem of Reciprocity in the NGO World'. *Annals of the American Academy of Political and Social Science* 554: 66-80.

Tsing, A., H. Swanson, E. Gan and N. Bubandt, eds. (2017). *Arts of Living on a Damaged Planet: Ghosts and Monsters of the Anthropocene*. Minneapolis: University of Minnesota Press.

World Bank (2011). 'World Bank Applies 2009 Debarment to China Communications
Construction Company Limited for Fraud in Philippines Roads Project'. Press
release. http://www.worldbank.org/en/news/press-release/2011/07/29/world-
bank-applies-2009-debarment-to-china-communications-construction-compa-
ny-limited-for-fraud-in-philippines-roads-project (accessed 2 December 2020).

Yao, R., M. Kotova and M. Zito (2014). Raise or Fold: Changing the Registered Capital
of a Company in China'. *China Briefing*, 30 July. http://www.china-briefing.com/
news/2014/07/30/raise-fold-changing-registered-capital-company-china.html
(accessed 2 December 2020).

Yeh, E.T. (2013). *Taming Tibet: Landscape Transformation and the Gift of Chinese
Development*. Ithaca, NY: Cornell University Press.

Yeh, E.T. (2016). 'Introduction: The geoeconomics and geopolitics of Chinese development and investment in Asia'. *Eurasian Geography and Economics* 57(3): 275-285.

Yeh, E.T., and E. Wharton (2016). 'Going West and Going Out: Discourses, Migrants,
and Models in Chinese Development'. *Eurasian Geography and Economics*
57(3): 286-315.

Zhou, L., and D. Leung (2015). *China's Overseas Investments Explained in 10 Graphics*.
Washington, DC: World Resources Institute.

About the authors

LUKE HESLOP is a Lecturer in Social Anthropology at Brunel University and
a Visiting Fellow at the London School of Economics and Political Science.
He specializes in trade, labour, and mercantile kinship in South Asia, and
infrastructure and connectivity in the Indian Ocean.

LAURA JEFFERY is Professor of Anthropology of Migration at the University
of Edinburgh. She works on healthcare at the intersection of gender and
protracted displacement, creative engagement with migration and displacement, and intangible cultural heritage and human-environment relations
in the context of protracted displacement.

8   Roads and the politics of thought

Climate in India, democracy in Nepal

Katharine Rankin and Edward Simpson

Abstract

The chapter presents the politics of thought as an analytical terrain through which to broach the themes at the heart of this volume: the inadvertent role of roads in reproducing and generating hierarchy, class inequality, and social disruption. In bringing together two major research projects led by the authors, we illustrate how roads have been engaged through critical social sciences as an epistemological as well as a material vector of change. By outlining methodological and conceptual approaches to large road and infrastructure projects in South Asia, we show how *ideas build roads.* The chapter draws attention to frequently overlooked aspects of road construction – such as how future environmental impacts are routinely ignored in the political processes and construction practices that constitute the making of roads.

Keywords: India, Nepal, Reunion, democracy, environment, methodology

Introduction

This chapter brings together two major research projects led respectively by Edward Simpson and Katharine Rankin: 'Roads and the Politics of Thought: Ethnographic Approaches to Infrastructure Development in South Asia'[1]

1   This project is funded by the European Research Council (616393). At SOAS, I am grateful to my colleague Marloes Janson and to those who worked on the project: Shaina Anand, Ilona Bowyer, Julia Brodacki, Carolyn Charlton, Khalid Chauhan, Srinivas Chokkakula, Niamh Collard, Sanjukta Ghosh, Liz Hingley, Laura Jeffery, Mustafa Khan, Luke Heslop, Debbie Menezes, Nicole Roughton, Kanchana Ruwanpura and Ashok Sukumaran. Views and errors in this chapter are mine (Simpson).

Heslop, Luke, and Galen Murton (eds), *Highways and Hierarchies: Ethnographies of Mobility from the Himalaya to the Indian Ocean*. Amsterdam, Amsterdam University Press 2021
DOI: 10.5117/9789463723046_CH08

and 'Infrastructures of Democracy: State Building as Everyday Practice in Nepal's Agrarian Districts'.[2] Simpson is an anthropologist, whose UK-based collaborative project worked comparatively across South Asia, but the contribution here is written with India centrally in mind. Rankin is a geographer trained in anthropology and planning, whose project works in partnership with Nepal- and Canada-based researchers and collaborators to explore road development in vernacular terms.

We start by considering how roads have been engaged through critical social sciences as a key vector of change, epistemological as much as material, before moving to discuss the key theoretical and practical aims of the research projects. The projects are centrally concerned with the overarching themes of this volume, namely the inadvertent role of roads in reproducing and generating hierarchy, class inequality, and social disruption; uneven experiences of road development amongst the people in its midst; and the articulation of road building with state building and sociopolitical and geopolitical relations. The projects consolidate around the politics of thought as an analytical terrain through which to broach these themes. Like the material and human resources as well as governance processes that build roads, ideas can be understood to constitute infrastructures upon which roads are built. Both projects used ethnographically oriented comparative methodology and treat ideas and politics in broad registers of culture and power in addition to political parties and the institutions of democracy. Among the projects' key findings, the chapter identifies climate change as an example of critical, globally significant issues that come into view and demand political attention when roads are engaged as a politics of thought. We specify the distinctive ways within South Asia that road building leads to an imperative to broach matters of environmental sustainability, as well as take stock of its implication in processes of uneven development.

Together the projects build an expansive understanding of political thought and make a case for careful investigation of how *ideas build roads*. Simpson's project focuses on planners, engineers and governments, and the office as a key site of knowledge production; he is concerned primarily with large-scale highway-building projects. Rankin's project orients to a farther-flung 'field' in order to encompass other agents of knowledge production

2   This project is funded by the Social Sciences and Humanities Research Council of Canada (SSHRC Grant no. 435-2014-1883, 2014-2020). The current project is being undertaken collaboratively with Pushpa Hamal, Elsie Lewison, Shyam Kunwar, Lagan Rai, Sara Shneiderman and Tulasi Sigdel. Community-based researchers have also contributed data and reflections; they are Durga Hasta, Samjhana Nepali, Yaman Sardar and Shanta Thapa. The chapter was vetted with core team members, and the errors are mine (Rankin).

– labourers, local contractors, and the cultural-political imaginaries of people in rural areas where smaller-scale but equally transformative motorable tracks (known as 'rural' or 'agricultural' roads) multiply at a staggering pace, with the aim of 'connecting' regions perceived as 'remote' relative to centres of governance and commerce. It is our hope that the considerations and insights arising from these long-term, collaborative investigations can serve as a frame and overview for the work discussed in other chapters of the volume (for example, Khan, Heslop and Jeffery, Huang, and Gohain can be read in relation to 'Roads and the Politics of Thought' and Sarma as well as Murton and Sigdel in relation to 'Infrastructures of Democracy').

Roads through the critical social sciences

The arrival and expansion of roads changes the ways in which space and time are conceived. The Romans famously saw roads as key to the growth and control of their empire, an idea suggestive of broad civilizing powers. In England of the eighteenth century, it was commonly thought that roads reduced the incidence of witchcraft. In the colonial nineteenth century, the road was considered the first change a 'rude country' must undertake to pass from poverty and barbarism. Roads recursively are forged by and bring with them ideas, politics, and ways of seeing. Roads, as the chapters of this volume have shown, structure and are structured by human relationships and geographies in particular ways, ways which are not 'natural' or given but made.

Several clusters of critical roads scholarship are discernable and have a bearing on how we have conceived the politics of thought in our respective work. Historians of colonialism have looked at the ways in which roads intersect with power and control. Road building was often instrumental in the formation of colonial knowledge and cultural systems (e.g. Mrázek 2002; Ahuja 2004). Roads allowed the passage of goods, troops and bureaucrats, and they also allowed the land and its people to be imagined and experienced in particular ways (e.g. as a vector of linguistic change). They also manifest some of the inconsistencies and uncertainties in the colonial project (Sinha 2012). Non-colonized states like Nepal engaged roads to thwart colonial incursion, building selectively on the interior but eschewing linkage across borders (Leichty 1997; Whelpton 1983, 2005; Rankin et al. 2017).

The anthropological literature on roads and infrastructure is not vast, but uncommonly high in its qualities. It regards roads as potent sites of meaning and culture in which ideas such as hope and desire, fear and danger (e.g.

Khan 2006), spirituality and witchcraft (Klaeger 2009; Masquelier 2002), nationalism and hatred (Dalakoglou 2012) are brought into sharp relief. Roads variously divide or shape communities; represent either the state or modernity; reflect the end of traditional ways of doing things by marking the onslaught of commodity fetishism (Mostowlansky 2011; Trankell 1993). Roads alter the shape of things and have qualities all of their own which exist outside the materials of their construction. In the anthropological work, we can clearly see the relationships between road building and power and control. While the witches of the road highlight an uneasy relationship to modernity, we can also see how roads become the sites through which history is made, notions of citizenship are forged, and where capitalism operates in its most extreme and enchanting forms. Roads cease to be anodyne or the neutral means to a destination. Rather, roads become artefacts of culture and politics, mediums of change and hope, and vehicles of state building, liberation, and oppression. Roads tie construction to notions of religion, time, and agency.

We have also been inspired by the ways that anthropologists have shown how power and ideas intersect with the compulsions and principles of bureaucracy and governance. Well known are Scott (1999), Ferguson (1990), and Li (2007) as well as Mosse (2004). In *Cultivating Development*, Mosse shows how distinct organizational cultures work to legitimate their own forms of knowledge practice in development contexts. Institutions inform what can be known about their activity through the use of language, aims and objectives and by existing in particular relations to other institutions.[3] Of particular significance for our purposes, Penny Harvey and Hannah Knox (2015) move the focus of the discussion towards cultures and language of engineering and bureaucracy, as well as the life worlds and thoughts of those who live in and along the new roads. In their work, we see how different perspectives and approaches to the world come together to produce direct and concrete action, however unlikely that might at times appear. Their scholarship has directly contributed to the critical theorization of infra-structure, the role of culture in the cost-benefit analysis of roads, the desire for connectivity, and roads as a form of contemporary governance. Harvey and Knox move to the methods of engineers and planners in emphasizing the unruly character of nature in their discourses and in their work to control nature. In this concluding chapter we follow this approach, to take

3   Similarly, Didier Fassin (2012) has examined the political use of compassion in international humanitarianism, showing how unquestioned words and ideas are at the heart of how we think about global injustice and moral hierarchy.

stock of some of the ways the ideas of those who build roads, including the perspectives not only of planners and engineers, but also of local contractors and labourers. Like many of the contributors to this volume, we ask, *What do the road builders believe they are doing when they build a road?*

In a general sense, road building has historical, cultural, and political momentum of its own. Following a different tradition of critical transport history, a new generation of economic and cultural historians of twentieth-century Europe have written wonderful and inspiring books about roads. Schipper (2009) has described how road building was central to the development of the European Union in the twentieth century: 'infrastructural Europeanism'. Zeller (2007) has shown how in Germany the National Socialists attempted to use autobahns as pathways to nature and to further their nationalist vision. Moran (2009) has traced the development of the motorway network in the United Kingdom, arguing, amongst other things, that the semiotics and fonts of Britain's roads were used to distinguish the country from its hierarchical Victorian past and the politics of continental Europe. Merriman (2007) has looked at the history of Britain's M1 motorway, paying particular attention to the subaltern dimensions of its construction and social life. There are many books written by engineers on roads which document the relationship with their craft and political and social ideas of the moment (e.g. Baldwin and Baldwin 2004). They show how fashions quickly change and how plans for building roads that in the 1970s looked like the future are seen as regressive and even foolish a decade later. We draw inspiration from this literature as accounts of power, culture, history and affect, alongside the anthropological interventions discussed above.

By both design and effect, roads are built for both improvement and obsolescence. Road building passes through technological phases and financial fashions. Roads are built because of the continued appeal of the story of individual freedom and movement and the grand narratives of modernization and progress. Roads are built because some people may think there is a need for them, to improve traffic flow, to temporarily reduce congestion, to bypass somewhere, to pass through somewhere else, to reduce the unit cost of transport. New roads may replace older and poorly maintained roads – roads always need costly maintenance. Other people may build roads to bring civilization to a rude country, to bring producers closer to a market, a village closer to a highway, a port closer to a city, or an army closer to a site of potential conflict ('closer' here means in time and with oil). Some people believe that roads bring peace; others think roads bring trouble (see Sarma, this volume). Roads may be part of an attempt to establish a democratic utopia or a society based on class inequality (see

Gohain, this volume). Some may build roads to add further lustre to their achievements (see Huang, this volume). Others may build roads because they were passed plans and instruction to do so. Many build roads for investment, seeing profits in tolls, kickbacks, rising land prices, and the corruption of land-acquisition orders or construction contracts (see Khan, this volume). Road building is thus a deeply political act, with historical drag and the profound influence of political ideas about individuals and societies.

In South Asia, road building has entered a new historical phase characterized by intensity and scale and the global reach of many of those involved. Deregulation is allowing, indeed encouraging, non-sovereign actors to influence the direction and spread of new roads (see Murton and Sigdel, this volume). Road building in today's South Asia involves chains and layers of organizations and subcontracts (see Heslop 2020). A large and under-examined part of building a road takes place in offices, in meeting rooms, and on paper. Engineering the landscape and laying the tarmac can be a relatively swift process in comparison, and certainly one that is more visible to critical scholarship. Knowledge and control of current road-building practices belong to a long list of interest groups in a wide range of locations. Many of these organizations have their own philosophical traditions, epistemologies, languages, and specific institutional aims and objectives. Financers, planners, engineers, contractors, labourers, and road lobbyists, for example, see themselves and their duties very differently in road building.

These are our road builders. The work in colonial history, anthropology of infrastructure, and critical transport history exemplifies how and why an ethnographic approach is well suited to understand the cultures of international organizations and road-building practices, and how different ideas about road building come together to make roads happen. They show how objects at the centre of an institution's discourse (development, humanitarianism – or roads) come to be clothed in particular enchanted ways of understanding; they show how such understandings have histories, which are held in place by identifiable individual and collective relationships; they are also able to trace how discourses about particular objects may shift through time and space and between relationships. They also show how the 'distributed cognition' (Hutchins 1996) or the division of labour between organizations tends to mean that there is no one with an overview. In different ways, our research set out to chase an overview, one that was, however, always disappearing round the next bend in the road because of the scale and complexity of our questions.

Road-building projects

Our projects share an interest in the infrastructure of ideas and underlying politics of thought that build roads. Simpson's project on 'Roads and the Politics of Thought' aimed directly to look at the interface between climate change discourse and policy and road building across South Asia. In South Asia, there is a great deal of institutional work being done on climate change, which happens in parallel but with no connection to road-building projects. In many parts of South Asia roads have become integral to the world – yet are seldom spared a thought other than as barometers of 'development' and 'government efficiency'. Consequently, it has been intellectually, institutionally, and morally difficult to link roads – as a way of organizing social, economic, and political life – to carbon politics and climate change. This difficulty has been compounded by the fact that over the last few decades, mobility has been promoted as the panacea for economic and political woes and these ideas have enormous institutional and popular momentum. These developments often take place as if there is no need to reduce carbon emissions in an era of global warming, although many of the same institutions that promote roads also have divisions dedicated to carbon reduction and climate change awareness. The chapter attends to two critical junctures in the articulation of roads research – the first identifying an imperative to attend to the politics of thought, and the second pointing to an imperative to interrogate road politics in relation to carbon politics.

Rankin's project, 'Infrastructures of Democracy', has focused on democratic transition in Nepal in relation to roads. While undertaking exploratory research on the meaning and practices of 'democracy' in rural areas of Nepal following the decade-long Maoist insurgency and civil war, and the subsequent institution of a multiparty democratic (and ultimately federal) republic, roads were continuously articulated as key sites of protest, claims making, profit, and territorial control. Post-conflict, these colliding claims manifested in a veritable frenzy of rural road building – sometimes dubbed a form of 'dozer terrorism' (Paudel 2018). Rapid track opening aimed at diminishing 'remoteness' sits in contradictory relation to a parallel, donor-led push to pursue 'green approaches' to infrastructure development aimed at achieving the twin goals of social and environmental sustainability. Given the stakes for governance and local claims, roads thus offer frameworks for probing the 'infrastructures of democracy' – the contested physical infrastructures underpinning state reconstruction, as well as the social and political infrastructures governing everyday life and claims for democracy. The chapter illustrates these frameworks first by considering several conjunctures, or 'regimes of territorialization', within which distinctive ideational formations emerged to shape the building of roads. It subsequently explores how the idea of 'green roads' in the current conjuncture articulates long-standing aspirations for modernization, political power, and economic development on the ground.

Roads and the politics of thought: Ethnographic approaches to infrastructure development in South Asia

In the briefest terms possible, this project has traced how roads have been produced historically by governments as metaphors and monuments for control and progress. In the twentieth century, roads were entwined with nationalist projects with their own institutions and peculiarities and embedded in popular political consciousness. In the twenty-first century, roads have been given to the market and 'off shored' as engineering spectacles and, as an asset class, roads now allow money to move as well as vehicles.

The historical and institutional history research we undertook compellingly showed how roads became an integral part of South Asian political thought.[4] We then 'collided' this material with climate change agendas. The importance of this move is demonstrated by two 'facts' derived from research with international road builders, mostly in consultancy firms and government departments concerned with 'development' elsewhere. First, road transport produces around a quarter of global carbon emissions (World Bank 2017). Carbon emissions continue to rise despite decades of negotiation conducted on the assumption that the globe is warming and the effects will be catastrophic (IPCC 2018). Second, planners and infrastructure specialists assume that new roads produce more traffic, rather than easing congestion in the longer term. New roads therefore have multiplier effects on mobility and on future carbon consumption. It is therefore salutary to learn that globally 25 million kilometres of new roads are anticipated by 2050 and that while it took a century to get the first billion vehicles on the road, the second billion will take a decade.

In India, the current targets set by the national government are 130 km of rural road and 50 km of four-lane highway every day. It might seem incredible, but no one is thinking through road building in a prognostic and anticipatory fashion. In India, recently there have been some attempts to

---

4   In this and the subsequent section, 'we' refers to the members of the two project teams; elsewhere, 'we' references co-authors Rankin and Simpson.

work out the carbon costs of building a road; but there is no mechanism or apparent will to think through the future implications of carbon consumption through silent multiplier effects.[5] Although this oversight is easy to point out, it took a few years of research to reach this conclusion. The following section outlines some of the steps taken in the research with a focus on one particular strand of the overall project.

In India, there is a massive and highly publicized rural road-building scheme called PMGSY (Pradhan Mantri Gram Sadak Yojana or the Prime Minister's Village Road-Building Scheme). This scheme claims to have added half a million miles of new rural road to the network since the turn of the century. The aim was to 'connect' tens of thousands of 'habitations' (a term used to include sub-settlements within entities classified as 'villages' in census data) to 'all-weather' or 'black-topped and asphaltic roads'.

Prolonged fieldwork with road men and bureaucrats within their institutions and pages of reports indicates that there is jubilance and pride in the structure and achievements of the programme. All this energy and enthusiasm notwithstanding, we were curious – given the size and certainty of the programme – as to why there was so little writing about PMGSY, particularly as the scheme has a budget of US$50 billion. Among the road men, we met with blank faces when trying to talk critically about PMGSY. The scheme was 'non-controversial' – many of these men asked, *What is wrong with building roads in rural areas?* Often, the language that came back mirrored the words used by the promoters of PMGSY, particularly the idea of 'connectivity'. We were dealing with truth so self-evident that otherwise critical minds did not see a question in the idea, at least in the way it was packaged as a particular form of claims and data. Building roads was progress, meaningful development, and an obvious priority in India. Srinivas Chokkakula, who was leading on this strand of the research, asked around among academic colleagues in Delhi for their response to the question as to why there was no critical debate about PMGSY. Memorably, he received a reply from a colleague: 'The uncritical responses may be due to the belief across the board, there is no counterfactual to building rural roads.'

The powerful phrase, 'no counterfactual' stuck with the project and we have used it often in our discussions as shorthand for how deeply embedded roads have become in popular thought in India. There are lots of shades of

---

5   When the project started in 2015 there was no literature. In the August 2019 edition of the *Indian Highways*, a publication from Indian Roads Congress, the editor noted in reference to India's commitment to Conference of Parties (COP-21) that: 'At present, there is no such system that can quantify the environmental footprint of upcoming and ongoing projects' (Nirmal 2019: 4-5).

opinion in India which revolve around the varying role and responsibilities of the state, ideas of welfare, and market forces. Among the experts, there are also differences of opinion about network modelling and efficiency in road networks. However, the broader question of whether roads are the best way forward is not one that can be meaningfully discussed in the present climate, where the government is stepping back from welfarism and providing roads, electricity, and water as a way of facilitating 'choice' among the electorate.

Simpson's project hosted a number of roundtables in India to discuss the pros and cons of road building with a range of practitioners and professionals. In these fora, too, the evidence discussed was equivocal and unconvincing and the statistics or sample sizes questionable. Often the claims made by road builders were assertions rather than evidence backed. It seemed as it there was no counterfactual because the history of the twentieth century had put road building at the heart of a nationalist project. The institutions and language of government had developed to focus on road building as a priority and as a gauge of its own success. The provision of roads had become as fundamental as health provision or education had been in previous decades.

Notions of development – as a rhetorical and strategic priority – and the centrality of the road to nation-building in India mean that there is little counter thinking. Therefore, to make the connection between roads and climate change in the offices of roadmen was often a matter of diplomatic hazard. In such environments, road building was an unquestioned imperative, national service almost. Climate change suggested the need to reduce carbon emissions. First, quite often, road builders did not see their work as being relevant to carbon reduction. Roads were generally not seen as polluting forms of activity; when they were, their self-evident need outweighed the cost of carbon emission. Some road builders suggested that to associate road construction in India with climate change was an example of neocolonial thought: a way of keeping India undeveloped and therefore less powerful in the world. This was until quite recently also India's position in international climate talks. At home, climate change remains a 'non-issue' in electoral politics (Dubash 2012). Internationally, India has consistently argued that the North and South have different responsibilities and obligations. In line with the international stance, the domestic focus has been on economic growth as a developmental ethos.

The project's way out of this impasse was to conduct research elsewhere, in this instance, the French island of Reunion, where climate change and road building have been hotly debated for two decades as a way of generating a counterfactual narrative. In that field location, Simpson looked at cars, roads, and climate thought on the island. The material again shows how roads have been produced historically by the French state as monuments to colonial domination over unruly nature and civilizational progress. However, here, in the late twentieth century, resistance to nationalist control and the presentation of an alternative to roads and cars was built on separatist, environmental, and leftist politics. In the context of a small island, positions on climate change responsibility became inseparable from competitive dynastic rivalries and therefore part of the reproduction of the social order rather than the catalyst for a radical new direction. The planned construction of a yet another new road, this time on a massive bridge out at sea parallel to the coast and high above the rising waters of the ocean, gives historical legitimacy to the recent political success of the centre right and firmly sediments French power in the post-colony. The material shows how climate change thinking becomes part of everyday struggles and concerns and carries with it the potential for metamorphosis as the relation between road infrastructure and climate change is reconfigured through argument and bitter contestation. In India, things are how they are, but they are not like that everywhere.

In Reunion, there is a struggle between political left and political right over the relation between human action and climate change. In short, the left wanted to end the hegemony of the car and the road as a way of life by introducing collective forms of transport such as trams. The winning right wanted roads that were adapted to climate change – built higher above the sea – so that business could continue as usual. In India, there is a struggle to determine if the state or the market should provide – but there is less disagreement about what should be provided, as roads remain beyond question. In some parts of the world, the feeling is now that we are rapidly heading towards climate extinction, while in other parts of the world this remains a 'non-issue'.

Infrastructures of democracy: State building as everyday practice in Nepal's agrarian districts

The link between democracy and roads emerged in the late 2000s when Rankin had begun working with colleagues Pushpa Hamal and Tulasi Sigdel in Nepal and Andrea Nightingale at the University of Edinburgh. We had been motivated by the sense of optimism that seemed to characterize the period of political restructuring immediately following the Comprehensive Peace Accord (2006) that ended the Nepalese Civil War, and particularly the commitments to redistributive justice that were being articulated by the Unified Communist Party of Nepal, the *janjati* (indigenous ethnic population), and other social movements in the context of a hard-won state-restructuring process. But we also could see like everyone else that despite the Maoists' ambitions to bring their revolutionary struggle within the ambit of liberal political institutions, the so-called 'post-conflict' period was already wracked with political stalemate. In this context, it seemed to us that subnational scales of governance were an important place to look for interesting political openings, as well as regressive closures.

The late 2000s was, in fact, an extraordinary moment in terms of local governance – there was no national constitution, no elected local government, and at the same time, a major decentralization of financial resources and governing authority, following on the mandate of the Local Self-Governance Act (1999). The latter had designated infrastructure as one of four key service sectors that would be devolved to the local state, supported by the requisite budgetary transfers. An 'all-party mechanism' had been designated to formalize local bureaucrats' informal practice of consulting with local political party leaders in the exercise of local governance.[6] Under these circumstances – decentralization plus an ad hoc local governance mechanism premised on the possibility of political consensus across multiple interests – the district (*jilla*) had become important to a range of actors: donors who want to bypass the dysfunctional national state and 'partner' with local community-based organizations; NGOs and consultants burgeoning to conduct the business of 'social mobilization' and programme monitoring and evaluation; party leaders who were finding that in the absence of viable national party organizations, authority derives from a capacity to collaborate with others to actually plan and get things done; and a politicized population recognizing that making claims on the planning function of the local state is the way to express a sense of entitlement to inclusion and citizenship (Rankin et al. 2018). Our work sought to develop an approach to determining what kinds of polities are being built from the ground up through everyday governance practices of these colliding interests.

What we did not anticipate was how this framework would lead to roads as a central topic of subsequent research (which consolidated as the 'Infrastructures of Democracy' project). The topical focus on roads derived

6   The All-Party mechanism was dissolved in 2012, under allegations of corruption, but in practice the style of 'consensus politics' that it sought to institutionalize has continued even after local elections in 2017 and the transition to a federal state structure.

foremost from the observations of Hamal and Sigdel in Mugu District of the Karnali Region in 2010. A national strategic road, the Karnali Highway, a dirt track all of 5.5 metres in width, had recently been blasted open through the precipitous mountains surrounding the Jumla-Mugu district border by the Nepal Army – an extraordinary feat of engineering by any measure. The inauguration of the Karnali Highway in the district capital by the Maoist prime minister marked an expansion of the national highway network into one of two districts remaining 'unconnected' from the national grid. Of equal note, albeit to less public fanfare, was the extensive 'track openings' branching off from district trunk roads to scale precipitous slopes and ford Himalayan rivers and reach the villages of politicians and businessmen who had the power to influence the allocation of budgets and resources – all to the incessant roar of bulldozers and excavators, with barely a hint of engineering or environmental rationality.

Based on these observations, the 'Infrastructures of Democracy' project has revealed the multiple ways in which roads have become a major focus for competing governmental ambitions – donors pioneering 'green' development; political parties gaming the market for local construction contracts; trucking syndicates seeking to control the terms of transport once the roads are built; NGOs and consultants in the business of social mobilization and evaluation; entrepreneurs seeking to trade in imported goods as well as expand markets in agricultural and forest products; and marginalized groups making claims to social inclusion and citizenship. Nearly everyone, it seemed, was enrolled in the project of road building; this trend was dramatically on display in Mugu where there had formerly been no motorable roads, but equally evidenced in the hill and Terai (southern plain) district. Thus roads came to furnish for our purposes a contested terrain of local governance through which competing political rationalities are revealed and contradictory political subjectivities are forged.

Given the dramatic imprint on the landscape unfolding before our eyes, it was tempting to marvel at the novelty. And yet the diversity of competing claims and renditions of 'what brings the road' and 'what the road brings', as Hamal (2014) puts it, also led us to wonder how the motorable road had figured historically and geographically in the making of the Nepali state and its official discourses and practice of development. We found, not surprisingly, that road building has always figured centrally in the political thought of planners and rulers in Nepal (Rankin et al. 2017). In fact, significant documentation already existed allowing us to identify three 'regimes of territorialization' through which roads have played key roles in territorial strategies for building the Nepali state and constituting political thought

(Wilson 2004). Mahesh Chandra Regmi (1977), John Whelpton (1983, 2005) and Mark Liechty (1997) show how managing roads served as a means to 'manage coloniality' during the period of national consolidation under the Shah monarchy, through to the end of a series of hereditary Rana prime ministerships (1950). On the one hand, Nepal's rulers sought to limit access of foreigners and thus British colonization by refusing to build motorable roads between India and Kathmandu. On the other hand, they sought to build and upgrade a postal road network within the country as a means of issuing orders, collecting revenues, and thus controlling the population within Nepal's newly constituted borders.

A second regime of territorialization, which we identified as 'integrating the nation' (1951-1970), corresponds roughly with Indian independence and the end of direct colonial rule in South Asia. At that time the Ranas lost their ruling status and a series of democratically elected governments operating alongside the restored Shah monarchy sought to establish the country's first formal and modern government bureaucracy. Nepal's rulers sought to ensure autonomy from India despite its longstanding integration into the British Raj economy (Tamang 2012), by engaging roads and transport as a means to forge national unity. Within a Cold War geopolitical context, roads also furnished a mechanism for building leverage with India, China and the US in international diplomacy – and the acquisition of bilateral aid. Finally, roads served as a popular developmental imaginary through which the modern Nepali state could win consent for a highly unequal path to modernization, as well as mobilize labour without recourse to illiberal modes of force and repression. Third, 'Building the Economy' (1970-1990) signals a shift towards regional economic planning. Within this regime of territorialization, economic development would no longer be assumed to result naturally from improved accessibility afforded by new roads. The economy would require spatial planning – which involved dividing the country into development regions, establishing a north-south axis linking mountains, hills, and southern plains, and strengthening east-west connections among regions for deeper national integration that would address wealth and population disparities (Gurung 1969).

Our research staked out a 'final' regime of territorialization corresponding to the post-1990 period. Not only our research, but the media and the development grey literature had become replete with accounts of 'dozer terrorism' by which motorable tracks were being opened throughout rural areas all over the country in conjunction with the devolution of governance authority and budgets, and ultimately with the crafting of a federal state structure. As they should, these accounts have raised the alarm about the intensity of rural road building. And yet, observing these developments in relation to the historical trajectory mapped above suggests that road building has long been imbricated in processes of state building. Thus the task becomes one of clarifying the politics of thought – and, we would argue, its articulation with politico-economic and cultural currents – governing particular regimes of territorialization.

We might characterize the contemporary regime of territorialization as 'restructuring the polity', in order to evoke the new forms of collective and political consciousness generated by the Maoist movement and subsequent trajectories towards political democratization (even as they have been criticized for falling short in achieving a meaningfully democratic state). Evoking 'polity' also troubles globally circulating currents of neoliberal economic ideology that dispel notions of state-led economic development in favour of local, self-help entrepreneurism and market making. As in previous regimes of territorialization, roads can be read as a trace on these developments. This is the time of devolution of road planning and budgets, mobilization of local users' groups for 'labour-based', 'green roads' construction. And it is also a time in which those seeking to challenge legacies of exclusion and marginalization regard the road as a key site for making claims and forging political judgement. Our project title, 'Infrastructures of Democracy', thus denotes the physical infrastructures (such as roads) underpinning post-conflict state restructuring as well as the social and political infrastructures (such as users' groups or political parties or *janjati* [indigenous ethnic population] associations), through which governance transpires and aspirations for democracy are pursued.

We are not alone in recognizing the significance of roads for the contemporary conjuncture in Nepal. Based on an analysis of Himalayan borderlands, Galen Murton (2016, 2017) has similarly investigated the co-production of roads, states, and 'spaces of social, political and economic interaction at multiple scales' (2016: 229-330). Engaging relational ethnographic approaches, and enriching a body of scholarship attending to Nepal's critical geopolitical tactics in relation to East and South Asian hegemons, Murton traces how various actors within Nepal leverage major infrastructure projects like highways and hydroelectric dams for political purposes; or, in other words, how politics articulate infrastructures at the same time as, vice versa, infrastructures articulate politics across a range of social and spatial scales. Dinesh Paudel and Philippe Le Billon (2018) similarly examine two trans-Himalayan road corridors connecting Nepal and China to consider the 'Geo-logics of power' – on the one hand, how Nepal's 'buffer state' status (between India and China) has contoured its participation in China's Belt and Road Initiative and, on the other hand, how geologic formations have a role to play in shaping these geoeconomic and geopolitical power dynamics.

As with the central focus of this volume, our research has eschewed a focus on mega-infrastructure developments in favour of more mundane rural road building and its articulation with the everyday lifeworlds of purported beneficiaries – a key terrain for the politics of thought. In this sense it takes inspiration from another long-term academic study investigating the impacts of road construction in rural areas of Nepal (Blaikie et al. 1980). That research engaged neo-Marxist dependency theory and multi-sited, mixed-methods research to argue that road building had exacerbated relations of dependency between the rural periphery and urbanizing centres – specifically by displacing populations, promoting rural-urban migration, inflating land values in roadside locations, generating a new broker economy of contractors and middlemen, and creating enhanced opportunity in commerce and transport for those with capital to invest and loss of livelihood for those who do not (see Cambell 2010). In so doing, it challenged long-held assumptions about the positive impacts of roads on economic development and spawned a major debate within Nepal about development rationality.

Our work takes many of these critiques as a starting point, and seeks to understand these ongoing politico-economic processes in relation to competing political rationalities for road building three decades later, and in the wake of a major revolutionary mobilization carried out in the name of rejecting relations of dependency. It engages ethnographic approaches to foreground the significance of cultural politics for tracing dynamics of consent, subversion, and critical political consciousness in relation to prevailing patterns of spatial and socioeconomic inequality and the politics of thought. For purposes of illustration, and in order to address the issues of climate change awareness raised by Simpson's project, we elaborate the concept of 'green roads', a donor-led formulation geared towards institution-alizing principles of sustainability that might be regarded as an 'alternative paradigm' for road development, if not the elusive 'counterfactual' raised in Simpson's project.

Like in India, it is certainly fair to say that carbon politics has failed to inform road building in Nepal or to animate Nepali popular imagination, enamoured as it also tends to be with the modernist allure of mobility, and especially of connectivity and accessibility within and between remote regions and difficult topographies. A politics of environmental degrada-tion most certainly has, however, deriving from the critical role played by Nepal in generating a global discourse of environmental crisis in the 1980s

(Lewison and Murton 2020). An approach to conservation was worked out in Nepal at that time (involving donors and Nepal-based forestry experts) to confront the dramatic evidence of human-induced forest degradation, which rejected foregoing Malthusian frameworks, to centre the viability of 'traditional' management systems (Gilmour and Fisher 1991; Eckholm 1975). Due in significant part to the presence of a vigilant and active federation representing forest users, Nepal went on to develop some of the most progressive community forestry laws in the world, which have since travelled through foreign aid circuits as models of best practice for blending social and environmental sustainability (Nightingale and Ojha 2013). A key feature of this socio-environmental approach was the institution of community forestry user groups (CFUGs), which ceded forest management to surrounding communities entrusted with balancing conservation and livelihood (Ojha and Timsina 2008).[7]

By the late 1980s, rural road building, dozer-terrorist style (known more formally as 'cut-and-throw'), seemed to be undoing many of the gains in community forest management, and the renewed scars of deforestation, landslides, erosion, and loss of agricultural lands were visible for all to see. Pioneered by the Swiss and Germans in the second half of the 1980s (Mulmi 2009), 'green roads' was consolidated as an approach that adopted commitments to environmental and social sustainability now normalized in the forestry sector, and applied them to road construction. Like community forestry, green roads were worked out in relation to global currents and politics of thought about environmental degradation and conservation – namely the principles of sustainability articulated in the Bruntland Report issued by the World Commission on Environment and Development in 1987 – and the experience in Nepal again proved critical for informing global strategy (Acharya et al. 1999; Banskota 1997; Shrestha 2009). The aim was to engage local labour, local resources, and appropriate technology to build roads in a manner that would reduce environmental and social vulnerability. Road-building users' groups would be formed by communities trained in bioengineering techniques and tasked with constructing sections of the road with hand tools. Livelihood benefits and social protections were promised in the form of minimum wage, equal pay for men and women, transparency in accounting, proper maintenance over time, land compensation, and public hearings for social audits. Green roads thus aim to build 'a sense of ownership' that would help ensure quality and maintenance over time, while

7   CFUGs organized to form the Federation of Community Forestry Users Nepal (FECOFUN), itself now a powerful force for indigenous and community rights on Nepal's political landscape.

bioengineering techniques would reduce the maintenance required. The political thought underpinning green road practices thus aligned well with the decentralization agendas of both the transitioning Nepali state and the neoliberal, good-governance, post-Washington consensus informing much of the development aid agenda.

How, though, has the politics of thought in this instance articulated on-the-ground politico-economic currents? How could we situate green roads conjuncturally in the districts where we are working? In the hill and plains districts, where longer-term and more lucrative employment options exist, residents typically opt against stigmatizing manual labour contributions. They may wish to contribute in other ways, such as through cash donations, or may even insist that roads are a public good that should be provided by the Nepali state. In such contexts, politico-economic relations and modes of political thought on the ground simply do not support the model. In more remote, high hills areas, participation is more robust, but residents comprising users' groups as well as an emerging cadre of local petty contractors notoriously 'game' the system in a context where power and opportunity tends to be concentrated amongst a nexus of political party leaders, senior government officials, businessmen, and leaders of third-sector organizations. In the 'green roads' register, users' groups come across as 'local labour'. In practice, users' groups tend to be led by those members of the local elite with the social capital to recognize and seize opportunity from the apparatuses of development. They have honed skills to harness benefits that would enhance their status while also generating benefits for those within their communities from whom they derive political support (as the two objectives often go hand in hand). They may, for example, record local labour contributions in green roads accounting rubrics, and then commit 'wage' payments to cover the costs of a bulldozer to surreptitiously open a track in a fraction of the time that manual labour could while distributing any 'wages' that remain among group members. Users' groups are able to hire bulldozers without official oversight because costs for their allotted road sections are small – falling below the threshold for formal contract tendering. Supply of petty contractors and heavy equipment has been facilitated by state-led construction of strategic and district roads involving contract tendering. Here, too, petty contractors have developed mechanisms for collaborating to subvert official tendering processes, so that contracts are rotated amongst affiliates of political parties, while ensuring that everyone enjoys some monetary remuneration for 'consensus bidding'.

Local politics of thought informing 'green' (and other) road construction, that is, goes a long way towards shoring up prevailing relations of class (and indeed caste and gender). As Murton and Sigdel also examine in this volume, users' group leadership as well as the 'winning' bids among local contractors are typically claimed by those who have prior access to other forms of power, such as by owning a business, holding a high-level post in the local bureaucracy or a contractor license, serving the leadership of a political party, or winning an elected office – or by being closely related to someone with one or more of these credentials. Such opportunities are typically brokered by caste, class, and gender status, and they primarily accrue to higher-caste men – with the recent institution of gender and minority quotas opening up some opportunities for women and low castes, usually those with influential relatives or patrons. Users' group leadership and contracting bidding forms part of a nexus of privilege, through which power and wealth accumulate. Sometimes users' group members or the wider public view these roles as rightful compensation for the effort involved in securing a project budget for the community, or even for the expenses of election campaigning – the logic here being that a party candidate might be promised compensation out of users' group funds. Patronage is another logic that sustains the system, as 'clients', those with less access to power and opportunity, hope to benefit by maintaining allegiance and reaping the benefits of patronage ties, whether as a kickback, a temporary job, or party recognition.

The politics of thought underlying green roads necessarily falls to the wayside when it comes up against these logics. How have donors and their government partners responded to such practices that compromise sustainability goals? Foremost, they have sought to clamp down on 'corruption', as these subversions of the model are commonly glossed. Thresholds for tendering requirements have been lowered in order to promote more transparency in contracting. The use of bulldozers would thus be managed by market signals – in favour, presumably, of sustainable cutting techniques, but also in recognition that in practice users' groups consistently opt against providing the requisite manual labour. In an effort to conjoin good governance and market making, a consortium of donors and government line agencies has also advocated that local bureaucracies contract out monitoring and compliance roles (World Bank 2013). The task going forward, then, will be to similarly account for how these politics of thought aimed explicitly at making markets in turn (and no doubt similarly) articulate politico-economic and cultural political dynamics, creating differential opportunity and inevitably straying once again from the intended political rationalities.

Conclusions

Roads are shaped by thought as much as by bulldozers, excavators, and cranes. Roads render abstract political ideas – modernity, markets, development, good governance, environmental conservation, climate adaptation (among many others) – as concrete, territorialized reality. This insight suggests that it is not just access to the infrastructure itself, but also access to the political arena of ideas that are at stake in road development. Given the experience in Nepal and India, how, we might ask, might the politics of thought about roads become more encompassing, more deliberative, more democratic? What are the conditions of possibility for more robust counterfactuals and alternative paradigms?

A first order of commitment might be to reassess ideologically 'loaded' keywords that have acquired considerable political potency in the governance of road building. 'Corruption' comes to mind as a liberal-economic vector of thought that directs practices of market making, and aims to curtail the latitude formerly accorded to civil society for participating in the development of infrastructure. Certainly, patronage practices intersect with material conditions in ways that divert resources away from their intended purpose of constructing roads in an environmentally sustainable manner. And yet, practices glossed as corruption also support enduring forms of social sustainability that enjoy widespread consent, even if they work to reproduce hegemonic cultural politics. Good governance strategies alone are unlikely to find much traction against these deeper dynamics. 'Mobility' and 'connectivity', too, are ideas that correlate unproblematically with growth in thought about roads. And yet burgeoning ethnographic research on roads points to the dialectics of mobility and immobility (e.g. Murton 2017; Harris 2013; Huang, this volume), as well as the challenges for viable livelihood posed by mobility itself. As many cases show, the road becomes a danger zone where children can no longer play safely, for example, or, as goes the common refrain, trucks arrive full but leave empty – creating dependency and gutting long-standing forms of socioeconomic and agricultural sustainability. Other terms to problematize might be 'sustainability' and 'resilience'. How, for example, might roads ever be sustainable, especially with the carbon outputs attributed to them?

Such reassessments could go a long way towards building alternative thought. They point to the imperative to seek out modes of judgement and forms of anticipatory thinking within the societies that are the intended beneficiaries of road building. How, for example, might existing practices of care for the environment inform more deliberative processes for linking

conservation and development (Singh 2018)? How might day-to-day evalua-
tions of justice and desired futures become a resource for a kind of planning
that would seek to go beyond 'good governance', to help catalyse collective
forms of political consciousness. What threads of revolutionary consciousness, even, can be salvaged in India and Nepal, through critical deliberation
over the meaning of roads in relation to planetary futures? Such modes of
questioning point to a more expansive politics of thought than that which
is linked to the visions of experts and politicians; and they forge a role for
research about political thought that goes beyond critical analysis to broach
terrains of advocacy.

List of works cited

Acharya, B.N., R. Aryal, B. Karmacharya and W.P. Meyer (1999). *Green Roads
in Nepal: Best Practices Report: An Innovative Approach for Rural Transport
Infrastructure Development in the Himalayas and Other Mountainous Regions.*
2nd ed. Kathmandu: Deutsche Gesellschaft für Technische Zusammenarbeit
(GTZ) and the Swiss Agency for Development and Cooperation (SDC).

Ahuja, R. (2004). '"Opening Up the Country"? Patterns of Circulation and Politics
of Communication in Early Colonial Orissa'. *Studies in History* 20(1): 73-130.

Augé, M. (1995). *Non-places: Introduction to an Anthropology of Supermodernity.*
London: Verso.

Baldwin, P. and R. Baldwin (2004). *The Motorway Achievement* (vol. 1). London:
Thomas Telford.

Banskota, M. (1997). 'Mountain Accessibility and Rural Roads: Innovations and
Experiences from Nepal'. Issues in Mountain Development 97/5. International
Centre for Integrated Mountain Development.

Blaikie, P.M., J. Cameron, and D. Seddon (1980). *Nepal in Crisis.* Oxford: Oxford
University Press.

Campbell, B. (2010). 'Rhetorical Routes for Development: A Road Project in Nepal'.
Contemporary South Asia 18(3): 267-279.

Dalakoglou, D. (2010). 'The Road: An Ethnography of the Albanian-Greek Cross-
Border Motorway'. *American Ethnologist* 37(1): 132-149.

Dubash, N.K., ed. (2012). *Handbook of Climate Change and India: Development,
Politics and Governance.* New Delhi: Oxford University Press.

Eckholm, E.P. (1975). 'The Deterioration of Mountain Environments'. *Science* 189:
764-770.

Fassin, D. (2012). *Humanitarian Reason: A Moral History of the Present.* Berkeley:
University of California Press.

Ferguson, J. (1990). *Anti-politics Machine: Development, Depoliticization, and Bureaucratic Power in Lesotho*. Cambridge: Cambridge University Press.

Gilmour, D.A., and R.J. Fisher (1991). *Villagers, Forests and Foresters: The Philosophy, Processes and Practice of Community Forestry in Nepal*. Kathmandu: Sahayogi Press.

Gurung, H.B. (1969). *Regional Development Planning for Nepal*. No. 1. Kathmandu: National Planning Commission, His Majesty's Government of Nepal.

Hamal, P. (2014). *Rural Road Construction in the Global South: How Does Process Shape Outcome?* MA thesis, Brock University.

Hamal, P. (forthcoming). *Road Building in Nepal: Social Relations, Community Development, and Learning*. PhD dissertation, University of Toronto.

Harris, T. (2013). *Geographical Diversions: Tibetan Trade, Global Transactions*. Athens: University of Georgia Press.

Harvey, P., and H. Knox (2015). *Roads: An Anthropology of Infrastructure and Expertise*. Ithaca, NY: Cornell University Press.

Heslop, L.A. (2020). 'A Journey through "Infraspace": The Financial Architecture of Infrastructure'. *Economy and Society* 49(3): 364-381.

Hutchins, E. (1996). *Cognition in the Wild*. Cambridge, MA: MIT Press.

IPCC (2018). *Global Warming of 1.5°C: An IPCC Special Report*. Edited by V. Masson-Delmotte et al. Intergovernmental Panel on Climate Change.

Khan, N. (2006). 'Flaws in the Flow: Roads and Their Modernity in Pakistan'. *Social Text* 24: 87-113.

Klaeger, G. (2009). 'Religion on the Road: The Spiritual Experience of Road Travel in Ghana'. In *The Speed of Change: Motor Vehicles and People in Africa, 1890-2000*, ed. by J.-B. Gewald, S. Luning and K. van Walraven. Leiden: Brill, 212-231.

Lewison, E., and G. Murton (2020). 'Geographical Scholarship in Nepal: Sustainability, Infrastructure, Disaster and Power'. *Studies in Nepali History and Society (SINHAS)* 25(1): 15-58.

Li, T.M. (2007). *The Will to Improve: Governmentality, Development, and the Practice of Politics*. Durham, NC: Duke University Press.

Liechty, M. (1997). 'Selective Exclusion: Foreigners, Foreign Goods, and Foreignness in Modern Nepali History'. *Studies in Nepali History and Society (SINHAS)* 2(1): 5-68.

Masquelier, A. (2002). 'Road Mythographies: Space, Mobility, and the Historical Imagination in Postcolonial Niger'. *American Ethnologist* 29(4): 829-855.

Merriman, P. (2007). *Driving Spaces: A Cultural-Historical Geography of England's M1 Motorway*. Oxford: Wiley-Blackwell.

Moran, J. (2009). *On Roads: A Hidden History*. London: Profile Books.

Mosse, D. (2004). *Cultivating Development: An Ethnography of Aid Policy and Practice*. London: Pluto Press.

Mostowlansky, T. (2011). 'Paving the Way: Isma'ili Genealogy and Mobility along Tajikistan's Pamir Highway'. *Journal of Persianate Studies* 4: 171-188.

Mrázek, R. (2002). *Engineers of Happy Land: Technology and Nationalism in a Colony*. Princeton, NJ: Princeton University Press.

Mulmi, A.D. (2009). 'Green Road Approach in Rural Road Construction for the Sustainable Development of Nepal'. *Journal of Sustainable Development* 2(3): 149-165.

Murton, G. (2016). 'Trans-Himalayan Transformations: Building Roads, Making Markets, and Cultivating Consumption between Nepal and China's Tibet'. In *Roadology: Roads, Space, and Culture*, ed. by Y. Zhou. Chongqing: Chongqing University Press, 328-340.

Murton, G. (2017). 'Making Mountain Places into State Spaces: Infrastructure, Consumption, and Territorial Practice in a Himalayan Borderland'. *Annals of the American Association of Geographers* 107(2): 536-545. DOI: 10.1080/24694452.2016.1232616.

Nightingale, A.J., and H.R. Ojha (2013). 'Rethinking Power and Authority: Symbolic Violence and Subjectivity in Nepal's Terai Forests'. *Development and Change* 44(1): 29-51.

Nirmal, S.K. (2019). 'From the Editor's Desk'. *Indian Highways* 47(8): 4-5.

Ojha, H.R., and N. Timsina (2008). *Communities, Forests and Governance: Policy and Institutional Innovations from Nepal*. Delhi: Adroit Publishers.

Paudel, D. (2018). 'Bulldozing Democracy'. *Nepali Times*, 6 July. https://www.nepali-times.com/editorial/bulldozing-democracy-2/ (accessed 28 September 2020).

Paudel, D., and P. Le Billon (2018). 'Geo-logics of Power: Disaster Capitalism, Himalayan Materialities, and the Geopolitical Economy of Reconstruction in Post-Earthquake Nepal'. *Geopolitics* 25(4): 838-866. https://doi.org/10.1080/146 50045.2018.1533818.

Rankin, K.N., A.J. Nightingale, P. Hamal and T. Sigdel (2018). 'Roads of Change: Political Transition and State Formation in Nepal's Agrarian Districts'. *Journal of Peasant Studies* 45(2): 280-300.

Rankin, K.N., T.S. Sigdel, L. Rai, S. Kunwar and P. Hamal (2017). 'Political Economies and Political Rationalities of Road Building in Nepal'. *Studies in Nepali History and Society (SINHAS)* 22(1): 43-84.

Regmi, M.C. (1977). *Landownership in Nepal*. New Delhi: Adroit Publishers.

Schipper, F. (2009). *Driving Europe: Building Europe on Roads in the Twentieth Century*. Eindhoven: Technische Universiteit Eindhoven.

Scott, J. (1999). *Seeing Like a State: How Certain Schemes to Improve the Human Condition Have Failed*. New Haven, CT: Yale University Press.

Shrestha, R.H. (2009). 'Harmonizing Rural Road Development with Mountain Environment: Green Roads in Nepal'. http://scaef.org.np/conference/conference/

pdf/Session-6/9.%20Hare%20Ram%20-%20Green%20Road%20-%20Theme.
pdf (accessed 1 October 2020).

Singh, N.M. (2018). 'Introduction: Affective Ecologies and Conservation'. *Conservation and Society* 16(1): 1-7.

Sinha, N. (2012). *Communication and Colonialism in Eastern India, Bihar: 1760s-1880s*. London: Anthem Press.

Tamang, S. (2012). 'Historicizing State Fragility in Nepal'. *Studies in Nepali History and Society (SINHAS)* 17(2): 263-295.

Trankell, I.B. (1993). *On the Road in Laos: An Anthropological Study of Road Construction and Rural Communities*. Uppsala: Uppsala University, Department of Cultural Anthropology.

Urry, J. (2004). 'The "System" of Automobility'. *Theory, Culture & Society* 21(4-5): 25-39.

Urry, J. (2011). *Climate Change and Society*. Cambridge: Polity Press.

Urry, J. (2013). *Societies beyond Oil: Oil Dregs and Social Futures*. London: Zed Books.

Whelpton, J. (1983). *Jang Bahadur in Europe: The First Nepalese Mission to the West*. Kathmandu: Sahayogi Press.

Whelpton, J. (2005). *A History of Nepal*. Cambridge: University of Cambridge Press.

Wilson, F. (2004). 'Towards a Political Economy of Roads: Experiences from Peru'. *Development and Change* 35(3): 525-546.

World Bank (2017). *Global Mobility Report 2017: Tracking Sector Performance*. https://openknowledge.worldbank.org/handle/10986/28542 (accessed 10 April 2021).

Zeller, T. (2007). *Driving Germany: The Landscape of the German Autobahn, 1930-1970*. London: Berghahn.

About the authors

KATHARINE RANKIN is a Professor in the Department of Geography and Program in Planning, University of Toronto, Canada. Professor Rankin is the Principle Investigator for the project 'Infrastructures of Democracy: State Building as Everyday Practice in Nepal's Agrarian Districts' and has published extensively on state reform in Nepal.

EDWARD SIMPSON is a Professor of Social Anthropology at SOAS University of London. 2015-2020 he led the European Research Council-funded project 'Roads and the Politics of Thought: Ethnographic Approaches to Infrastructure Development in South Asia'.

Authors notes

SWARGAJYOTI GOHAIN is Assistant Professor of Sociology and Anthropology at Ashoka University, Haryana. Dr. Gohain has done research in Northeast India and the Himalayan region on borders and the state, culture, migration and infrastructure. She is the author of *Imagined Geographies in the Indo-Tibetan Borderlands* (Amsterdam University Press, 2020).

PENNY HARVEY is Professor of Social Anthropology at the University of Manchester (UK). Prof. Harvey's major works in this field are *Roads: An Anthropology of Infrastructure and Expertise* (with H. Knox) and *Infrastructures and Social Complexity* (with C.B. Jensen and A. Morita).

LUKE HESLOP is a Lecturer in Social Anthropology at Brunel University and a Visiting Fellow at the London School of Economics and Political Science. He specializes in trade, labour, and mercantile kinship in South Asia, and infrastructure and connectivity in the Indian Ocean.

LAURA JEFFERY is Professor of Anthropology of Migration at the University of Edinburgh. She works on healthcare at the intersection of gender and protracted displacement, creative engagement with migration and displacement, and intangible cultural heritage and human-environment relations in the context of protracted displacement.

MUSTAFA KHAN is a social anthropologist researching the state, infrastructure, and contested borderlands of South Asia. Prior to coming to anthropology, he worked as a lawyer within the infrastructure development sector for over a decade. He obtained his doctorate in Social Anthropology in 2020 from SOAS, University of London.

GALEN MURTON is Assistant Professor of Geographic Science at James Madison University in Harrisonburg, Virginia, US. His work is primarily concerned with the politics of large-scale infrastructure development throughout the Himalayas and especially in the borderlands of Nepal, India, and the Tibetan regions of China.

YI HUANG is an independent scholar. He graduated with a BA from Fudan University and an MA in Social Anthropology from SOAS, University of London. He works in the NGO sector teaching anthropology and ethnographic research methods to development workers in China and as a consultant on Chinese development projects.

KATHARINE RANKIN is a Professor in the Department of Geography and Program in Planning, University of Toronto, Canada. Professor Rankin is the Principle Investigator for the project 'Infrastructures of Democracy: State Building as Everyday Practice in Nepal's Agrarian Districts' and has published extensively on state reform in Nepal.

JASNEA SARMA is a postdoctoral research fellow at the Institute of South Asian Studies (ISAS), National University of Singapore (NUS). She works on borderlands, ecologies, and resource frontiers in India, Myanmar (Burma), and China.

TULASI SIGDEL is Senior Director of Studies at Nepal Administrative Staff College. He is also associated with research project entitled 'Infrastructures of Democracy: State Building as Everyday Practice in Nepal's Agrarian Districts'. His areas of research interest are cultural politics, democracy, governance and administration in Nepal.

EDWARD SIMPSON is a Professor of Social Anthropology at SOAS University of London. 2015-2020 he led the European Research Council-funded project 'Roads and the Politics of Thought: Ethnographic Approaches to Infrastructure Development in South Asia'.

Index